Out of the
Blue

The Fall of
the Tory
Dynasty
in Ontario

Out of the Blue

The Fall of the Tory Dynasty in Ontario

Rosemary Speirs

Macmillan of Canada
A Division of Canada Publishing Corporation
Toronto, Ontario, Canada

Canadian Cataloguing in Publication Data

Speirs, Rosemary, date.
    Out of the blue : the fall of the Tory dynasty
in Ontario

Includes index.
ISBN 0-7715-9897-1

1. Progressive Conservative Party of Ontario.
2. Ontario – Politics and government. I. Title.

FC3076.2.S64 1986   324.2713′04   C86-093813-1
F1058.S64 1986

DESIGNED BY William Fox/Associates
EDITED BY Patricia Kennedy

Macmillan of Canada
A Division of Canada Publishing Corporation
Toronto, Ontario, Canada

Printed in Canada

For my mother, with gratitude

Contents

Acknowledgements

Out of the Blue is based largely on interviews – both those done at the time and those conducted later – that allowed me to glimpse the motives and manoeuvres behind the events on the public stage. Many of those involved gave generously of their time and insights, even though they knew that this record might prove painful. Because feelings on all sides, but particularly, of course, among Conservatives, are still so tender, the interviews were largely confidential. Whether or not the main actors are pleased with my final version, I hope they will feel it is true to the facts.

I would like to thank, but absolve from all blame, the following people, for enduring what often turned into lengthy and repeated interview sessions:

The premiers, past and present, William Davis, David Peterson, and in particular, Frank Miller, who talked to me many times about this most difficult period in his life; party leaders Larry Grossman and Robert Rae, who will no doubt hope my forecasts prove faulty once again.

The premiers' aides John Tory, Clare Westcott, Sally Barnes, Les Horswill, Michael Perik, Joan Walters, James Anthony, Hugh Mackenzie, Hershell Ezrin, Gordon Ashworth, Vince Borg, Tom Zizys, and George Hutchison; senior civil servants Ed Stewart, Tom Campbell, and Brock Smith; former and present cabinet ministers Dennis Timbrell, Alan Pope, Roy McMurtry, Robert Elgie, Bette Stephenson, Sean Conway, Robert Nixon, Elinor Caplan, and Ian Scott; MPPs Ross McClellan, Elie Martel, and Richard Johnston.

Political heavyweights Eddie Goodman, Norman Atkins, Hugh Segal, Brian Armstrong, David McFadden, Patrick Kinsella, Lou Parsons, John Laschinger, Paul Weed, Michael Kirby, Don Smith, Mary-Ellen McQuay, and Robin Sears; pollsters Allan Gregg, Ian McKinnon, Martin Goldfarb, Michael Adams, Peter Regenstreif, and Michael Marzolini.

Those who worked behind the political scenes: Alan

Schwartz, John Bitove, John Balkwill, George Boddington, Bob Harris, Janet Ecker, David Melnik, Tony Brebner, Ross Mc-Gregor, and Gerry Caplan; political groomer Gabor Apor; ministerial aides David Allen, John Guthrie, Warren Gerard, and Sean Goetz-Gadon.

I am indebted to colleagues at the *Toronto Star*, in particular Alan Christie and Denise Harrington, for additional material on events for which I was not present. Ottawa columnist Carol Goar assisted with insights into Brian Mulroney. The *Toronto Star's* managing editor, Ray Timson, gave me a four-month leave of absence to write the book, and let me rummage through the newspaper's library and photo files.

Key figures in all parties read the manuscript, or relevant parts, and provided helpful criticism, but I hesitate to name them for fear their peers would consider my interpretation to be theirs.

Lastly, I would like to thank some people who were not political players or newspaper colleagues but were helpful in other ways: my friend Libby Burnham, who knows politics at first hand; Douglas Gibson, who had the idea; political scientist Graham White, who read the manuscript and found mistakes; and Pat Kennedy, the editor of the book. And of course my husband, John Deverell, who read the rough manuscript, and was an invaluable help in making it less rough.

INTRODUCTION

Out of the Blue

On the day Ontario's venerable Progressive Conservative government officially expired, workmen stretched a white banner emblazoned with a red maple leaf above the arched front entrance at Queen's Park. The banner had been hastily borrowed by the incoming Liberals from provincial functionaries organizing for Canada Day celebrations on July 1. The victorious Grits hung it high to flap all that summer on the pink sandstone façade of the old Parliament building – symbolically proclaiming that smug, complacent "Tory" Ontario had at last changed the old pattern. The tentatively expressed will of the electorate, and an unanticipated alliance of Liberals and New Democrats, had toppled one of the country's oldest and most powerful political dynasties. On Wednesday, June 26, 1985, the last custodians of the Tory legend mournfully submitted their resignations. And for the first time in nearly forty-two years, a Liberal government took office in Ontario.

In the scurrying excitement around Liberal leader David Peterson, aides cast about for a special way to convey the historic import of the swearing-in. Peterson would be the first Liberal premier since 1943, when Harry Nixon held office for a brief three months at the end of Mitchell Hepburn's turbulent administration and then lost the government to the gentlemanly colonel George Drew. The passage of the successful Conservative regime which Drew founded was to be marked four decades later only by a black-bordered announcement from Lieutenant-Governor John Black Aird saying he had accepted the resignations of the last Tory premier, the right-winger from Muskoka, Frank Miller, and his ill-fated cabinet.

Peterson decided that Aird would swear in the new Liberal

cabinet in the early summer air, a public event that would herald a new open and accessible government. In keeping with Peterson's recent run of good luck, June 26 was warm and sunny. About five thousand people gathered on the Queen's Park lawns to watch the province's twentieth premier as he and his cabinet took the oath on a raised platform erected in front of the steps. Peterson, following a careful script, arrived on foot through the crowd. Although he had attained a fragile grip on power by means of a deal with the third-place New Democrats, his planners wanted to make it look as if Peterson was the choice, not just of the legislature, but of the people.

Dressed in a dark-blue suit, sporting his trademark red tie, and with his actress wife, Shelley, by his side, Peterson strolled up the walk from Queen's Park Crescent while a band played and the spectators cheered. He stopped frequently to greet people in the crowd. Behind him came the very political Peterson clan: his father, Clarence, had been a municipal politician in the family home town of London, Ontario, and his brother Jim was a former federal Liberal MP.

On the platform the new cabinet sweltered in the sun, all of them attempting to look suitably solemn but barely repressing their excitement. The new treasurer, Robert Nixon, kept breaking out in grins that stretched from ear to ear. Nixon was the son of Harry Nixon, who had reigned so briefly, and was himself a former leader of the Ontario Liberals who had lost in 1967 to John Robarts and in 1971 and 1975 to Bill Davis. Now fifty-six, and one of the oldest members of Peterson's cabinet, he was finding the Tory desolation particularly sweet.

In his brief speech, Peterson spoke of his hopes for opening up the governing process. He had been shaken by the cynicism he'd discovered among voters in the recent election – a widespread belief that government was beyond reach, that the ordinary citizen's voice was not heard, and that Tories would always be in charge at Queen's Park. "All of you who were kind enough to join me this afternoon are helping to symbolize the kind of government to which Ontario is entitled: a government without walls, without barriers," he proclaimed.

Then the new premier and the lieutenant-governor stood side by side at the entrance, shaking hands with the crowd that Peterson had invited inside to sip apple juice, nibble strawberry tarts, and have a look around his office. "This is your day, your government, and your building," Peterson had told the spectators. "Please come in and meet them." Newspaper photographs and television screens showed hundreds of people jamming into Peterson's office and inspecting the cabinet rooms – the inner sanctum of government opened to men and women off the street. Clever public relations created an event which looked very much like a people's celebration.

For all the sunshine and balmy breezes, however, many in Peterson's entourage were feeling emotions akin to panic that day. Elinor Caplan, a North York alderman until her surprise election victory in the Toronto riding of Oriole, had been flabbergasted the previous afternoon when Peterson told her she'd be chairman of the management board of cabinet and minister of government services, both weighty responsibilities that usually went to senior ministers. Now Caplan stumbled from the platform and peered frantically around through contact lenses made dry and opaque by the hot sun. The new minister was carrying a small box containing the Great Seal of Ontario. She'd been told she was custodian of this historic treasure as minister of government services, and she was searching for the staffer from the premier's office, to whom she'd been introduced only that morning, who was to take the Seal to the legislature's vault. Among the blurred faces in front of her, Caplan spied one that seemed familiar and handed over the Seal.

Two days later, at a dinner with deputy ministers, Caplan's deputy, Glenn Thompson, leaned over to ask, "Where is the Great Seal of Ontario?" The premier's office was upset because the Seal was nowhere to be found, and Thompson had been told it was his responsibility. Fortuitously, even as the horrified

Caplan was confessing her blunder, the mystery was being solved. An amused Walter Borossa, chief of protocol for the government, walked into the premier's office with the Seal. Caplan had handed him the treasure, and, after waiting long enough to cause alarm, he'd come to put it back in the vault.

Caplan's misadventure was one of many that would be endured by the new politicians in office. Out of Peterson's forty-eight-member caucus, twenty-five were first-time MPPs. Their experience of provincial politics consisted of the election campaign and a few short days on the Opposition benches watching the Conservative government's dying gasps.

Ten ministers in the new cabinet came from this untried group. The day before the swearing-in, Peterson had warned his caucus that some of the older hands were going to be disappointed, but that it couldn't be helped. He needed the neophytes to give his cabinet the representative mix which his rural-based caucus had lacked. Newly elected MPPs made up the cabinet's Metro representatives, its two women, its one black, one minister of Italian origin, and two Francophones. The Liberals, it was clear, had made a good beginning at opening their leading ranks to elements of the population who had felt excluded in the past. It was precisely what Larry Grossman, the former Conservative treasurer, had struggled – too late – to persuade his party to do.

With the swearing-in on June 26, the new ministers were suddenly on stage. As they stepped down on to the lawns, they were circled by scrums of reporters asking what they intended to do about extra billing by doctors, rent controls, separate-school funding, and environmental clean-up. Liberal party flacks pushed in behind, distributing biographies, to help reporters identify cabinet ministers who were virtual unknowns.

As they escaped from the reporters' clutches, the ministers headed for the Amethyst Room on the first floor of the legislature, where, as is normal, they were given briefing books with capsule explanations of the major issues facing each ministry. What was not standard practice was the distribution of maps. Each minister was given a mimeographed guide to

Queen's Park to help him, or her, find the right office in the scattered complex of provincial government buildings. "This is how new we are," Caplan said, as she set off, map in hand.

For the Liberals, the chance to govern had literally come out of the blue. Only short months before, the Progressive Conservative party of Ontario had appeared invincible. Over a span of more than four decades, five different Conservative premiers – George Drew, Tom Kennedy, Leslie Frost, John Robarts, and William Davis – presided over one of the most successful political organizations in Canadian history. The Tories rode a golden tide of economic prosperity from the end of the Second World War until the mid-1970s. They were easy times for a government to win a reputation with the voters as good managers.

When the economy began to stall, the dynasty shuddered. William Davis, after a comfortable election win in 1971, was reduced to minority government in 1975 and again in 1977. But his Tories proved adaptable, imposing restraint where once they'd been expansive, while selling the voters the idea there was still no better place to be than Ontar-i-o. Davis's image as a reassuring father figure for difficult times grew on the electorate. When he handed the succession to Frank Miller in January 1985, all the polls said the government party was more popular than ever.

The party's subsequent abrupt downfall is a clear illustration of the old political adage that governments are not defeated, they defeat themselves. During the few short months Miller occupied the premier's office, it became obvious that the supposedly invincible organization he inherited was wracked with internal division. An administration that had been carried through the previous few years by Davis's personal popularity was aging and lacked the will to respond to new social pressures. Miller himself, in a series of classic bungles, roused public concern that he and his government were abandoning the moderate traditions of the past forty-two years. The voters lost faith in the province's long-time managers and began to look elsewhere.

That is when all the lucky stars began sparkling in the

Liberal sky. Up to then, David Peterson, a 41-year-old London lawyer and businessman, had not appeared to be a compelling alternative. In the three years since he'd been chosen party leader, Peterson had languished ineffectively in Opposition and, in a series of caucus defections and by-election defeats, had lost many of his front-benchers. Commentators said the Liberals appeared destined for third place, behind the New Democrats.

But in the months before the election, Peterson had come out of his corner fighting. He dragged his party's right-wingers with him and put together an attractive and progressive campaign platform. On the election trail, he turned in an unexpectedly strong performance – he was handsome, modern, and energetic. By comparison, the 57-year-old Miller appeared worn and outdated, while the New Democrats' Robert Rae, for all his sincerity on the issues, was curiously aloof and lacking in socialist fire.

In the last days of the election, when the Tory vote was in free fall, Peterson, and not Rae, proved the more effective magnet. The Conservatives plummeted to 52 from 72 seats, the barest of minorities in a 125-seat House. The Liberals took 48 seats, up from 28 when the legislature dissolved. The New Democrats rose only three, to 25 seats.

Then, in an extraordinary series of negotiations, the New Democrats signed a formal pact with the Liberals, assuring them of at least two years in office in return for an agreed agenda of legislative reforms. Miller's Tories were defeated in the House on June 18, and Lieutenant-Governor John Black Aird became one of the few Queen's representatives in recent years to decide a government's fate. He called on Peterson to name a cabinet.

Now, on June 26, watching the swearing-in from the sidelines, Bob Rae and a handful of New Democrat MPPs were torn with pride and jealousy. They were pleased with their crucial role in toppling the Conservatives. On the other hand, they had to watch as Liberal MPPs were sworn into portfolios they longed to hold themselves. Rae clenched his teeth and said the right things to reporters about the constructive opposition role his party would play in the legislature. Some of his caucus-mates were less restrained and moaned that they should have demanded some cabinet seats as the price of support for Peterson's Liberals.

Many Conservatives were still in a state of shock. Former ministers had taken their limousines for the last time that morning, after spending the evening before moving boxes from their spacious ministerial offices to the cramped quarters of the Official Opposition. Their salaries dropped overnight from $71,998 to $46,494, and their large staffs were slashed to two or three aides. The privileges of travel and the satisfactions of influence slipped away. Most could not bear to watch the swearing-in. The only visible Conservative was John Tory, the unflappable red-headed son of a communications magnate, and principal secretary to Bill Davis in his final years, who was on hand as a television commentator. Frank Miller kept himself busy, and away from Queen's Park, by calling a meeting at his Toronto apartment in the Sutton Place Hotel, ostensibly to discuss how the Conservatives would handle their first days in Opposition. Hugh Segal, Eddie Goodman, Sally Barnes, Tony Brebner, Bette Stephenson, and Larry Grossman shuffled their feet until the man who'd just lost the premiership said: "As chairman of the Question Period group, it is your meeting, Larry." Grossman jumped – no one had told him – then realized the meeting was just a pretext to give the group something to do on a day they were all finding difficult. So he rambled on in general terms, and after a while the meeting broke up. Miller and the others wandered away, and Grossman sat awhile in Miller's apartment, pondering the irony of a 42-year-old regime ending in such a desultory fashion.

The Tories found it hard to accept the loss of power. Some, like former consumer minister Robert Elgie, a neurosurgeon, might never have given up their private-sector lives for politics if they had contemplated the possibility of not sitting in cabinet. Others were young enough never to have known any life other than being part of the party in office. The redoubt-able Bette Stephenson, despising the snivelling, said, "We are not bloodied. We are not bowed. I do not hurt." But most of her fallen comrades reacted as though a *coup d'état* had taken place, instead of a legislative defeat. Miller, who had occupied the premier's office for only 139 days, reviled the "unholy alliance" of Liberals and New Democrats who had "hijacked" his government. It was as if the Tories had run Ontario so long, they had come to believe it was theirs. The loss, as Elgie said, was followed by a period of grieving.

The Tories were not alone in their assumptions. So long had been their tenure in office that in recent years commentators had come to regard them as inevitable governors of a cautious and unimaginative people. From 1905 to 1985, there were only two interruptions of Tory rule, once for the United Farmers from 1919 to 1923, and the second time for Hepburn's Liberals from 1934 to 1943. Observing the pattern, political scientist John Wilson of the University of Waterloo labelled Ontario a "Red Tory province", whose citizens valued order, stability, and continuity more than anything. Wilson argued that as long as the Conservatives provided those qualities, they could go on forever.

Still, the possibility of defeat had long been there. Through all the Tory decades, there was always another Ontario waiting. During those forty-two years, the Conservatives never once captured the loyalty of a majority of the voters, not even during Frost's commanding majorities in the 1950s. Twice in the mid-1970s, Bill Davis was returned with minority governments. In his last election in 1981, only fifty-eight per cent of voters bothered to go to the polls, and Davis's renewed majority was fashioned from only forty-three per cent of that vote. The continuation of Conservative hegemony depended on voter apathy and a divided Opposition.

It depended also on the long domination of the federal government by the Liberal party of Canada. Voters elected the Conservative Davis as a counterweight to Prime Minister Pierre Trudeau. Both men and their parties appealed to the same middle-class Ontario constituency – as many as a third of the people who voted Liberal federally switched in provincial elections to the Ontario Conservatives. Once Brian Mulroney swept into office nationally in September 1984, the old voting pattern was threatened. Change at the federal level appeared to bring a mood for change provincially too.

Historic patterns are deceptive, however. It could so easily have been different. What if William Davis, after nearly fourteen years as premier, had not decided to resign on Thanksgiving Day, 1984? Then, surely – and even Frank Miller agrees – the popular Davis would have won the next election handily. Peterson, too much like Davis to be comfortable fighting him, would probably have suffered the fate so many anticipated for him. He'd have been just another lacklustre Liberal who had been defeated by the Tory juggernaut, and then thrown out by his party for his failures. Bob Rae would likely have become leader of the Opposition, and surely would have preferred that to being co-signer of an accord with the Liberals. The fall of the Tory dynasty in 1985 was far from inevitable.

Yet, questions of inevitability aside, history provides some interesting comparisons between the August 4, 1943, election in which Drew trounced Harry Nixon, and the election of May 2, 1985, which brought Miller's downfall. As Nixon had done before him, Frank Miller called an election within weeks of being chosen leader, but Miller hastened to the polls without Nixon's excuse that time was running out. For both, the pre-election omens were good, but the election itself was disastrous, because neither had devoted enough time to first winning the people's confidence. And, like Nixon, Miller's fall from power, and into political oblivion, was due as much to the sins of his predecessor as to his own mistakes.

There are parallels for the winners, too. David Peterson in 1985, like George Drew in 1943, had an attractive, vigorous election platform to offer voters. Drew's twenty-two points of "practical reform" even included denticare, one promise that his Conservative successors never kept and that the Liberal Peterson was able to put forward again four decades later. Peterson, like Drew, took office with a minority, and with another party poised to take over should he slip. But while Peterson's biggest threat was from the fifty-two Conservatives he'd just toppled from office, Drew's predecessors, the Liberals, were reduced to a rural rump, and a fledgling socialist party came out of obscurity to official Opposition status. The Conservatives won 38 seats and the Liberals 16, and 34 seats went to the Co-operative Commonwealth Federation, forerunner of the NDP.

The sudden growth of the CCF marked the birth of the modern three-party system which was so to benefit Drew and his Conservative successors. Drew's dependence on CCF support for his fragile minority in 1943 committed him to reform measures. Thereafter the socialist alternative helped keep the Tories "progressive", or sufficiently so that the population enjoyed incremental reform over most of the forty-two years. But while the effect on the Tories was long-lasting, the CCF surge brought socialists only a brief taste of success. In the 1945 election, the CCF was reduced to 8 seats, while Drew's Conservatives won 66 seats and the Liberals 14. From that date, the Conservatives ruled by the grace of a divided Opposition. Neither the Liberals nor the New Democrats were able to take a permanent lead. The two Opposition parties remained locked in a see-saw struggle over second place for four decades.

Drew, however, had given his party more than a divided Opposition. With his winning 1943 platform he had put the Conservatives on the path of flexible response to the new forces of change. His twenty-two points of progressive labour legislation, subsidized housing, assumption of half of school costs to lighten property taxes, and medical protection made Hepburn's tired Liberals look like reactionaries and stole thunder from the CCF. Drew's successors learned from him the importance of honouring the progressive as well as the conservative side of their tradition. They built their success in the moderate middle ground of politics.

The Drew formula – cautious reform – enabled the Conservatives to guide Ontario through forty-two years of rapid change. During the Tory years, the population doubled from 4.1 million to 8.9 million. Accelerated growth in the economy was accompanied by dramatic technological change as the railway and radio gave way to airplanes and television. With the influx of two million immigrants, a largely Anglo-Saxon, Protestant, and still noticeably rural society became urban, polyglot, and multiracial. By 1981, more than one-third of Ontarians were Roman Catholic. The majority of working women held jobs outside the home. In response to new pressures, the province's role had mushroomed. Provincial spending of $300 million in Leslie Frost's first budget had grown to $26.8 billion in the last Davis budget of 1984.

Frost, who became premier in 1949, after the brief caretaker administration of Tom Kennedy, developed the governing style that proved so reassuring to Ontario electors. He was the first of the prudent managers. Government was business, Frost said, and common sense. The newspapers called Frost "Old Man Ontario" – the wise and wily small-town lawyer, presiding over the building of roads and Hydro plants which were the foundation for the province's modern industrial economy. Ruling against pitifully weak Opposition parties, Frost knew the only way he could lose government was by rousing strong passions in the electorate. Like Bill Davis two decades later, he made no waves. His style was to smooth over differences and find the moderate way. Donald MacDonald, then leader of the Ontario CCF, dubbed him "The Great Tranquillizer". Frost even reconciled the Ontario Tory party with the federal Liberals, with whom Drew had waged bitter battles. Détente made political sense: the Ontario Conservatives and the federal Liberals appealed to many of the same elements of the Ontario electorate.

John Robarts, who succeeded Frost in 1961, was a gravel-voiced corporate lawyer from London, Ontario, who described himself as a "management man". In his blue pinstripes, the handsome, greying Robarts was the chairman of the Ontario board – the epitome of staid respectability. Outwardly sober, he was in private a robust "man's man", a lover of outdoor sport, whisky, women, and beefsteak. He is best remembered as the Ontario premier with sufficient national stature to call the Confederation of Tomorrow Conference in 1967. Like Leslie Frost, Robarts governed in economic times that were mainly good, and rode the tide. As he saw it, government's job was to provide a stable political environment that would encourage private investment at home and attract capital from across the border.

Robarts undertook the reorganization of the Ontario government, and began the amalgamation of local school boards and municipal governments which fitted the province for modern times. Yet the role of administrator bored him, and Robarts retired, confiding that he felt uncomfortable with the huge bureaucratic government he had helped to create. Bill Davis would handle it better, he said.

Davis, however, proved a mixed blessing for his party and his province. Outwardly he was the most successful of the Conservative premiers, staying in office for fourteen years and retiring at the height of his personal popularity. Yet, within weeks of his departure, the Conservatives were locked in internecine warfare that snatched victory from the grasp of his successor, Frank Miller, and destroyed the Ontario Tory dynasty. Watching from the sidelines, Davis was deeply hurt by Miller's failure – he was confident that under him the Conservatives would have made no such mistakes, but he was also aware, despite all his denials, that he must be partly to blame. His apparently healthy party had really been in a dangerously weakened condition – which is the untold story of the Davis years.

1

Bill Davis Steps Out

Until Premier William Davis walked into the cabinet room with his wife, Kathleen, beside him, his hastily assembled ministers and the reporters crowding the corridor outside thought he had called them to announce an election. Ten days earlier, the *Toronto Star*'s front page said Davis was leaning towards retirement. But so fierce were the denials from Davis's close friends, and so loud the warm-up rumbles of his election organization – the famous Big Blue Machine – that it seemed unthinkable the leader would quit.

Davis was, at fifty-five, the undisputed political boss of Canada's largest province. His personal popularity was at an all-time high. His party believed he was poised to increase the majority with which the Tories held Ontario. Only personal burn-out could prompt a resignation, and the reticent premier had successfully hidden his fatigue from all but a few of his closest associates.

Still, the *Star*'s signal couldn't be ignored entirely. The media dogged Davis for a week as he escorted Queen Elizabeth to Bicentennial festivities around Ontario. Davis immersed himself in the formalities, using the royal presence to conceal his debate with himself. When reporters finally cornered the premier outside his office, he was his usual evasive self. In exasperation, CITY-TV reporter Colin Vaughan thrust his microphone into Davis's face and demanded, "Would you give us a straight answer for once?" Davis smiled benignly and replied, "Colin, why, after all these years, should I change?"

Then it was Monday, October 8, 1984 – Thanksgiving Day. The legislature was about to return, and it was the premier's last chance to call a fall election. The *Globe and Mail* headlined the pack wisdom: "Davis meets aides today; election likely."

So there was palpable shock among the waiting reporters when Davis arrived at 3 p.m. and walked into the hastily called cabinet meeting with his wife and his 28-year-old son Neil in tow. Reporters looked at one another in startled realization: Davis wouldn't bring family to announce an election; this must mean retirement. There was an instant scramble for the telephones. As the word spread, confusion mounted throughout the legislative building.

On the floor below, David Peterson, leader of the Ontario Liberals, had assembled a group of nominated Liberal candidates and their supporters to give an appearance of vigour and eagerness for the election trail. The Liberal candidates milled about uncertainly, trying not to look foolish but afraid to leave until they knew just what Davis was telling his cabinet behind closed doors.

Inside the cabinet room, Kathleen Davis later said, "it was like sitting in an electric field – everyone was so charged and full of emotion." She and Davis both wept when he told his surprised ministers that after almost fourteen years as Ontario's premier, he was stepping down. In the tributes that flowed then from his old friends in cabinet – and continued to flow for weeks after – there was little evidence of the alarm lurking in some stout Tory hearts.

Not until months later, after the collapse of the 42-year-old Ontario Conservative regime, did Conservatives say publicly that Davis's resignation had set them up for defeat. Bitter party members blamed him for waiting so long; for saddling his successor with a divided, indebted, yet complacent party; and, worst of all, for leaving behind the volatile emotions unleashed by his recent decision to extend full funding to Roman Catholic separate schools.

Davis had been warned of the harm his resignation might do the Tory cause. Hugh Segal, his former principal secretary and confidant, had privately forecast disaster unless the premier stayed on for one more election. Voters had a "comfort level" with Davis, Segal argued. They would trust him to steer the economy through a fragile recovery and handle the social divisions of an increasingly polyglot society. More importantly, only Davis had enough personal popularity to get away with extending funding to the separate schools without serious political damage to his Conservative party. Segal said history would judge Davis a success only if his successor won the next election, and, as Segal saw it, all of the likely successors were potential losers.

Other trusted advisers had pooh-poohed Segal's Cassandra cries. Toronto lawyer Edwin Goodman, a friend of more than a decade, Hugh Macaulay, Davis's former chief organizer and appointee to the chairmanship of Ontario Hydro, and Senator William Kelly, the Ontario party bagman, all argued that party and province were both in good shape and Davis should do what was best for himself. He could leave in good conscience at the pinnacle of his career, before his lustre dimmed. The party, they said, would be stimulated and renewed by the contest for leadership occasioned by his departure.

Davis reflected that confidence at the news conference that followed his dramatic meeting with cabinet. With Kathleen and Neil, eldest of their five children, sitting in the front row, reporters jammed in the seats behind, and cabinet ministers and trusted retainers lining the media studio walls, Davis said he had told party president David McFadden to arrange a leadership convention at the earliest opportunity. He was sad, but composed. "It has always been my wish to leave the party and the government in as strong and dynamic a circumstance as possible," Davis said. "With both the party and the government in very good standing with the public, with the tremendous strength of our organization, and with the support and co-operation we can expect from a new Progressive Conservative government in Ottawa, I believe that the party is extremely strong."

Although he didn't cite the figures, the reason for his optimism was well known. The Decima Quarterly poll, the country-wide survey by Tory pollster Allan Gregg, in the fall of 1984 once again gave the Ontario government the highest public-approval rating of any provincial government in Canada. A private Tory party survey by the same firm in September 1984 put the Conservatives at a high 53 per cent, the Liberals at 22 per cent, and the New Democrats at 25 per cent.

Davis mentioned a few personal accomplishments of which he was proud – notably the Canadian constitutional accord of November 5, 1981, in which he played a leading role. But his legacy, he said, was not single deeds. It was years of "humane and competent government". The nation's industrial heartland was leading the rest of the country in recovery from a severe economic recession. The province's standards of education, health care, and social services had been maintained so that Ontarians were able to enjoy a high quality of life. Even the school question appeared to be resolving itself more smoothly than Davis had anticipated when he'd announced full funding for Roman Catholic separate schools in June. The premier's political estate seemed to be in order.

If Davis had not retired that Thanksgiving Day, his party might well have been able to finesse the school controversy with a minimum of difficulty. After nearly fourteen years in office, the premier had built a reputation as a consensus leader who could keep the lid on the most volatile questions on the public agenda. To diffuse confrontation, Davis always appeared calm and in charge, listened at length to what all sides had to say, and played opponents off one against the other while enveloping himself in clouds of pipe smoke and political bafflegab. The premier seldom talked specifics, and never speculated publicly on the consequences of his actions. "Politicians," he'd explained to the legislature that April, "never get into trouble until they open their mouths."

Davis himself spoke a lot but seldom said anything. He was the quintessential middle-class Protestant product of the comfortable small town that Brampton had been when he was growing up. His press secretary, Sally Barnes, used to joke that Davis's idea of a naughty dessert was a bowl of vanilla ice cream, and that when he was really having a blowout, he'd order caramel sauce on top. "The average Ontarian is a moderate," he was to say on Global television a year after the retirement. "He is not to his left or his right. That has been the history of Ontario. Success lies in the middle of the political spectrum."

With the passage of years after 1971, Davis's personal maxim "moderation in all things" degenerated into the uninspiring "never rock the boat". Ed Stewart, his long-time deputy, used to say that the Davis devotion to tranquillity matched the mood of Ontarians – the people, he argued, like the careful, cautious approach.

Clare Westcott, Davis's executive assistant and behind-the-scenes trouble-shooter for many years, was not convinced that Ontarians wanted caution carried to the point of paralysis. He often needled the premier about his indecisiveness, once presenting him with a ruler inscribed: "Maybe . . . and that's final." At a farewell roast for Davis at the Royal Canadian Yacht Club, Westcott was to sum up the Davis style as no one else dared: "He has made procrastination a vital and important instrument in the running of a government. He has literally turned it into a science. Taking quick action is considered sinful. When he's asked, 'Do you have trouble making up your mind?', his answer is, 'Well, yes and no.'"

At the end, Davis's hesitations over his own future undermined his party and government. His style remained relaxed and assured, but he was less and less inclined to action. A growing array of decisions remained on perpetual hold: compensation for the mercury-poisoned Indians at Grassy Narrows; removal of the radiation-contaminated soil at homes in the Malvern area of Scarborough; freedom-of-information legislation; a spills bill which finally passed the House but wasn't proclaimed because polluters didn't want to be made fully liable; control of toxic substances in the workplace; resource-planning in the vast, over-exploited reaches of northwestern Ontario; a ban on extra billing by doctors to bring Ontario into conformity with federal law; extended public funding for day care; and labour reforms to encourage equality for women in the workplace. Davis's government was suffering the peril of the aged: hardening of the arteries.

Davis himself was tired. Four years earlier he might have followed his party's tradition by retiring – thus allowing the

Conservatives to repeat their ten-year ritual of shedding the
old leader and emerging renewed under a younger man.
Instead, he summoned a final burst of energy and forced
himself out on the election trail. His gruelling pace in the
March 19, 1981, election was fuelled by the knowledge that
this was his last chance to regain majority government – a
majority that would be based on Davis's own personal popularity, by now his party's greatest asset.

Davis was driven by the legend of the Tory dynasty. His
advisers urged him to prove to himself, and to history, that
he was not the author of its decline. Six years of humbling
minority government had made Ontario Tories hunger for past
triumphs. Among Davis's predecessors, only George Drew had
been returned with a minority government – and that had been
at the very beginning of Conservative rule. In subsequent
elections Drew, Frost, and Robarts basked in the authority
that winning a majority in an election gives a party over the
legislature and the bureaucracy.

When Davis won his first election as premier with a
smashing majority in 1971, he had seemed a worthy successor
to the dynasty. The party's then rudimentary polling had
forecast Conservative losses following the inaction of Robarts'
final year, and Davis had known he was entering a risky battle.
In preparation, he launched a hundred days of government
activity aimed at recapturing the voters' hearts. He pleased
urban liberals by stopping the Spadina expressway in Toronto,
and placated his party's WASP supporters by refusing a demand
from the Roman Catholic school system for full funding. He
assembled the famous Big Blue Machine by wooing organizer
Norman Atkins from the camp of his recent leadership rival
Allan Lawrence to be chairman of the election campaign.
Atkins brought with him an energetic band that injected new
life into the crowd around Davis. Atkins, brother-in-law of
Tory guru Dalton Camp and president of Camp Advertising,
excelled at putting a campaign organization with winning
chemistry into the field. He borrowed American electoral
techniques to give the Ontario Tories their first highly polled,
carefully controlled campaign based on the maximum exploi-

tation of television. A hand-picked squad of advancemen ensured that every moment of the Davis tour went like clockwork. The airwaves were flooded with catchy jingles and reassuring messages. The campaign cost $4.5 million and produced a harvest of 78 Conservative seats – to 20 for the Liberals and 19 for the New Democrats.

With majority firmly in hand, the young premier quickly displayed an impolitic arrogance. His government was ham-fisted in imposing regional government on municipalities, and was rocked by scandals over apparent favouritism in granting government contracts. Davis's own integrity remained unsmirched, but he retreated into a closed circle of his mandarins. Aloof, hidden by bureaucrats, he appeared a technocrat premier caught up in trendy schemes for model communities, futuristic mass-transit systems, and government land-banking of thousands of rural acres set aside for planned urban growth. He'd been schooled in an expansive, and expensive, style of government which was becoming unsuit-able as prosperity gave way to leaner times.

Davis paid for his lack of the common touch in 1975 when his party won only 51 seats. The New Democrats under the spellbinding Stephen Lewis, son of former federal NDP leader David Lewis, became the Official Opposition with 38 seats and the Liberals dropped into third place with 36. Davis was so shaken that he considered resigning. But he determined to stay and fight. He grabbed for majority again – too soon – in 1977; he learned patience and waited for a better chance.

It was fortunate for the Conservative party that he stayed. None of the likely successors, especially the impatient and high-handed Darcy McKeough, could have handled minority government as well as Davis did between 1975 and 1981. He put aside his technocrats and listened to advisers with a better feel for the people: lawyer Edwin Goodman, his new deputy Ed Stewart, a colourful and youthful Hugh Segal, and press secretary Sally Barnes. They taught Davis to introduce his speeches with a half-mocking line of patter, singling out figures in his audience for special mention and teasing. They talked him out of his ill-fitting three-piece suits and floppy haircut into casual tailoring and a suitable mature styling of his silvering hair. They carefully balanced every progressive initiative with symbolic gestures to tradition – when the party began muttering he was too pink, Davis showed he could be blue too by ordering schools to reinstate the Lord's Prayer and vowing his undying allegiance to the Queen. They invited the press to take pictures of him playing baseball, or rough-housing with his dog. Premier William Davis became "Brampton Bill".

In the legislature, Davis proved himself a master of accommodation, avoiding defeat, restraining spending in step with the economic slowdown, always responding at the last moment if the uproar grew too loud. He skilfully sowed division between the Liberals and the New Democrats, painting the former as less liberal than himself and the latter as well motivated but ideologically misguided. Davis publicly disdained the Liberal leaders Robert Nixon, Stuart Smith, and later David Peterson, but he carefully nurtured a mutual-admiration pact with Stephen Lewis, and, after they both stepped out of politics, successfully recommended Lewis to Prime Minister Brian Mulroney for the post of Canadian ambassador to the United Nations. Davis's treasurer Frank Miller, less a diplomat, once discussed the Tory/NDP relationship with the *Gravenhurst News* (June 22, 1983), admitting that "The biggest problem for the Progressive Conservative party is to keep the New Democratic Party artificially strong so as to split support between the Liberal party and the NDP. This strategy is one of the reasons we have stayed in power so long."

Whether it was because of Davis's wiles or their own healthy fear of forcing an election, the two Opposition parties seldom combined for votes in the Tory minority years. When they did, Davis backed off. He gave up on a proposed Ontario health insurance premium increase – to the chagrin of his treasurer, Darcy McKeough, who resigned months later – abandoned health minister Frank Miller's plan to close certain small hospitals, sidetracked property-tax reform, froze the move to more regional governments, forced cancellation of the proposed federal airport in Pickering because local voters didn't like it, imposed rent controls when NDP leader Stephen Lewis made headlines with stories of rent gouging . . . and survived.

Davis handled the brokerage politics of minority so well that by the time of the 1981 election he was extremely popular. The premier himself was the Tory ticket to future success. In Conservative headquarters, the 1981 campaign chairman, Norman Atkins, hung a sign reading "Majority is the Priority". There was no purpose beyond the slogan that Atkins was prepared to articulate. It was just something he wanted to do for his friend "Billy". Davis himself had no fresh vision to offer. He ran on the strength of his personal popularity – the known quantity, bland, unexciting, solid, someone people could trust to mind the store. And he held out the Big Carrot, an election platform known by the acronym BILD, a \$1.5-billion grab-bag of economic projects for every corner of the province.

BILD had been born in the fall of 1980 at a dinner called by Davis in a private dining-room at Toronto's La Scala restaurant. Invited to the political brainstorming session of senior cabinet ministers were treasurer Frank Miller and industry and trade minister Larry Grossman; their deputy ministers, Rendell Dick and Red Wilson; bright bureaucrats Duncan Allan, Brock Smith, and Bernie Jones; and advisers who made no bones that this was an election-strategy meeting – Eddie Goodman, Hugh Segal, Bill Kelly, and advertising expert Tom Scott. With the arrogance of nearly four decades in power, the Conservatives presumed it was their right to use deputy ministers and other bureaucrats as an arm of the Conservative party.

Segal set the agenda by rhyming off polls that showed the public expected that the provincial government could do something about unemployment and industrial restructuring. Goodman said a big program was needed – something worth at least \$1 billion – if it was to have an impact. Brock Smith and others had been working on an industrial strategy for Grossman, who anticipated just such a meeting, and proffered a string of advanced technology centres to be located in different communities of the province. The technology centres were good local politics, and they were a public demonstration that the provincial government was moving to meet the high-tech challenge. Davis wanted more such ideas and assigned staff from different ministries to work on BILD.

The premier unveiled the bureaucrats' offerings at a pre-election ceremony on January 27, 1981. Most of BILD was a repackaging of highway and other projects which the ministries would have undertaken in the normal order of business. A few ideas were genuinely new, such as the technology-sparking IDEA Corporation. IDEA later foundered in a morass of mismanagement caused by the confusion surrounding its original mandate. For political purposes, the corporation was launched prematurely and without adequate planning.

Still, BILD suited the premier's immediate electoral needs wonderfully. Davis travelled across the province dispensing largesse from his goody bag – a new ski resort here and better storage sheds for cabbages there. But a professional bureaucracy once famed for its competence was embarrassed at being used so openly for partisan ends, and began to lose some of its enthusiasm and creative edge.

The media greeted BILD with open scepticism. The electoral bribery was too crude to escape comment. The discouraged Liberal leader, Stuart Smith, watching himself being overwhelmed by the manipulative Tory campaign, spoke bitterly of the voters as sheep sleepwalking to the polls. And, despite the size of his personal victory, even Davis didn't enjoy the election. He was exhausted rather than exhilarated and told his closest advisers that he would not run again. The Tories settled in to govern with 70 seats, while Smith's Liberals stood still at 34 and the New Democrats, under Lewis's plodding successor, Michael Cassidy, dropped sharply to 21. Davis had his majority, but it was a victory won in a climate of public apathy. Only 58 per cent of Ontario voters had bothered to take part in the March 19 ballot. The Tories understood the danger, although they pretended the mood was one of contentment, rather than indifference.

Around Davis, after the mad dash for a majority, there was

a sense that he'd achieved the goal and couldn't imagine what to do next. The legislature lost its excitement. With a seventy-seat Tory majority, there was no possibility of a political upset – even should the Opposition combine, as it had only occasionally dared to do during the six previous years of minority government. When New Democrat or Liberal MPPs protested their inability to use the committees or the legislature to press issues, Davis repeatedly reminded them in the House that "the realities of March 19" had freed him from the trammels of the Opposition. The beaming faces on the crowded Tory benches provoked cries from the Liberal and NDP seats against the bland self-satisfaction of the government. But Davis, rising in his seat, held out his arms as if to embrace his majority and crowed, "Bland works."

Behind the monolithic façade of majority, however, there was trouble brewing in Tory ranks. The public got the first glimpses of that in the fall of 1981 when the premier decided to pump $650 million into a minority interest in Suncor Incorporated, the Canadian subsidiary of the Sun Company of Radnor, Pennsylvania. What was revealed was the growing separation between Davis and his cabinet, his caucus, and the party rank-and-file as he relied more and more on the advice of an inner circle of unelected advisers to make major decisions. The debate over Suncor turned a spotlight on the yawning split between the conservatism of small-town Ontario and the urban Red Toryism of the Davis clique, which was apparently oblivious to its own isolation.

Despite deep recession and tight budgets, Davis had been secretly shopping for an oil company partner for a year. The search began after Hugh Segal, who had good connections with the federal Liberals, saw some research prepared for the prime minister's office by Liberal pollster Martin Goldfarb. The attitude survey explained the difficulties Joe Clark's short-lived Conservative government suffered over its plan to sell off Petro-Canada. The federally owned oil company was immensely popular. The string of Petro-Canada gas stations with their red-maple-leaf credit cards was good advertising for the re-elected Trudeau government which ousted Clark in early 1980: the demand for credit cards had exceeded expectations, and thousands of Canadians were on the waiting-list. Segal, the exuberant idea man of Davis's court, dreamed of Tory-blue gas stations, of road signs and credit cards emblazoned with the Ontario trillium, and station attendants outfitted in blue and white.

Segal and Eddie Goodman also wanted to make Ontario a major player in the national energy game. World oil shortages in the 1970s had swung economic power west. As Alberta's Conservative government under Peter Lougheed warred with Prime Minister Pierre Trudeau over oil pricing and the national energy program, Ontario found itself on the sidelines. In western newspaper editorials and cartoons, Davis was pilloried as the smug premier of a fat-cat province which had exploited western resources in the past and persisted in demanding low prices for western oil when the world price was sky-high. Segal and Eddie Goodman convinced Davis that Ontario could get along better with the oil barons by becoming one of them. Ontario, in effect, would buy a place at the table with the other big-stakes players in the oil game.

Ontario's search for an oil company purchase was dubbed Project Phoenix, a hush-hush affair known only to a half-dozen people. Goodman originally pushed for an Ontario investment in Gulf Canada. The idea appealed to his Canadian nationalism, and, at the time, to a shrewd expectation of big profits. But the Gulf purchase didn't materialize. Other companies were considered but didn't meet Segal's, and by now Davis's, top criterion of a string of gas stations which could bear this Ontario trillium. Little did they know that by the time they settled on Suncor, the oil market would be on the verge of a crash.

To Davis and Segal, Suncor looked like a winner. The Sun Company of Radnor, Pennsylvania, of which Suncor was the Canadian subsidiary, needed Canadian partners before it could take advantage of national energy-program incentives for arctic tar-sands exploration and development. Satisfying the partisan political requirement for trillium retail outlets, Suncor also owned 553 Sunoco gas stations in Ontario and another 339 in Quebec. Days before the public announcement, treasurer Frank Miller and industry minister Larry Grossman were informed of the plan. Ontario would purchase 25 per cent of Suncor shares for $650 million. Miller's private-enterprise philosophy and his treasurer's thrift were so offended that he considered resignation. His advice to back out was ignored. Larry Grossman warned that the expenditure was too big in relation to the expected political gain, but he too was ignored.

On October 13, 1981, Davis stunned his cabinet, his caucus, and the legislature in quick succession with the news of the Suncor purchase. He said Sun Company would quickly find other private Canadian partners and raise Canadian ownership in the company to 51 per cent. But the plan for majority control, and with it the blue trillium propaganda scheme, soon collapsed. The private companies with whom the government had been negotiating – Noranda Mines Limited and Hiram Walker Resources Limited – backed out because the price was too steep.

Meanwhile, Davis resorted to closure to force the legislature to approve the purchase, overriding Opposition objections that the money would be better spent on social programs, and ignoring rumblings in the normally docile Conservative back bench. Davis said the Suncor shares were a good long-term investment that gave Ontario a window on the western oil patch, and partnership in the national energy program. Instead, the investment quickly became a liability: it didn't make Ontario an influential oil player, and the failure to find other Canadian partners meant it contributed little to Canadianizing a key resource.

The Suncor debacle didn't excite public opinion greatly, but it sparked real anger among grass-roots Conservatives. That became clear when the party met at its first policy conference in many years on October 24 and 25, 1981, at the Holiday Inn in London, Ontario. Party president David McFadden had argued that party members, who had worked hard in the March 19 election, deserved a voice in the formation of party policy. Meeting in private caucuses, the

350 riding delegates churned out recommendations on energy policy and the economy. The media quickly tuned in to the sour mutterings of rural and small-business conservatives who believed in free enterprise and minimum government. Many of them disapproved strongly of the government meddling in the private sector that the Suncor purchase represented. They were the same people who, the next month, were to be offended again by the sight of their Ontario Conservative premier hand in glove with a Liberal prime minister as Davis and Trudeau wrung the constitutional accord from the other provinces. In the Tory-blue reaches of his party, Davis got little credit for what he regarded as his crowning achievement. The right-wingers felt that their premier was getting much too pink.

The most militant among them were the campus youth, greatly agitated by labour minister Robert Elgie's Bill 7 amendments to the Human Rights Code, giving human-rights officers broader powers to investigate and settle workplace and accommodation disputes arising from racial, religious, or sex discrimination. "What does the social activism of this Bill have to do with a Conservative or Progressive Conservative philosophy?" the youth demanded in a flyer distributed at the meeting. "Can you sell this Bill to the voters in your riding? Do you want to?"

Bill 7 offended party sensibilities – as did Suncor and as would the constitutional partnership with Trudeau – but these were just lightning-rods to a deeper, emotional discontent. Many in the Tory hard core felt that what they represented, and valued, was being pushed aside for trendy liberalism. In fact, it was. The Davis Conservatives believed, probably correctly, that the right-wing drift of their party core would quickly destroy the government if allowed free rein. "The Conservative party survived in the 1970s and early 1980s because Bill Davis was not a small-c conservative," Hugh Segal has argued. "If he had been, we'd have been off the radar screens."

But whatever the political justification, the right-wingers found Red Toryism hard to swallow. The rank-and-filers said bitterly that their toil and votes were accepted but their views ignored by Davis, who closed himself off at his Tuesday-morning breakfasts with Toronto admen and pollsters who rode high on the party's back. The resentment focussed on Segal and Norman Atkins. At about this time, Segal left the premier's office to head a subsidiary of Camp Advertising called Advance Planning Limited. Camp Advertising, led by Atkins, annually won the Ontario tourism account and other major government contracts. Advance Planning provided consulting services to the government and was on contract for the Ontario Bicentennial celebration. It was widely believed in the party that Atkins became wealthy through the government contracts. In fact, he is not a millionaire and often contends he would have been a richer man if he'd devoted more time to business and less to Ontario politics. Still, his influence in the party excited widespread envy.

To close the policy conference in London, the premier brought in Allan Gregg, of Decima Research, the party pollster who'd helped him to his victory in 1981. Gregg, flamboyant and long-haired, and wearing one gold earring, presented an unsettling message. With a slide show of charts on demographic and public-opinion trends, he lectured the largely white, largely middle-aged, Protestant, and Anglo audience on the growing ethnic diversity of the province, the surge of women entering the work force, and the dangers of straying from the political middle. Bill Davis had been achieving a careful balance between the competing interests of old and new Ontario – and by doing so kept the Tories in power. Davis himself pleaded with the delegates to ignore the siren call of the new neo-Conservative ideology: "Let's not be caught up in theology that is counterproductive and leads us away from our responsibilities to all the people. . . . Progressive Conservatives in Ontario are not the same as the Conservative Party of England or the Republican Party in the United States." If party workers wanted to go on winning elections, he warned, they'd better not expect their leader to become a Margaret Thatcher or a Ronald Reagan.

In the chatter of the backrooms, the premier's press secretary, Sally Barnes, referred to the pro-Reagan youth as "little Hitlers". For their part, the youth knew that the senior bosses of the party held them in contempt, and responded with defiant offers of jellybeans – Reagan's favourite candy. The discontented youth wing and its right-wing elders were in no position to challenge Davis openly, however. His election victories had given him mastery of the party, forcing party members to swallow resentments that were personal as well as ideological. For, despite his strengths as a political leader – his reassuring style and his ability to project himself as a man of decency and human values – Davis lacked the personal touch. He could greet people by name in all corners of the province, but he always kept a distance. An associate as close as Segal only once called him "Bill", and deduced from the ensuing icy silence that he'd better stick to "Mr. Premier". Only old contemporaries like Atkins dared familiarity, and that not often.

Davis left the operations of the party to his lieutenants. It was typical that he arrived late at the London policy meeting and spoke from the platform, rather than table-hopping as Larry Grossman did, shaking hands with all and sundry. The premier preferred the regal style, sweeping into meetings in the centre of an entourage, strobe lights flashing and music pounding. Like bland, it worked.

Davis had inherited a badly organized party in 1971 when he'd discovered to his dismay that Robarts' neglect of Frost's old party network had allowed local riding associations to collapse. Still, the popularity Davis built in his first few months of action as a new premier, the momentum of the newly hatched Big Blue Machine, the focus on leadership, the massive advertising, and the media concentration on his central campaign overcame the lack of proper grass-roots organization. The poor state of the Conservative party organization wasn't really revealed until 1975, when party demoralization, public doubts, and economic malaise plunged Davis into the minority years. Party organizer Ross de Geer, aware that constituency organizations were moribund, had assigned David McFadden, then fifth vice-president, to investigate and then to head a committee to rebuild the party. The party hired a staff of permanent field organizers and mounted campaign schools for local party executives, putting stress on poll and canvass organization. By 1981, the organizational resurrection paid off. In 1975 no more than 10 per cent of the provincial ridings had been totally canvassed by Conservative workers. In 1981, the Tories were out doing door-to-door canvassing in every constituency.

But while the party had changed its style, Davis hadn't. In 1981, he again ran a highly advertised leader's campaign, an "umbrella" campaign in which everything focussed on him. At Decima Research, pollster Allan Gregg churned out the daily tracking data which enabled Davis to pitch his policy announcements, and his handouts, to precisely chosen targets. This centrally controlled campaign, a triumph of organization and technology, left the party $3.6 million in debt. It also left the people who'd done so much of the constituency donkey-work feeling left out, as became apparent at the London conference.

In the fall of 1983, McFadden called a second membership policy conference, this time at Toronto's Skyline Hotel. There were few contentious issues: the government was tired, and anxious to avoid a repeat of the internal wrangle of 1981. There was no reason to expect one. Although the rank-and-file felt rebuffed by the fact the government had pursued Suncor, its anger had, in fact, dampened the progressive impulses within the party. McFadden, still anxious to improve internal relations, told Davis's office to be sure the premier was there to take part in the deliberations. Once again, Davis showed briefly to deliver a prepared text and then departed. To many delegates, it appeared that the leader wasn't interested in their opinions. The resentment against the Davis inner circle was to fester and become, in 1985, a crusade by the party's small-town roots to oust the Big Blue Machine.

As long as Davis remained unambiguously committed to leading his party, its internal divisions likely would have remained underground. But, in the spring of 1983, Davis began flirting with the notion of a run for the national leadership of the Progressive Conservative party. This interlude was bizarre, not because the experienced and popular Ontario leader wanted a chance to be prime minister of Canada, but because he paraded his dilemma in a prolonged, public, agonizing way. Davis became "Willy or Won't He" to the media.

The temptation was strong. Davis thought that pulling together the fractious national party and giving it responsible, moderate leadership was a task he would do rather well. Unfortunately, he spoke no French, had been condemned in Quebec for his refusal to make Ontario officially bilingual, and in much of Western Canada was disliked for denying the producing region the benefit of high world-oil prices. Also, certain federal Conservatives still weren't ready to forgive him for undermining Prime Minister Joe Clark in the 1980 election by opposing Clark's proposed gas-tax increases.

The Big Blue Machiners thought these disabilities could be overcome. The federal party, disappointed by Clark's failure to hold on to power, wanted a winner. Davis was a proven winner, and an experienced manager of government. Richard Hatfield of New Brunswick would support him, as would a small group of Quebecers led by Marcel Masse. Hugh Segal had scouted B.C. premier Bill Bennett and Saskatchewan's Grant Devine and hoped they would be positive, or at worst neutral. Ontario's delegates had been picked over by the other candidates, but party leaders thought at least fifty per cent would vote for Davis. Atkins and Segal insisted that though there was no guarantee of winning, Davis had a strong chance.

The premier's old friend Eddie Goodman disagreed with that assessment, however, and threw all his prestige against the candidacy, determined to spare Davis the humiliation of defeat. On May 3, 1984, the day Davis was to decide, Goodman drove to the premier's yellow-brick Brampton home a couple of hours earlier than the hawks in the Davis crowd, took him aside for a private chat, and told him to stay put in Ontario. Goodman said it was finally time for Davis to have a private life. If he ran for the federal leadership, Goodman advised, he probably wouldn't win, and such a setback at the end of a long, successful career would be an awful blow. To support his dismaying analysis, Goodman had brought ammunition with him: a poll taken for him by Michael Adams of Environics Research Group and paid for by the Ontario Conservative party. The poll said Davis would get almost no votes from western delegates and few in Quebec. He was likely to place third or even fourth behind Joe Clark, Brian Mulroney, and John Crosbie.

Shortly after, the rest of Davis's confidants – Segal, Atkins, Tory, Kelly, and a handful of others – arrived in the rain at Davis's home, and were shown into the "rec" room. Atkins and Segal were infuriated by the poll results. They felt its findings were deceptive because the poll didn't show second-ballot choices and the kind of strength Davis might develop as other contenders dropped. Michael Adams' figures made a strong impression on Davis, however, and Norman Atkins has never fully forgiven Eddie Goodman, formerly a close friend, for commissioning the poll which helped keep Davis out of federal politics.

Goodman's view was corroborated by a private telephone conversation between Davis and Grant Devine, Saskatchewan's Tory premier. Davis already knew that Alberta's Peter Lough-eed was hostile to his candidacy because of Davis's opposition to higher prices for Albertan oil. William Kelly, Davis's long-time fund-raiser and head of an Arctic gas-exploration com-pany, and Ontario party president David McFadden, both men with strong contacts in Alberta, were still hoping to change Lougheed's mind. That week, McFadden had called Lougheed's chief of staff, Bob Giffen, in New York to ask whether there was room for hope. Giffen said that there wasn't, and that a Davis candidacy could divide the federal party. To be certain, Kelly and McFadden had chartered a private plane and were ready to make a final pitch to Lougheed over breakfast in Washington the next morning.

But, as they sat in Davis's downstairs recreation room, it became clear the plane wasn't needed. Davis said that Devine's attitude was the touchstone for his decision, and that during their telephone call, Devine had indicated he was no longer prepared to go against Lougheed. Devine, too, would oppose Davis if he ran for the national leadership.

Aside from the numbers, other factors weighed in the balance. Davis was hurt by the suggestions his candidacy would be divisive. He'd been reluctant to challenge Clark because he'd long made loyalty to the leader a virtue in his own wing of the party. He knew his wife, Kathleen, would support him, but she wouldn't really enjoy moving to Ottawa. And his absentee parenting of five children nagged his conscience. His children were mostly grown now, but he wanted to be a better grandfather than he'd been a father. Davis told the men who'd been drumming up support for him to turn it off – they had no candidate.

The next day, Davis told a news conference that he'd decided his candidacy would be divisive, and he would not run. He seemed sincere when he said cheerfully that his life was in Ontario.

A couple of weeks later, however, at a private dinner with supporters at the Albany Club, Davis was suddenly overcome by his emotions. The Albany Club on King Street in downtown Toronto was the home-away-from-home for the Red Tory crowd, and was full of memories for Davis of his years of victory. He began to weep, and continued to do so openly through large parts of his speech in which he thanked the men who had supported his federal hopes. Several of his guests said later they were stunned by the premier's display of feeling, because they hadn't realized until then how desperately Davis had wanted the national leadership. From that moment, Opposition MPPs at Queen's Park began saying that the life had gone out of Bill Davis – that he was operating on automatic. The premier became increasingly remote, and policy initiatives were on hold.

The Big Blue Machiners who'd been working so hard to persuade Davis to go national were understandably deflated. But the effects spread beyond the inner circle. The whole provincial party, held on standby in case Davis decided to run, now found itself out of the main game, its leader rejected.

The Ontario Tory dynasty had no candidate acceptable to the rest of the country at a time when the federal government was within Conservative grasp. As provincial party leaders and workers dispersed to support several different federal candidates, the ties that bound them to Davis and the Big Blue Machine were loosened.

More significantly, Davis's prolonged flirtation with the federal leadership had fanned the hopes of his would-be successors. For some years, Larry Grossman, Gordon Walker, Dennis Timbrell, and Frank Miller had been jockeying for position by forming their own organizations and building support across the province. At the party's 1982 general meeting, the unofficial candidates paraded their stuff for the party like a bevy of beauty contestants. The election of party officers became a struggle to see who could put most adherents on the executive. Frank Miller claimed victory by a slim margin.

When it appeared Davis might leave in 1983, the rivalry became intense. Davis, in fact, took another year and a half to resign, and in the interval everyone around Queen's Park, including the media, made sport of the activities of the pretenders. When Frank Miller decided to give up his ambitions that fall, he confessed to reporters that the circumstances were ludicrous. "How," he asked, "do you drop out of a race that doesn't exist?"

Miller's decision did little to reduce party tensions. His key workers simply offered their services to Dennis Timbrell, and the unofficial race simmered on. Most right-wingers who had clustered around London's Gordon Walker until he ruined his own chances by running too openly, and then around Miller, now focussed their hopes on Timbrell. He became the standard-bearer for all who felt slighted over the years by Davis's powerful inner circle. Meanwhile, the Big Blue Machine types remained hopeful that Davis would go one more election. If that was not to be, they inclined to Larry Grossman or Roy McMurtry. Davis periodically moved to squelch the pretenders. The confidants who carried his messages were received with bitterness by Millerites who felt Davis closed his eyes to the organizing activities of others while clamping down on their man Frank. What had been one party – a patchwork coalition of right-wing Conservatives, moderate Tories of the Davis ilk, and many who were really Liberals but gravitated to the party in power – became an internally warring camp.

Davis kept on publicly insisting the divisions were largely figments of the press's imagination. But he too was affected by the internal wars. They explain why he waited so late before announcing his separate-school-funding decision, and told no one, keeping even education minister Bette Stephenson out of the game until the last moment. His key advisers worried about the restlessness in Tory ranks. Goodman and Segal felt there were two huge outstanding issues on the Davis agenda – official bilingualism and full funding for Catholic schools – but they warned Davis he could only hope to get away with one without stirring outright rebellion at the local level. Davis procrastinated out of worry, and simply because glacially slow decision-making was his style.

In his biography *Bill Davis*, published by Methuen in 1985, *Toronto Sun* columnist Clare Hoy offered a stark version of what happened behind the scenes to impel Davis to reverse his position on Roman Catholic school funding. Hoy said that, after the election of 1981, Davis gave his word to Emmett Cardinal Carter, Roman Catholic Archbishop of Toronto, that he would extend tax funding to the senior grades of the Catholic system before the next election. Roman Catholic bishops had been making the request for additional money in twice-yearly private meetings with Davis ever since his 1971 rejection of their demand. The province was already financing Catholic schools to the end of Grade Ten, in accordance with special constitutional rights acquired at the founding of the nation more than a century before.

In 1863, the Scott Act guaranteed minority education rights as they then existed in Canada West (Ontario), and the British North America Act of 1867 reaffirmed those rights. Basically, that meant both Protestants and Roman Catholics had the right to public support for their elementary schools. Grades Nine and Ten later became part of the court-approved understandings, but in Catholic schools, these two grades were funded at a lower level than in the public high schools. What Hoy says that Davis promised to Carter was full funding for all five grades of Catholic high schools. However, says Hoy, when Davis mentioned his promise at a strategy meeting in May 1984, called to contemplate a snap election that year, his political advisers were thunderstruck. The idea of heading into an election with such a controversial issue hanging over their heads horrified them, and they told Davis to explain to Cardinal Carter that once again he'd have to wait at least until after the vote. Carter, however, insisted Davis keep the original deal, threatening opposition from Catholic pulpits during an election if he reneged. Davis, Hoy says, then dropped the idea of an early summer election and the next month announced the extension of separate-school funding.

Davis has since vehemently denied having any deal with Carter or being threatened by him. At a September 20, 1985, hearing of the legislative committee studying Catholic school funding, Davis testified he'd acted on the basis of conscience. "The Cardinal never threatened the first minister of this province," he insisted. Davis said his 1971 pre-election decision not to extend full funding to Catholic schools had bothered him ever since. In a statement against full funding written for him by Dalton Camp, Davis had argued: "We would inevitably be obliged to proceed throughout all our educational institutions; to fragment and divide both our young people and our resources, from kindergarten through post-graduate university studies." Looking back, Davis told the committee: "I believed in what I said at the time, but I was never totally comfortable with the position I had taken." At the time, Carter, then a bishop, wrote to the premier expressing deep distress and disappointment at the decision, because he felt he and Davis had had an understanding that funding would proceed. Once the 1971 election was over, the Church renewed its demands, but in private. Carter and Davis formed a relationship of mutual respect and liking in those private dialogues, and Carter became a regular fixture at Conservative party functions, giving his blessing from the head table.

These public signs of harmony reflected growing under-standing between the two men. When Davis says there was no deal, it's probable that there was never any explicit promise. But Carter had come to know Davis well, to understand the naggings of his conscience, and to feel that the premier would eventually set an old wrong right. Carter and Davis, and later principal secretary John Tory, were alone with the secret, however. Only a few in the premier's inner circle favoured Catholic funding – among them cabinet ministers Tom Wells and Roy McMurtry. The rest were either violently opposed, like Eddie Goodman, Hugh Segal, education minister Bette Stephenson, and Ed Stewart, or neutral in the fashion of Larry Grossman, willing to follow the premier's lead.

From time to time, Davis hinted to his cabinet they'd have to face the issue some day. With a few ministers – one of them Frank Miller – the premier held private discussions and urged them to prepare to defend a future change in policy. And at that May 1984 strategy meeting, where Davis discussed, and eventually rejected, an early-summer election, he warned his top campaign organizers that separate-school funding was coming and would be an issue percolating when the govern-ment went to the people.

In early 1984, a Goldfarb poll prepared for the cabinet office showed that for the first time more than half the citizenry supported extension of full funding to Catholic schools. Decima Research was also monitoring the issue, and reported to Davis that more than sixty per cent of the public would accept extended funding, although Protestant opinion was evenly split. The figures were improving, but it was clear that, by extending funding, Davis risked angering large numbers of voters and offending the core of his own party. Still, he felt that the short-term risk had diminished greatly since 1971 and was outweighed by potential long-term political gains. Failure to fully fund the schools was a continuing irritant in relations between the Conservatives and the Catholic community, which by then had grown to represent more than one-third of the entire electorate. More important, the Catholics constituted a strong majority in certain west-end Toronto ethnic ridings where both Liberals and New Democrats did well and the Tories were stymied. By extending funding to Catholic schools, Davis hoped to change the image of his party and break down barriers between it and other cultural communities.

In November 1981, the Roman Catholic bishops of Ontario had presented Davis with a formal brief on the question of funding for separate high schools. Davis feared the public response if the brief were released to the media and the issue were opened for widespread debate. He asked Carter and the bishops to keep the brief private for three months, and promised "constructive consideration" of their request when he met with them again.

Naturally, with Davis "consideration" took time, but by early 1984, the bishops felt an announcement was pending. Davis knew that either he or his successor would be calling an election in late 1984 or 1985, and that failure to live up to his commitment to the bishops would force them to go public with an issue that could split communities in an election. Davis didn't want Catholic demonstrators harrying his party at election events across the province. Then, too, Davis was convinced that the separate-school system was thriving and would go on growing – which meant every year that passed put a burden on more Catholic parents.

In April, during his annual dinner with the bishops, Davis indirectly acknowledged he was ready to move by saying that there were several intricate problems related to funding that now required solution: protection for teachers who were laid off in the public system; the degree of access for non-Catholic students; whether religious education would be compulsory for non-Catholic students attending Catholic schools; and the transfer of school buildings and property. Subsequently, on Davis's behalf, John Tory held a series of meetings with Catholic bishops and officials in the education ministry on these topics. Davis himself talked many times to Carter to ensure that the legislation would be acceptable to the Catholic Church.

As the announcement date drew closer, Joan Walters, who had succeeded Sally Barnes as the premier's press secretary, became aware of what was afoot, and wanted to leak it. She felt that by breaking the news without preparing the cabinet, the caucus, or the public, Davis risked a backlash. Davis, however, believed the decision was so important it had to be presented and explained in his own words – a fait accompli. By the time he finally made the announcement, on June 12, 1984, it came too late to allow for the preparation and passage of legislation in the fall session. Had Davis been ready even a month earlier, he could have defended and passed the new law himself – instead of bequeathing it to a successor who was uncomfortable with the change and therefore not credible defending it.

As with the Suncor decision, Davis did not invest the time and energy to win the support of his own party. When he broke the news to cabinet, hours before the announcement, only eastern Ontario's Norman Sterling dared to disagree, and to insist that his opposition be officially recorded in the cabinet minutes. Most members of cabinet and caucus were dubious, but hid their feelings. Caucus, indeed, gave Davis a standing ovation.

The premier may have been lulled by their apparent acquiescence, and by the absence of any immediate public outcry. There was no sign of backlash during the five by-elections that autumn. Indeed, private polling by Decima Research in the fall put Davis's government at fifty-three per cent, more popular than at any time in more than a decade. The poll showed that Davis's announcement had broken the Catholic community's historic allegiance to the Liberals, and indicated that the Conservatives could expect a significant increase in support from Catholic voters. Larry Grossman says now that during the fall the Conservatives were the victims of their own success. They appeared to be doing so well that they assumed the sailing ahead would be smooth.

Segal was less sanguine. In the final days before Davis retired, he argued vehemently that the conservative-liberal coalition that had governed Ontario for so long was coming unstuck. With the addition of the separate-school decision, he saw a recipe for disaster. In his view, only Davis's personal popularity – his association with smooth management of the issues – stood between the Conservatives and potential political losses.

Davis was shaken by the vehemence of the protests from Segal and then from his cabinet associates when he finally made his retirement intentions known. Many Tories understood after the 1981 election that he didn't intend to run again. But when Davis left his decision so late, they thought he'd changed his mind. Surely he wouldn't deny the party his enormous popularity at the last moment?

Norman Atkins, chief engineer of the Big Blue Machine, had been spending most of his time in Ottawa, where he'd just assisted Brian Mulroney to a smashing national election victory. With his attention thus diverted, Atkins didn't realize his old friend Bill Davis was thinking about pulling out of politics. Hugh Segal, Atkins' partner, was left home to mind their mutual interests in advertising and provincial politics. Segal had pounded the party drums furiously for a fall election, knowing that that would make it impossible for Davis to retire. Much of the party, however, was reluctant to rally to Segal's call. Ontario Tories had been through a federal leadership contest and a federal election. They were tired, and for those who didn't know what was bothering Segal there was no obvious reason to be stampeding Ontario to the polls during the harvest season.

As we have seen, Davis's oldest friends – Eddie Goodman, William Kelly, and Hugh Macaulay – supported his retirement decision. This trio believed Davis owed nothing to any but himself, and should retire at his peak. However, when the *Star* signalled the premier's impending departure, Davis found himself under siege from a frantic party. In cabinet, horrified ministers suddenly faced a next election in which their chances were greatly lowered if Davis were no longer at the helm. Led by intergovernmental affairs minister Tom Wells, a handsome white-haired veteran from Scarborough, and by craggy George McCague from Durham, chairman of management board, the cabinet members in turn begged Davis to stay, if only for the election. This became the question over which Davis agonized until the last moment before his public announcement. Segal, in particular, argued there was nothing wrong with his winning the election and then retiring. But Davis replied that the first thing the media would ask him, should he announce an election, would be how long he personally intended to stay. And, although Davis possessed an unmatched ability to waltz, jig, sidestep, and mislead and evade reporters, he was not in the habit of telling lies.

Treasurer Larry Grossman followed Davis out of the October 8 cabinet meeting and into the premier's private office to urge Davis to stay on awhile. Grossman's reasons, like those of other cabinet ministers who urged him to stay, were selfish. Grossman didn't believe he could win the leadership without more time to prepare. He needed another year as treasurer, proving he could be a frugal manager, to win the respect of Conservatives who regarded him as a free-spending Red Tory. And he needed at least another year to build a campaign organization to rival what Dennis Timbrell already had in the field. Grossman asked Davis to stay through the election, promising that he and other key ministers would thereafter carry the government. Davis replied simply that he was too tired. He had seen and done it all and he wanted out.

Yet, even after his frank talk with Grossman, Davis continued to waver. His wife, Kathleen, found that the retirement decision they'd discussed together for long months was coming unstuck. The premier, preserving his options to the end, told his principal secretary, John Tory, to prepare two press statements, one announcing retirement and the other calling an election.

Davis was worried about the state of the Conservative party. In the three years since the 1981 election, Kelly had failed to clear away the debt. He and Davis had been unwilling to take the political flak for the obvious solution: an amendment to the decade-old Election Financing Act to increase the $4,000 limit on contributions from wealthy individuals and corporate supporters. Also, the Big Blue Machine had become complacent about its grip on power, and didn't regard fund-raising as an urgent problem. Few contemplated what a burden the party's debt, now $2.8 million, would prove if the Conservatives failed to return to office after an election.

Davis was less concerned about the debt than about the ossification the debt implied – the lack of new members, new partisans, new donors. Davis hoped his retirement would bring a breath of fresh air to the organization. Certainly a new leader would have a freer hand to bring new faces into cabinet. Davis himself was very reluctant to face another cabinet shuffle. Many of his ministers were old associates – people like Bette Stephenson, Frank Drea, and Robert Welch – to whom a new premier would not owe the same debt of loyalty. Davis found the strong emotions aroused by cabinet demotions difficult to handle. He had been deeply unhappy, for example, about criticism of his previous decision to drop Doug Wiseman of Lanark from his cabinet. Newspaper stories said Wiseman, a prudent right-winger, had been sacrificed after he clashed over the letting of contracts with his high-spending deputy, Alan Gordon, who just happened to be an old member of Davis's staff in the cabinet office. Davis always denied he had chosen the bureaucrat over the politician. He had other reasons, which he refused to spell out because he detested giving personal hurt. Now he didn't want to face dropping ministers again.

In the end, during Thanksgiving weekend with his family at their cottage on Townsend Island in Georgian Bay, Davis decided he could not face another four years in office. He rejected the cynical notion that he should use his popularity to win a personal mandate from the people and then hand power to another. John Tory called, and the premier instructed him to make the arrangements for his retirement announcement the next day. He later gave the same instructions to his deputy, Ed Stewart.

It was all very untidy. When Davis resigned, the Ordersin-Council had already been prepared for an election call. Davis's procrastination misled even party president David McFadden, who was at headquarters on Dundas Street preparing for yet another election warm-up school when Tory called to say a resignation letter was on the way. Davis himself had no idea what he would do next. His personal staff members, like John Tory and Ed Stewart, had planned to move on, but in the uncertainty they stuck by loyally, and now were left to the mercies of the next premier. Frank Miller, who had stepped out of the leadership race and dismantled his team, suddenly had to decide whether he could resurrect his candidacy.

After resigning, Davis had made some provisions to smooth the transition. In the four months before a new leader would be chosen, he called five by-elections to replace four Liberals and one New Democrat who had contested the summer's federal election rather than continue the hopeless battle against an invulnerable provincial machine. With the by-elections over, his successor wouldn't have to face immediate tests before the people unless he chose to do so. The premier also promised to announce provincial transfer payments for 1985 to the hospitals, school boards, universities, and municipalities, whose annual needs account for seventy per cent of the provincial budget. However, Davis reminded ministers in a memo to pare the transfer payments to the bone, because otherwise his successor could face possible loss of the province's Triple-A credit rating. The memo fell into the hands of the media – and so did the story of a hitherto secret trip which Davis and Grossman had made in August to persuade Standard and Poor's, the big New York bond-rating house, to maintain the credit rating. Davis and Grossman had promised strict restraint and a reduction in the provincial deficit. In the ensuing debate about whether a New York credit house or the legislature should decide Ontario's payments to hospitals and schools, Davis reached another characteristic non-decision. He would let the school boards and other institutions proceed into 1985 without knowing their revenues, and leave the task of telling them – somewhere down the road – to his successor.

It is impossible, of course, for any premier, or prime minister, to retire without leaving some political trouble in his wake. And Davis, retiring at his peak, also left his party some substantial assets. The provincial economy was on the verge of a sustained recovery, which augured well for a leadership transition. He had maintained reasonably intact the Tory reputation for sound management of the provincial economy. His own reputation for personal decency had submerged memories of past scandals. The by-elections, held before his official stepping-down, in which the Tories gained one seat and the Liberals lost two, gave no indication that the government was in trouble.

The Opposition appeared to pose no threat. David Peterson seemed weak and without profile, and Bob Rae was deemed too young, cold, and wedded to unpopular union causes. Realistically, the Tories knew their remarkable strength in the polls would slip with a new, untried leader and once an election was under way. They knew, too, that having a Conservative rather than a Liberal government in Ottawa was going to hurt, since many voters don't like to have all their eggs in one party's basket.

Nobody, and certainly not Davis, foresaw the extent of the Tory slide. The Davis legacy contained the seeds of trouble. It took a complacent leadership convention, and bungling by the chosen successor, to bring them to full flower.

2

Frank Miller Wins – and Loses

Frank Miller kicked off the race to succeed Bill Davis two weeks after the premier's Thanksgiving announcement – and immediately took the lead. He was a candid, intelligent, experienced politician, and former treasurer of the province, and he spoke utilitarian French learned on the job in Quebec. He was a serviceable candidate for the premiership, well liked and good-humoured. Still, he was hardly political dynamite. He was fifty-seven years old, had suffered a major heart attack, was often lost in the crowd because he was small in stature – at five feet seven inches barely a half-inch above his rival Larry Grossman – was pale of complexion, and had an unruly tongue that periodically uttered outdated views.

Miller's handlers tried to curb his habit of saying what he thought. Miller told reporters that his campaign managers "chewed me out" early in the campaign for identifying himself as a right-winger, so now he was calling himself a small-c conservative. "They said I was speaking more from the heart than is wise," Miller unwisely told the press. His managers tore their hair, but Miller could only keep to a script so long. He was frank to a fault.

However, this didn't much worry his party, because most Tory delegates assumed whomever they chose was an automatic winner. The new premier didn't have to have charisma, because neither of the Opposition parties looked sufficiently threatening to be taken seriously. Since the real struggle for power was within the Ontario Progressive Conservative party itself, the delegates paid little heed to public polls showing that Ontario preferred the other contenders, Larry Grossman or Roy McMurtry or Dennis Timbrell. They were absorbed in choosing a leader who best reflected their vision of Conservatism – and that was Frank Miller.

The party rank-and-filers at last had a chance to express their will. This time they didn't have to march the middle road. They didn't have to stand by while slick Toronto pollsters told them how to win. In the previous two years they'd helped dump pink Tory Joe Clark and put Brian Mulroney, who then appeared more right-wing, into power in Ottawa. In the United States and in Britain, Ronald Reagan and Margaret Thatcher had established durable, successful right-wing administrations. A neo-Conservative tide appeared to be sweeping the western democracies, and the hard-core of the Ontario Tory party felt now it could safely afford to choose a leader close to its own heart.

Miller appealed to large sections of the party that had felt unappreciated during the Davis years. Miller himself, although he had held major cabinet posts, had never really made it into the inner Tory circle at Queen's Park, and his feeling of exclusion rankled. He was right-wing and small-town, but there was something more indefinable that kept him from belonging. Unlike Davis – or for that matter David Peterson and Bob Rae – Miller didn't regard political office as part of his birthright. He was the son of a tool-and-die maker who had died when Miller was a boy. His mother then moved her family of five from west-end Toronto back to her native Gravenhurst. Miller won a scholarship to McGill University, took a degree in chemical engineering, worked for the Aluminum Company in Arvida, Quebec, but then moved restlessly through a series of jobs, teaching at St. Andrew's College in Aurora, and running a branch company in Montreal and a General Motors car dealership in Bracebridge. He was operating Patterson-Kaye and Tamwood tourist lodges when he first ran for the legislature in 1971 and became MPP for Muskoka.

During his first days in the provincial Chamber, Miller listened to Bob Nixon talk about his father, the former premier, and Stephen Lewis boast about his father, David Lewis, then leader of the federal NDP. Miller rose and allowed that he had no political background. "My father died when I was thirteen. I do not recall him telling me which party he supported. So, unlike the other two, I was able to choose the right one." But, although he made a joke of it, he later repeated the same jest so often that it was obvious he was galled by pedigrees. Miller liked to relate his life experiences as a Horatio Alger rags-to-riches story. He held a deep belief that anyone with brains who works hard can achieve power in America, a point of view that made his eventual failure to stay at the pinnacle all the harder to bear.

Miller came into politics an unvarnished free-enterpriser, but as a member of the Davis cabinet he soon learned the politics of pragmatism. When he became health minister in 1975, Davis wanted him to curb the growth of the health-care system and cut costs. Miller and his ministry bureaucrats came up with a plan to close some smaller hospitals and concentrate hospital services in larger centres. Miller sold the cabinet on the general idea, but when it came to closing actual hospitals, he found himself fighting his colleagues as well as the public. The cabinet found there were too many local votes at stake and withdrew support. Miller suffered a heart attack during that stressful battle, and he learned that what appears rational may be lousy politics. Miller often said this was one of his stiffest lessons in compromise.

In the succeeding years under Davis, he often had to swallow his principles. He came closest to resigning over the Suncor purchase, which offended him because, in his view, government had no business doing the job of the private sector. Miller let his criticism leak to the media, which seemed unwise and indiscreet. But, even in 1981, he was already anticipating the premier's departure and fostering right-wing support for an eventual run at the leadership of the party.

Three years later, when Davis finally took his exit, Miller's genial nature, his straight-shooter style, and his right-wing philosophy, quickly won the support of the majority of cabinet. Nearly all the right-wingers, led by education minister Bette

Stephenson and housing minister Claude Bennett, climbed on board. But Miller also recruited the interventionist young minister of natural resources, Alan Pope. The media discounted Pope's allegiance and dubbed the Miller ministers "the dinosaurs", whose common cause with Miller was career self-interest. Frank represented for them a chance to continue in their long-held portfolios, whereas a younger leader would pasture them to give a more youthful face to his cabinet. As for Pope, they said, he backed a fellow northerner, and an older man, with a history of heart trouble – a choice thoroughly consistent with his own future leadership dreams.

Miller, the only candidate from outside Toronto, profited from a party executive decision to cut off voting memberships as of the date of Davis's retirement announcement. The party was trying to avoid the unseemly episodes of delegate-stacking and meeting-packing that had marred the recent federal leadership race that chose Brian Mulroney. But in doing so too crudely, the party blocked a badly needed influx of new blood. The enormous advantage conferred on Miller became clear in January when a disloyal Miller worker leaked to Timbrell's camp – and Timbrell's people promptly passed to the media – a fat wad of photocopied documents from Miller's campaign. Among them was a quick profile of the 1,711 convention delegates, written by Michael Perik, Miller's director of campaign operations, from his computer data: 73.5 per cent were Protestant, 63.9 per cent were of European, and mainly British, extraction, 60 per cent made more than $40,000 a year, and 53.8 per cent were over the age of forty.

Many of the delegates came from ridings still in the hands of Old Orange Ontario. They were small merchants, pharmacists, doctors, insurance agents – a small-town elite in a big-city province with large immigrant populations and an average industrial income of only $20,000 a year. Only 15 per cent of the delegates were in the 25-to-40 age group, the so-called Big Generation of Young Urban Professionals to whom Miller's younger rivals, in particular Grossman, were pitching their appeal. At Grossman's convention rallies, the music played was by rock king Bruce Springsteen. At Miller's parties, they sang "I want a girl just like the girl that married dear old Dad".

From the first, the prize was Miller's, unless he stumbled. He broke fast from the gate, lining up a dozen cabinet ministers to proclaim his virtues to the media. He released a poll done by Pope's people which showed him moving fast on first place. He already had a catchy campaign jingle called "Miller's Ontario" – and a pitch to go with it: "Miller's Ontario won't be a radically different place. It will be a place where we accept an old truism that an economy has to be able to pay the bills for the services government provides. It's a place where we try to give lots of opportunity to the small entrepreneur, so there will be someone to pay the bills. But it is not a place where we suddenly cut off services, or forget to help those who really need it." The advanced state of Miller's preparations came as a nasty surprise to the other contenders, since only a year before, Miller had disbanded his team and declared himself out of the race.

But Miller had been in the field a long time, and the spadework paid off. His designs on the premier's office went back almost five years. In 1978, Miller hired Jan Westcott, the son of Davis's executive assistant, Clare Westcott, ostensibly as his executive assistant, but Jan Westcott's real job was to talk Miller up as a potential successor to Davis. A bright young friend of Westcott's, Michael Perik, was only twenty-one years old when he started working the next summer at party headquarters as an assistant to executive director Patrick Kinsella. Perik and Westcott together began planning a leadership organization with the help of several of Miller's friends: David Melnik, a lawyer with aspirations to be a behind-the-scenes political mover, who was introduced to Miller by Norman Atkins; Hugh Mackenzie, a friendly, talkative Huntsville newspaperman, who worked on Miller's Muskoka campaigns; and Tony Brebner, a Toronto businessman who offered level-headed advice when the others got carried away.

The group agreed they needed a plan, so Perik spent the fall of 1979 writing a detailed, step-by-step strategy paper, modelled on Jimmy Carter's 1976 nomination campaign, and anonymously titled, in case it should fall into the wrong hands, "Donald Duck for Leader". The American president had won his nomination at the delegate-selection level, and that was how Miller's strategists planned his victory, too. By 1980, Perik had displaced Westcott in Miller's office and become the new executive assistant. Perik had a second office as well, a cubbyhole above the St. Clair subway station in Toronto paid for by money raised at a dinner for Miller and by contributions collected by Melnik. Here Perik installed a computer, and on it he kept the names of all the people Miller met in his extensive travelling and speaking engagements across the province. Perik mailed copies of Miller's statements and speeches out to everyone on the list. He also persuaded Miller to go to New York for some expert coaching in putting more feeling, and less teaching, into his speeches. Perik soon became Miller's unofficial campaign manager, a veritable encyclopedia of political lore and an indefatigable worker, but with one great flaw – a youthful inexperience that he hid behind a rigidly correct decorum.

Miller's little team soon had three other key additions: Ted Matthews, a tough delegate-tracker, or "legman", whom he met on the trail in Sudbury; John Balkwill, an Ottawa dentist and vice-president of the federal party, who built networks of eastern Ontarians and Tory youth during the fight to oust Joe Clark; and Jim Anthony, a policy adviser and speech-writer. All three were attracted to Miller for his right-wing views and their common distaste for the exclusive club that made up the Big Blue Machine.

Early in 1982, Perik travelled to Washington to study U.S. techniques of political organization and sought out Tom Donilan and Tony Corrado, young strategists whose techniques he had admired in his study of the Democratic campaigns of Jimmy Carter and Walter Mondale. He hired Corrado, who was pursuing a doctorate in political science at Boston University, on a fee-for-service basis to refine Miller's strategy. Fearful of adverse publicity about an American politico in Miller's camp, Perik carefully kept Corrado backstage.

Then, in the fall of 1983, to the dismay of the whole team,

Miller suddenly dropped from the race. He felt time was passing him by, and that Davis was not going to retire in the near future. He'd been chastised by John Tory for organizing too brazenly after he recruited the party's eastern Ontario organizer, Larry Keech, to his un-campaign. This, and other reproaches, explained Miller's feeling that the Davis crowd were clamping down on him more than on others, and would do their best to keep him from the succession. The internal play upset him. And he was embarrassed at holding an organization in readiness without knowing when the main event would come.

Miller thought that for him the great game was over. But Davis had always held Miller in personal affection, if disagreeing with his right-wing tendencies, and in a gesture of friendship a year later, he rekindled the minister's hopes. When Miller went to Davis to tell him he wouldn't run in Muskoka riding in the next election, Davis surprised him by suggesting he hold on. As usual, the premier was not explicit but hinted strongly that his retirement was near. Davis said that he had a mental list of successors and that Miller's name belonged on it. After that little nudge, it took only Davis's actual announcement on Thanksgiving Day to tempt Miller sorely. With pressure from Perik and Balkwill, and telephone calls from cabinet and caucus mates – including some who told him he was the only candidate who could stop Larry Grossman – Miller was back in the race.

Miller's revival dealt a cruel blow to Dennis Timbrell, the 37-year-old agriculture minister. Timbrell was so circumspect in style that he'd been labelled a Davis clone by the media wags. But, unlike Miller, who'd entered politics late and disclaimed high aspirations, Timbrell had been quietly aiming at the premiership all his life. Party elders claimed that he presented himself at a Conservative campaign office when he was ten years old, saying he wanted to learn how to become prime minister. There he spoke to Paul Weed, a warhorse of many Tory campaigns, who was enchanted and became the young man's mentor.

When a cabinet shuffle was pending in 1982, Timbrell, then

in cabinet, asked Davis for an apparent demotion – from health minister to agriculture minister – because it gave him an opportunity to organize his leadership campaign across rural Ontario. However, Davis left him in the obscurity of agriculture longer than he had envisaged. To Timbrell's dismay, the media began writing him off. But patient rural organizing, plus his strength as a Metro member for Don Mills riding, made Timbrell still the front runner in the unofficial leadership struggle – until Miller's re-entry threw his organization into disarray. Both depended on the party's right wing for support, but, worse for Timbrell, both now also shared key organizers.

When he stood aside, Miller had let his best people – Balkwill, Matthews, Anthony, and Perik – rally to the Timbrell cause. Timbrell's line was attractive to them – in private but not yet in public he talked of stagnation at the top of government ministries and his conviction that the Big Blue Machine was a closed club that had to be opened to fresh faces. The Miller people packed their computer lists and joined Timbrell's campaign manager, old pro Paul Weed, who by now had thirty federal and provincial campaigns under his belt. On arrival, they found Weed was at war with some of Timbrell's close staff in his ministries, notably his executive assistant, George Boddington, for control of the campaign. Timbrell didn't make choices, nor would he agree to accelerate organizing to top speed. Timbrell didn't believe Davis was ready to leave either.

At one point, Weed quit temporarily, in frustration over Timbrell's lack of action. Discouraged by Timbrell's fumbling, the Miller originals decided they'd be better off with their old candidate – now that he was back in the race. Timbrell, who to that point had hoped that Miller himself would be his campaign chairman, watched in shock as his key people deserted to the Miller bandwagon. Even Weed talked to Miller. He told Timbrell he was just scouting, but he was in fact attempting to negotiate a possible change of camps as campaign manager. When he failed to reach agreement with Miller, Weed stayed with Timbrell, where he was to prove a mixed blessing. His experience was important in pulling the shattered campaign together. But his hard-nosed personal style – he'd once been a collection agent – drove other useful people from Timbrell's side.

Passing up Weed, Miller turned to Lou Parsons, a real-estate agent, chairman of Go-Transit, and former regional chairman of Peel. As campaign chairman, Parsons was little involved in the actual mechanics of Miller's campaign, but in Miller's words he "wasn't a hurter", and he kept headquarters functioning smoothly. Parsons was an excellent foil for Perik, whose strengths were an encyclopedic knowledge and concentration on detail, but whose brusque impatience made him a poor handler of people.

With Miller implicitly – and Timbrell openly – promising a shake-up of the party backroom, the forces of the Big Blue Machine rallied to the two other candidates, Larry Grossman and Roy McMurtry. McMurtry, at fifty-two a big, tired, hound-dog-eyed man, was a former trial lawyer, a football chum of Davis's, and for a decade his attorney general. He was running because he felt he had no real future in Ontario politics without Davis, unless he took over himself. McMurtry began his campaign as the natural heir to the Davis legacy – the moderate middle-of-the-roader who could best carry the mantle of Tory success. "He is the one who follows in the tradition of Frost, Robarts, and Davis," pronounced his old friend Norman Atkins.

But McMurtry was a long shot, and both he and Atkins knew it. He'd done no organizing or fund-raising when he announced his candidacy on November 2. The other three candidates were literally years ahead of him, and he could win only if the delegates were so unimpressed by what they were already offered that they were prepared to switch allegiance.

Grossman, forty-one, a scrapper from a downtown Toronto riding, whose father had been Ontario's first Jewish Conservative cabinet minister, might easily have come forward as the standard-bearer for the party's Red Tory faction. But Grossman's pollsters, too, read the party's mood as right-wing or at best centre-right. For the previous year, in the treasury portfolio, he had been attempting to recast himself as a responsible fiscal conservative. Trying to be all things to all delegates produced a performance that was too rehearsed and too smooth. Still, Grossman presented a stronger challenge to Miller than anyone would have guessed.

In the "out" circles of the party, there was bitter muttering that what the Big Blue Machine was doing was running two horses, McMurtry and Grossman. Grossman, the theory went, was too hard-edged a candidate to win on his own. People either liked him or hated him. So McMurtry would pick up as many votes as he could among the undecided, and then deliver them to Grossman.

Norman Atkins, Davis's legendary campaign manager just back from federal triumphs as head of Mulroney's election team, was chairman of McMurtry's campaign. He'd rallied instantly to McMurtry, a friend of two decades, the man who introduced him to Davis, and a co-founder of the Big Blue Machine. Atkins, tired from his federal campaigning, opened the party contest while vacationing on the tennis courts in Antigua. He left day-to-day McMurtry operations in the hands of his cohort, Brian Armstrong, another of the so-called Eglinton Mafia who'd once worked for Atkins' brother-in-law Dalton Camp in his abortive 1965 try for the federal Eglinton seat.

Atkins' business partner at Camp Associates, Hugh Segal, former principal secretary to Davis, was supporting Larry Grossman, along with a clutch of other Big Blue Machiners, including campaign manager John Laschinger, and Tom Scott, head of Foster Advertising. For all these long-time backroom boys, Miller's impending win meant the end of influence. The Ontario Tory standard was about to fall into infidel hands.

Late in December, Bill Davis held a Christmas party for his cabinet at Fenton's restaurant in Toronto. At the end of the lunch Grossman and McMurtry ended up sitting at the table alone talking. McMurtry told Grossman, "I sure don't like the look of Miller's Ontario." Then the two spent several minutes exchanging anecdotes about the tactics of the Miller campaign and sharing their fears that Miller would win.

Grossman hoped that McMurtry would become the "hit man", taking on Miller on the campaign trail. But McMurtry wasn't ready to admit that his only remaining role was to play the bad cop. Susan Fish, who'd been lingering, joined them. As the trio left the restaurant, a newspaper photographer snapped a picture of the two last-place runners, laughing together, arms around Fish's shoulders – three Toronto Tory musketeers.

By this time both Grossman and McMurtry knew from their own polling that they were behind Miller and their only chance of winning was to shake up the party. Their problem was that the grass-roots delegates didn't believe the party could lose the next election no matter who was premier and so would choose the man they liked best. McMurtry and Grossman had a chance only if they could crack the complacency, and to do that, ironically, they had to attack the legacy of which they were the truest heirs.

McMurtry's tactics stirred the greatest public interest. Initially he had stressed the importance of sticking with the successful Davis formula of moderate pragmatic government. But as the weeks passed and his campaign failed to catch fire, his strategists realized the party didn't want just more of the same old thing – that in fact the party had become bored with Davis's blandness. McMurtry began talking of himself as an emotional and passionate man. He attacked his own government's "scattergun" approach to the problems of unemployed young people. He said the Davis regime had become immobilized in setting its priorities and was reactive instead of active. McMurtry provided a few sparks in an otherwise lack-lustre campaign – and won a few standing ovations for doing so – but his emotional appeal did not convince the delegates. He hadn't talked like that for the last ten years, and his ersatz passion failed to melt the party's heart.

Larry Grossman's assault on party lethargy was more analytic. Throughout the campaign he kept telling party delegates that they had to erect a "bigger tent", embracing not just more Ontarians but different kinds – immigrants, women, youth. He urged them to select a contemporary leader with a progressive urban outlook. He alluded to his "difference", attempting to make an asset of a religious background that was hurting his chances in some sections of the party. Workers for his rivals whispered to the delegates about Grossman's lack of "electability", code language that presumed Ontario wouldn't vote for a Jew. Grossman dealt with the issue by pointing to his appeal to a multicultural electorate. He was no Old Ontario WASP, but a Jew raised on the street politics of a downtown, largely immigrant riding. Grossman found his party difficult to rouse, however. The delegates were sleeping, he told reporters.

In January, less than two weeks before the vote, Grossman's campaign released a policy paper called "The Realities: Ontario's Changing Political Culture" in a final attempt to snap the party awake. Based on Allan Gregg's polling, and written largely by Hugh Segal, the document warned that changing demographics and recent economic hard times were producing an electorate that wanted a change from traditional approaches. Adherence to yesterday's solutions under an old-fashioned leader (Frank Miller) would doom the Conservatives to political oblivion. The Conservatives needed energetic, enlightened leadership (Larry Grossman), and a continuation of a moderate progressive approach on the issues. The paper warned that the party's traditional base among Protestant, married males living in small communities no longer corresponded to Ontario realities. Without Bill Davis's ability to attract voters of liberal outlook, the core vote for the Conservative party was only twenty-three per cent.

As well, the paper pointed out, with a strong new Conservative government in Ottawa, voters would no longer feel they had to maintain Tories in power at Queen's Park. Given the Liberal party's apparent collapse nationally, and its weak Ontario leadership, Gregg forecast possible major gains for the NDP. "If the voter is offered a Tory leadership that appears more insensitive, or tied to views that, while clear, have little to do with the public opinion context that now shapes Ontario politics, the NDP will be the beneficiary," the paper warned.

By the time the paper appeared, the Opposition parties

were absolutely delighted with what was happening in the Conservative leadership race. "McMurtry gets his loudest applause when he says things about the government we've been saying for years," Rae crowed. Peterson took hope from signs of polarization in the Conservative party. "The Big Blue Machine is taking on Miller because if he wins they risk losing the levers of power in this province," the Liberal leader said.

Inside his party, however, Grossman's paper had little impact. Coming so late in the leadership convention, at a time when the losers were obviously desperate, the warnings were dismissed. To be credible, they ought to have been sounded earlier. After it was all over, Grossman acknowledged that the main chance had been blown by late November, when the final date passed for selection of the voting delegates. The Millerites had won the early crucial rounds through superior organization.

That was largely the doing of Perik, Balkwill, and Matthews – following Corrado's "five-stage" strategy for influencing the delegate-selection process. The Miller campaign hired full-time co-ordinators for each region of the province, got their hands on delegate lists for each riding, set up regional phone banks, set quotas for the number of delegates each organizer had to win, and every night called for reports on the 125 ridings. The blanket techniques won riding after riding. In Hastings-Peterborough, for instance, the eastern Ontario trackers used an Ottawa office arranged by Balkwill to call a list of 700 potential Tory delegates, find out who the Miller people were in that pool, and ask them to help him win. Once the nomination date was set, the Miller supporters were called again, told when and where to go, and given the names on the Miller slate so they'd know who to vote for as delegates. Miller supporters were asked to speak to friends in the riding association and make sure they got there too. From head-quarters, Perik blanketed the party membership with letters from Miller, directing special pleas for assistance to those identified on the Miller computer list.

Perik later estimated that Miller pulled eighty to ninety per cent of his potential support during delegate selection, whereas Timbrell came in badly below his potential because his local "on-the-ground" organization was poor. Grossman's campaign operated more efficiently, but from too narrow a base of potential support. And McMurtry entered too late to be effective at this stage. By the time delegate selection was over, Miller's trackers estimated he had a 160-to-170-vote lead.

The race, for all real purposes, was over, but the candidates still had two months to flog themselves through a series of dreary policy debates. Davis's resignation was supposed to bring new life and new ideas to refresh his party. But he kept a repressive hand on the process. Shortly after the candidates declared, he persuaded them in cabinet not to diverge from the official line on four politically sensitive issues: full financing of Roman Catholic separate schools; official bilingualism; rent controls; and Ontario's purchase of the Suncor shares. Miller described the "no-controversy" pact on November 6 when reporters asked him about Suncor. He wasn't so daring as to call it a muzzle: they were simply all cabinet ministers observing cabinet solidarity. "The contender will be free only when their leader is not in office," Miller explained. Davis was protecting the party from a public display of internal cabinet division. He was particularly concerned that separate-school funding could potentially be an emotional, divisive issue at the convention. So the outgoing premier told the candidates that if anyone wanted to diverge from cabinet solidarity, he should quit his cabinet post. None of the four wanted to make that sacrifice for the sake of ideas.

Reporters who covered the debates found them boring beyond belief, and so did the audiences of Tory faithful. The candidates were so circumspect it was difficult to detect any differences among them. McMurtry was the only candidate to talk about people, and then only to make vague promises that under him the government would really tackle issues like youth unemployment. Timbrell at one point said he was pro-life and would not change the present abortion law, but immediately backed off when women supporters protested. He explained weakly that he was not really pro-life in the ideological sense – he just wasn't pro-abortion either. Miller, the supposed right-winger, was moved to demur on the issue, saying certain areas of the abortion law should be liberalized. And he demurred again when Grossman promised to balance the budget in a couple of years. Miller, a former treasurer, said such a quick balancing couldn't be achieved without cutting social programs. Miller himself created a couple of flurries by suggesting that environmental programs hurt jobs, and that he'd oppose pending legislation for the equal division of mutual business assets when a marriage breaks down. The hair-splitting made headlines because the four debaters were all potential premiers – not because it was news that made the pulses race.

This was a party so devoted to the status quo that it imposed self-censorship. Davis had told them to keep to the official line, and when anyone diverged, the others were quick to punish. When Dennis Timbrell suggested rent controls might be repealed once the apartment vacancy rate in Ontario reached three per cent, the other three jumped on him. Miller was most blunt: he shared Timbrell's reservations about rent controls, but thought removing them would be politically dangerous. None of the three defended rent controls on policy grounds. They talked expediency.

The dilemma of all four lay in what their polls told them about their own party. The vast majority of delegates identified themselves as centre or right on the issues. That put them out of touch with the general public. There were huge public issues in the air: separate-school funding, the effects of financial restraint on the province's schools and hospitals, the need for an environmental clean-up, child care, and equal pay for women workers. But party polls showed that the Conservative party was lagging behind the public in recognizing the need for change.

The issue of equal pay demonstrates this clearly. By convention rule, half the delegates were women, but those women included strong urban feminists as well as many who, in Frank Miller's words, were "more conservative on women's issues than the men". As a result, women delegates had no organized clout at the convention. Indeed, there appeared to be a tacit female silence. When their concerns failed to get a proper airing at the debates, environmental and women's groups attempted to canvass the candidates by letter to find out where they stood. The written replies were listless defences of the current do-nothing party positions. The progressive dimension of the PC political formula was dormant: regeneration was not working.

In the absence of any excitement over issues, the only hope for the three candidates who were trailing lay in behind-the-scenes deals. An alliance of Timbrell, Grossman, and McMurtry could beat Miller if quiet agreement could be reached. McMurtry and Grossman, both considered Red Tories, had an obvious common interest. There was the partnership of Norman Atkins in McMurtry's camp and Hugh Segal in Grossman's. Another pair of business partners split between the two camps were Allan Gregg, pollster to the Big Blue Machine, who was polling for Grossman, while his vice-president at Decima Research, Ian McKinnon, was doing the same job for McMurtry. Grossman maintains this apparent double-harness was simply a natural result of having in the race two ministers who both had long connections to the Big Blue Machine.

Both men also deny that they ever shook hands and agreed to support each other. A formal deal, and possible exposure of it, weren't really needed. Segal and Atkins were in daily touch anyway. When it was all over, McMurtry said there had never been more than a tacit understanding. However, on the convention floor the Grossman and McMurtry forces wore identical colours and carried signs indistinguishable in style and colour. The only difference was in the names.

The problem for Big Blue was that Timbrell, no friend to the Atkins crowd, was in second place and so seemed in the best position to lead the charge against Miller. In early January, Paul Weed, Timbrell's campaign manager, began manoeuvring to line up with Grossman – and, through him, with McMurtry. Weed spread the word that Timbrell would never make Miller king because he could not forgive him for what he regarded as the ultimate dirty trick. Timbrell maintained that Miller had not really dropped out of the unofficial race in the fall of 1983. Instead, he had faked his withdrawal and infiltrated the Timbrell campaign. Then Miller pulled his supporters back, leaving Timbrell in disarray.

Timbrell himself, however, was a bit reluctant to enter a deal with Grossman. To do so was tantamount to admitting he wasn't the front runner. Weed had been maintaining Timbrell's morale, and that of his team, by showing them optimistic delegate-tracking results that made Timbrell believe he was ahead of Miller. This tactic enraged John Bitove, a businessman who was Timbrell's fund-raiser. Bitove attempted to warn Timbrell that he was misinformed, and backed his contention with polling evidence from federal Liberal pollster Martin Goldfarb, who had been following the race for private clients. Timbrell was wary of a warning coming from a Liberal pollster. But he now decided to negotiate with Grossman, on the assumption it would be Grossman, and not himself, who would have to cross the convention floor.

Grossman's strategists, counting on an alliance with McMurtry after the first ballot, saw a chance to catch up to the unsuspecting Timbrell and carry him along as an ally for a final round with Miller. They figured they'd get seventy-five per cent of McMurtry's vote and rocket ahead of Timbrell, taking him by surprise because Timbrell was convinced he, and not Grossman, would be in second place and leading the charge. Grossman's campaign manager, John Laschinger, fostered friendly relations in regular lunch dates with Weed. They shared polling information, and agreed that an alliance was the way to beat Miller. On January 9, at Weed's instigation, the two sides met at Grossman's home and reached a mutual-support pact. Whoever was eliminated first in the balloting would throw his support to the other. In return, the loser was guaranteed second place in the new administration.

The deal was cemented further both in a meeting at the home of lawyer Alan Schwartz, Grossman's close friend and negotiator, and in the heat of the convention when deal-makers for both sides met behind the bleachers. Both camps meanwhile denied press reports of a mutual understanding. To admit to it would betray their strategy and might upset some supporters. Both Timbrell's and Grossman's camps began preaching a common theme however: Miller was too old, too much a Reagan-style right-winger, and too out of touch to lead the Conservative party in the 1980s. In their desperation, they ignored Bill Davis's instructions that they avoid bloodying each other. Personal attacks on a potential premier, he had argued, would only hurt the party in the public eye.

Miller was aware of the danger that the other three would combine against him. He defended himself against the charge that he was a Ronald Reagan of the north – a phrase he'd made the mistake of using himself early in the campaign – saying in a *Toronto Star* interview on January 24: "I'm like Ronald Reagan only in the sense I make people feel good, give them confidence. The other guys would like me to be Attila the Hun but I'm not. Sure I'm on the right of them and very comfortable there. But my earlier right-wing views have been tempered by experience." Miller quietly dispatched David Melnik, president of Vanguard Trust and a long-time adviser both on financial policy and on his leadership chances, to act as his negotiator. Melnik had plenty of private-sector experience, but he was a neophyte in politics. He learned some hard lessons, got bruised in Miller's service, and later was to admit he felt as though he'd been worked over by experts.

Melnik and Grossman's negotiator, Schwartz, were neighbours and casual family friends. In conversation, Schwartz led Melnik to believe that while Grossman couldn't agree to support Miller he was unlikely to go to any other candidate. Melnik reported to Miller that Grossman would sit tight after being eliminated in the balloting and would free his supporters to go where they pleased.

Grossman's man Schwartz also told Melnik to call Jim McCallum, a lawyer working for McMurtry. Melnik got some reassurance from Miller there, too. McCallum said McMurtry believed he had a chance on his own and would not therefore make deals with anyone. Only hours before the actual voting started, Miller talked to McMurtry's camp and was told that McMurtry still didn't want to make any arrangements. The fix was already in, but Melnik and Miller didn't know it.

Melnik also talked to Ralph Lean, in Timbrell's camp, and was told that Timbrell's people would get back to him. They never did. So on all three fronts, while Melnik felt he was being led to hope, he was in fact being outmanoeuvred. Grossman already had deals – firm or tacit – with the other two. Melnik lacked the party connections that would have warned him of the way the winds were blowing. And so, strangely, did Weed in Timbrell's camp. Weed had once been a member of the Big Blue Machine but had fallen out with Norman Atkins years earlier. In the last ten days before the voting, he made frequent attempts to contact Atkins in McMurtry's camp, but his telephone messages went unanswered. Whatever suspicions he entertained, he didn't know that Grossman and McMurtry were in alliance and that Timbrell's second-place standing was in danger.

In Miller's camp, however, some of the experienced pros were aware of the growing pact between the other three. Balkwill, Perik, and Matthews paid little attention to Melnik's assertions that no deal was on. They simply assumed that the Big Blue Machine would follow a strategy they'd observed in national leadership races – to back more than one candidate and telescope support behind whoever remained on the final ballot.

Balkwill and Perik had tracked the delegates carefully, and had a fair idea who each delegate would support – and not just on the first ballot. They had assessed each person's probable second choice if his or her man was knocked off. In Timbrell's camp, the majority said they'd go to Miller if Timbrell was eliminated. In Grossman's camp, there were many fewer second ballots for Miller. Clearly, Miller wanted to be facing Grossman rather than Timbrell in the final run-off. He would win against Grossman with the help of delegates from the Timbrell camp. Against Timbrell, Miller would lose, or at best squeak by, because most of Grossman's people would go to Timbrell, the younger man.

Miller's man Balkwill worked hard on the youth delegates, arguing that if they couldn't support Miller they should go to Grossman. Never mind the ideological differences, the two were the most able to lead the party. Balkwill's strategy was to bolster Grossman's strength so that he, and not Timbrell, would face Miller on the final ballot. It worked so well that Balkwill was to regret it months later, when Miller had resigned and Balkwill was working for Timbrell. Many of the former Miller youth delegates then simply switched to Grossman, and Balkwill couldn't get them to consider Timbrell. However, in January, when nobody contemplated a second leadership convention in a year, it looked like clever stuff.

Melnik, meanwhile, was disturbed by media reports of a Timbrell/Grossman alliance to block Miller. A couple of days before the convention, he called Schwartz at the Royal York Hotel, Grossman's temporary headquarters, and bluntly asked whether the stories were accurate. Schwartz knew that if he spoke truthfully, or even hesitated before lying, he'd be giving away important strategic information. He quickly replied, "It's not true." As Schwartz hung up the telephone, his wife asked what was wrong and Schwartz told her what he had done, adding: "David will never understand." Melnik learned on the convention floor that he'd been lied to, and that by trusting Schwartz, he had misinformed Miller. He did have trouble forgiving. The incident contributed to the bad blood between Miller and Grossman once the leadership contest was over.

The convention opened January 24 on the grounds of Toronto's Exhibition Place with an embarrassingly lifeless night of tribute to Bill Davis. Davis was an icon in his party, but outside his loyal circle few delegates felt strong emotional attachment to him. Davis spoke overly long, aware this was supposed to be a poignant moment and trying to wring the appropriate response from the crowd. But the delegates weren't in the mood for lionizing the past leader. They shuffled their feet, impatient for the real action. The party presented

Davis with a $5,000 cheque to endow a university scholarship in his name. Many felt this was a paltry gift for a premier who'd been in office nearly fourteen years. But the Ontario Progressive Conservatives were deeply in debt – $2.8 million was owed the banks at the end of December – and chief fund-raiser Bill Kelly had ordered party president David McFadden to make sure the convention broke even.

Most of the action quickly shifted out of the draughty, ugly Exhibition Coliseum, which had been designed for horse shows, to warm downtown hotels and watering-spots. At the Royal York Hotel, the leadership candidates moved from one policy session to another, giving their spiels and fielding questions. For Miller, the ad hoc sessions were dangerous ground. Fearing the candidate's unruly tongue, Perik had been trying to control possible damage by fobbing off the reporters pursuing his man. Miller's responses at the policy sessions had been carefully vetted beforehand, but Miller had made mistakes anyway, raising delegates' doubts. By the last week, he was starting to lose momentum, while Roy McMurtry, in particular, was picking up strength.

With one day to go, Miller stumbled badly. He'd been getting advice on Metro issues from Paul Godfrey, the former Metro chairman and then publisher of the *Toronto Sun*. Godfrey was promised to his old friend McMurtry on the first ballot, but in the end would go to Miller. Before the convention, Godfrey sat down with Miller and Perik and ran through a half-dozen Metro issues and the appropriate responses. Well down the list he mentioned Toronto city school board's then defunct gay liaison committee and suggested it was time someone took the board to task for having set it up. Perik later warned Miller not to raise the issue. But in a policy session, Miller talked of the Metro Toronto school board, remarking that "any school board with a gay liaison committee isn't my kind of board." The remark flew around the hotel as reporters and delegates rushed to repeat it to others. Miller immediately regretted what he'd said, although later he suggested he'd gained as much as he'd lost by displaying an anti-homosexual attitude. To many delegates, however, the comment revealed ignorance – he got the wrong school board – and an intolerance unsuitable in a man who wanted to be premier of all the people. Perik thanked his lucky stars that many of the weekend filing deadlines for the media had already passed. For that reason, the damage came late.

When voting began on Saturday, January 26, the first-ballot results threw everyone's calculations slightly askew. The surprise was Roy McMurtry's first-ballot strength. McMurtry had picked up momentum in the last days of the race with his populist-style attacks on the Tory record, but polls by the three other camps showed him trailing badly and likely to pull at most only 200 delegates. There had been, however, a final intervention by some of the old palace guard around Davis. They'd started a quiet movement to save McMurtry from embarrassing defeat and were contacting people in other camps asking for a first-ballot vote for Roy. Hugh Macaulay, formerly Davis's party organizer, was pulling every available string. These efforts, plus McMurtry's own fighting style in his convention speech – "they will never take the passion out of Roy McMurtry" – gave him 300 votes on the first ballot. Grossman captured 378 votes, Timbrell 421, and Miller 591.

McMurtry had done much better than anticipated and was saved from humiliation, but still had to drop from the ballot. Miller's team and Timbrell's were both unsettled. They'd done worse than expected. Timbrell was particularly chagrined. Weed had said he'd get 700 or more votes. But at 421 he was not far enough ahead of Larry Grossman to ensure he wouldn't be the next to drop.

Next came the manoeuvres which brought Grossman into second place and won Miller the convention. Shortly after the first ballot was announced, Grossman rose and went to McMurtry's box. McMurtry raised their clenched hands in the traditional signal of alliance. McMurtry asked his supporters to follow his example on the next ballot and vote for Grossman. His loyalists obeyed, even when, as was the case with cabinet minister Frank Drea, they were clearly unhappy. Drea explained to the television cameras that he was doing as McMurtry asked for one ballot only, then would be off to Miller. Others bolted ranks at once.

Timbrell's camp seethed with worry and bitterness. Timbrell and his people felt that the party hierarchy's campaign to save McMurtry from embarrassment had been a ploy to steal first ballots. Worse, by leading his delegates to Grossman, McMurtry now threatened Timbrell's second-place position. Timbrell was being robbed of victory.

Around Miller, frantic calculations were being made. From the first, Miller's strategists hoped he'd face Grossman, not Timbrell, on the last ballot. That now seemed a real possibility. A group of Miller's eastern Ontario riding supporters approached John Balkwill as he stood at the front of the Miller benches. They'd heard the strategy talk and suggested some of them could vote for Larry Grossman on the next ballot and leapfrog him ahead of Timbrell.

Balkwill's mind was in turmoil. On the first ballot, the Miller polling had been off by at least fifty votes, and he didn't know exactly where things now stood. Throwing too many votes to Grossman could rob Miller of momentum if he failed to gain enough strength on the next ballot. Switching too few votes wouldn't do the job. Balkwill decided to take the chance. He told the delegates that not more than ten should transfer their vote to Grossman; anything much more could prove too dangerous. Other Miller delegates were apparently having similar thoughts. Later, one Miller supporter, Grey-Bruce delegate Bill Davis, a farmer from Paisley, said Alan Pope, too, had been orchestrating a movement to throw second-ballot votes to Grossman. Pope, however, denied it.

Just how many Miller people made that critical one-ballot switch will never be clear, but it was just enough. This was one of the turning-points in the Tory fall from power. If Balkwill had guessed wrong and moved too many people, there's a slim chance Miller might have lost momentum and succumbed to the Grossman surge. If he had sent fewer to Grossman, in all likelihood Timbrell would have been the ultimate convention winner. The imponderable question is whether

Dennis Timbrell would have dealt more effectively than Miller with the problems he faced from the first day in the premier's office.

As it turned out, of course, Timbrell didn't get the chance to try. On the second ballot, he suffered the anguish of losing by a hair's breadth. Miller received 659 votes this time, Timbrell 508, and Grossman 514. A delighted Balkwill turned to Miller and said, "Congratulations, you just won." Miller relaxed and began composing his victory acceptance speech. He knew from his delegate-tracking that enough Timbrell people would come over to make him the next leader.

Grossman's people, crying with relief and shouting, rushed the Timbrell benches to try and win the support that would put their man over the top. Grossman knew better. He'd seen the delegate-tracking data just as Miller had and knew he wouldn't win. He quietly told his people not to get overly excited.

Timbrell was stunned. No one had really prepared him as Grossman had been prepared. John Bitove had attempted to tell him he was in trouble a few weeks before, but Timbrell had remained confident of victory. He was beginning to realize that his organization was far weaker than he'd known, but he wasn't quite ready to accept it. He wanted a recount.

In the back offices of the convention centre, John Laschinger for Grossman and Paul Weed for Timbrell were at loggerheads. Laschinger was trying to avoid a delay that would slow Grossman's charge, but Weed was still fighting for Timbrell's fast-fading chances. Weed demanded a new vote. When the other camps refused to consider holding the ballot all over again, Weed next demanded a recount. With a difference of only six votes – and the premiership at stake – he felt Timbrell was entitled at least to that. Miller's strategists liked the idea of the extra time to work on the Timbrell delegates. So the recount was on and the Timbrell/Grossman mutual-support pact was wobbling.

Miller's strategists made a final attempt to reach Timbrell and woo him to their benches. Clearly Miller was going to win and Timbrell could ensure himself a seat by the throne by moving to him then. David Melnik sent messages to Paul Weed and was told to go to a certain room under the stands and knock on the door. Weed would be there to meet him. When he got there, no one was waiting. Standing there alone, Melnik started to laugh, feeling rightly that he was taking part in a charade. In the adjacent corridors, he later learned, Grossman and Timbrell people already had stapled together stacks of their signs and were ready for a show of mutual support. Miller's organizer, Balkwill, talked to Peter Weed, Paul Weed's son, pleading with him not to let Timbrell walk to Grossman. Some Timbrell supporters agreed – among them Tory warhorses Paul Kates and Alan Eagleson – and began buttonholing delegates to go to Miller.

But Timbrell himself was firm about keeping his word. Paul Weed informed the Grossman team the deal was still on. In the back corridors, Timbrell and Grossman met and renewed their pledge. Then the recount came in, with the same second-ballot results. Grossman walked over to Timbrell's benches and the two raised hands. Timbrell kept his promise, knowing that by doing so he backed the loser and not the winner.

With all his rivals arrayed against him, Miller still kept the majority of delegates. Nine hours and forty-four minutes after the balloting began, party president David McFadden announced the final tally: Miller 869 votes or 53.3 per cent of votes cast, and Grossman 792 or 47.7 per cent.

The split in the party was revealed nakedly for everyone to see. Miller's band struck up his jaunty campaign song: "We are Miller's Ontario, We know that we're Strong. . . ." Behind him, smiling, cheering small-town delegates marched on to the stage. Lou Parsons dubbed them the "Tartan Train" that had outraced the fabled Big Blue Machine. A side of the party that had felt left out now revelled at putting one of its own in power.

Larry Grossman, his wife Carole sobbing helplessly beside him, took the stage to move the traditional motion of unanimity, the healing gesture by which parties are supposed to put aside internal rivalries and unite behind the leader. Grossman had warned the Conservatives they must choose a younger, contemporary leader. Now he swallowed his words, saying, "We have chosen very well indeed."

But gallant gestures on stage made little difference in reality. Two bitter rivals were now king and pretender – a scenario fraught with danger for Miller. Most Metro Toronto delegates had voted for Grossman, as had most of the youth. And while Miller had some staunch female supporters, he'd created deep worries among high-profile women delegates who suspected him of retrograde attitudes. "A lot of women will be worried with Miller as premier," Jane Pepino, a lawyer who'd been McMurtry's women's-issues adviser, told the newspapers.

Miller marched in triumph from the Coliseum, his followers full of excited plans. First on the agenda was a purge of the Davis-era backroom boys, a shake-up of the senior bureaucracy to bring government back to life after its long wait for a new master; then an election to give Miller his own mandate as premier. As for public policy, Miller himself said he would change directions only modestly. Miller's Ontario would encourage small private entrepreneurs to be the engine of the economy, and would maintain social services with greater efficiency. His statements did not suggest any radical departure from the Davis years.

The convention had done much, however, to prepare the public to believe that Miller *was* different, and to create unease about his intentions. In a long, bitter campaign, rival contenders from his own party had described Miller as too old, too out of touch, too right-wing. The contest had been covered by the media with an assiduity seldom devoted to party leadership races. The reason for this was that after forty-two years of Conservative rule, news directors on the newspapers and at television stations across the province assumed this race mattered even more than an election. The Ontario Progressive Conservatives, and not the people, were remaking the government. The process therefore deserved full coverage.

The Conservative party accepted the media interest as its due, assuming the convention excitement would only add to its commanding lead in the polls. In fact, although Conservative standing in the polls rose briefly, the party had suffered considerable damage in the public's estimation. Hadn't it been Roy McMurtry, attorney general for the past decade, who had said that Conservatives didn't care enough? Hadn't it been treasurer Larry Grossman who'd said that if the party chose Miller it could lose the next election? Some portion of the public chose to take the cabinet ministers at their word.

Two of the biggest beneficiaries of the convention coverage were the Opposition leaders, David Peterson and Bob Rae. As commentators on television during the long hours of voting at the Coliseum, both surprised viewers by their reasonable tone. Nothing they said was any worse than the Tories had already said of themselves. They were articulate, knowledgeable, urbane. They were also younger than Miller, livelier, and more engaging than the Conservatives playing out their struggle on the small screen.

What else had Ontarians seen? They had watched an unrepresentative convention, whose delegates were older, richer, more rural, and more homogeneously white and Protestant than the province at large, choose the candidate who did less well than either Grossman or McMurtry in the public polls.

They'd seen a series of claustrophobic leadership debates. They'd seen the imperial style of a party so long in office it assumed it governed by divine right; a party already $2.8 million in debt whose leaders poured more than $5 million into their lavish pursuit of the premier's office. They read in newspaper reports about McMurtry and Grossman accusing Miller of dirty tricks, about candidates buying votes by paying delegate expenses or promising patronage jobs. Worst of all, Ontarians had seen a party split and divided by internal bitterness. Dalton Camp, the Conservative columnist, mused in a perceptive column in the *Star* three days later that the party had emerged polarized: city versus rural, left versus right, and older versus younger. "This was a peculiar convention . . . and I am not sure that it was as beneficial to the party as these things usually are," Camp wrote. Miller had won, but the struggle had wounded the party he now led.

3

David Peterson's Luck

It was a ridiculous Saturday afternoon scene in the ring of Driftwood Boxing Club in September 1983 as David Peterson, leader of the Ontario Liberal party, T-shirt falling out over his boxing shorts, boxed three rounds with a former Canadian middleweight boxing champion, Joe Henry. The match was to raise money for a boys' boxing club in the low-income Jane/Finch corridor of north Metro Toronto. It was also uneven. Joe Henry was, in Peterson's words, "one tough guy", while the tall, slender Liberal leader has never been a natural at sports. He'd had to practise hard to achieve respectability as a college boxer – light heavyweight – in his days at the University of Toronto. As he aged, Peterson joined the morning ranks of keep-fit joggers. But that hardly prepared him to be in the ring with Henry.

However, Peterson has an insouciant attitude to adventures, even those with a potential for mortification. When Henry proposed a fund-raising match as Peterson was politicking in the Jane/Finch area one day, the Liberal leader agreed to take him on, and then went around for some days recounting the tale of his own folly. As fight day loomed nearer, he began warm-up training, only to suffer three cracked ribs at the hands of an overly enthusiastic sparring partner at a downtown gym. When he finally climbed through the ropes to meet Henry, Peterson's ribs were taped. He wore a T-shirt to conceal the injury, and *sotto voce* asked Henry to lay off the body. Henry showed mercy, and Peterson emerged from his hands unscathed, reflecting happily that Henry could have killed him. He'd done it for fun, he allowed later with a grin.

Peterson's political fortunes hadn't then fallen to the nadir he was to experience in the polls, among his own caucus-mates, and in the media during his worst political year – 1984. He'd earlier held the limelight for a couple of glorious months during the so-called trust-company affair – the notorious sale and resale of 11,000 Metro apartments by fast-buck artists within the trust industry. Then Peterson's financial expertise, backed by good party research, was displayed to good effect, but when the excitement of the scandal fizzled, so did Peterson's performance. By the time he tangled with Joe Henry, he was already viewed as an ineffectual political leader going nowhere in particular. His media adviser, George Hutchison, relished the idea of newspaper pictures of Peterson, pugnacious in boxing gloves, but Hutchison was well aware of the dangers of the stunt. A Liberal leader down and out on the mat wasn't the image Hutchison was aiming for. As it turned out, Peterson didn't go down, and he displayed a game quality that suggested that the contempt in which the governing Conservatives held him was misplaced.

There was, in fact, a competitive facet to Peterson that New Democrat Richard Johnston had already noted. While others in Bob Rae's socialist caucus, including Rae himself, dismissed the Liberal chief, Johnston was saying that Peterson, pushed into a corner, would come out fighting. And to the astonishment of nearly everyone, that's exactly what happened when the crucial May 1985 provincial election was called.

As George Hutchison was to say later, "All the stars crossed in the skies for us" before and during the campaign that shook Tory rule. But the best luck in the world would have meant nothing if the Liberals had not been well positioned to take advantage of the opportunity. It was David Peterson, and not Bob Rae, who filled the vacuum when the Conservative grip on power weakened, and no single analysis of federal-provincial voting trends can account for that result. The explanation lies in what had been going on behind the scenes in the provincial Liberal party for the last several years.

Peterson didn't arrive in politics looking as sleek and handsome as he does today, in dark suits accented by the ever-present red tie. The premier, with his silvering temples and glamorous actress wife, has been through a careful and extensive professional political grooming.

In 1975, when he first entered the legislature, Peterson was tall, and moderately good-looking, but his overall appearance was unimpressive, with his heavy glasses, long black side-burns, petulant mouth, and a five-o'clock shadow. He was no television star, and, beyond that, he was powerless and inept at platform oratory. He lost his first leadership bid in 1976 to Stuart Smith because of the inadequacy of his convention address. His subsequent success in February 1982 was based on good organization and personal inoffensiveness. "He's ordinary enough to relate to ordinary people" was the strongest accolade his boyhood friend Ted McGrath, who ran Peterson's London riding campaigns, could muster in defence of the new Liberal leader's style.

Peterson is at his best in small groups, with an easy, friendly manner, an enthusiasm for life and adventure, and consid-erable skill in telling humorously edged stories about himself and the people he's met. No matter what the circumstances, even in his darkest hours, Peterson will tell visitors he's having a "terrific time". Reporters who talked to him about his troubles as leader of the Opposition came away suspecting he was oblivious to reality. But he once explained that he had learned to appear carefree while boxing: "You learn how to hide your injuries. When you're hit, you don't want to show pain."

Toward his wife, Shelley, a fragile beauty, Peterson shows a protective side. Shelley shares his friendly warmth, but is uncomfortable in large crowds. Peterson's eye is always on her, and when she gets squeezed he knifes through the crowd. Once Shelley is secure, Peterson, a stroker of egos, works a crowd with effortless flattery. Davis's former deputy ministers still laugh when they recount how Peterson "hustled" them to his side when he became premier.

From the time of his first appearance at Queen's Park, the consensus was that Peterson was a nice guy, but no fireball. He was an unsteady performer in the legislature, alternately too soft or too personally nasty. His sharp tongue periodically revealed his resentful side, as when he referred to Prime Minister Pierre Trudeau as a "millstone" around the Ontario party's neck, or sullenly remarked, when reporters questioned him about the defection of Sheila Copps to the federal Liberals, that "the graveyards are full of indispensable people." At other moments he was a little too offhand and glib about serious questions. His one-liners were sufficient for television but left print reporters dissatisfied.

Peterson in those days was on the right wing of his party. Davis loved to twit him in the legislature because Peterson's wife is the daughter of London developer Donald Matthews, a former national president of the Progressive Conservative party. The Liberal leader's heart was really conservative, Davis suggested.

Peterson trained as a lawyer but was basically a business-man, president at age twenty-six of C. M. Peterson Company Limited, the wholesale electronics company founded by his father. He is said to have increased the sales six hundred per cent within six years of taking over. The financial state-ments of privately owned companies are not published, so Peterson's personal wealth is not a matter of record. He has declined to estimate his worth. He rents a house on Forest Hill Road in posh north-end Toronto, and retreats on weekends to his country home, an old three-storey stone farmhouse on the outskirts of London. His close friends say he was a hard-nosed company president, who put the bottom line first.

Peterson happily plugged into the business world power network. He joined the Chamber of Commerce's Young Pres-idents' Club, that self-promoting group composed of company presidents who have made their companies a million before they are thirty. He was president of the London Canadian Club, and introduced the first joint meetings of the men's and women's branches. Business gave Peterson a taste for being in charge, managing things, doing deals, which has since proved an asset in his role as premier but didn't fit him well for guerrilla warfare as chief Opposition leader.

Still, he'd been immersed in political ideas from childhood.

His father, Clarence Peterson, came of a Saskatchewan farm family and saw enough misery in the prairies during the Depression to sign the Regina Manifesto, the 1933 program of the Co-operative Commonwealth Federation. Clarence married a Regina schoolteacher, then moved to London to found the family business. David says his parents took their duties to their children seriously, leading them in dinner-table discussion of current affairs and taking them swimming at the Y every Saturday night. Clarence's views mellowed into liberalism. He became a London alderman and controller and ran for the federal and provincial houses. His son remembers working on both those campaigns.

In one campaign – in 1955 for the provincial seat of London North – Clarence pitted himself against a young Tory backbencher named John Robarts, and, of course, lost. Seventeen years later, when Robarts committed suicide in despair over the impairment to his health caused by a series of strokes, David Peterson, as leader of the Opposition, eulogized the former premier as "a big man in every sense of the word; a man of stature and importance, yet one who had time to recognize and acknowledge a young man like myself, the son of his opponent in the game of politics."

Jim Peterson, the eldest of the three Peterson brothers, became a federal MP, but lost his seat in the 1984 election and now is manager of the family business. He and the Liberal premier are close and still talk politics regularly. Jim managed David's unsuccessful 1976 leadership bid, and Heather Peterson, Jim's wife, helped run David's 1985 election campaign and now dispenses government appointments from the premier's office.

His friend Ted McGrath, another London lawyer, urged Peterson to run in London Centre in the 1975 election. As part of his insouciant pose, Peterson tells interviewers he fell into politics by accident when McGrath happened to ask him. But, if pressed, he concedes that a lifetime interest made his candidacy inevitable some day. After winning a riding considered a Tory bastion, Peterson served his party as critic of several ministries – energy and the Treasury among them – reflecting a stronger interest in the financial than in the social side of government.

A few months before his selection as party leader, Hugh Winsor of the *Globe and Mail* wrote that Peterson sounded like a classical nineteenth-century liberal, espousing the virtues of free enterprise and individual liberty. Winsor noted Peterson's university service with Frontier College, teaching English to a rail gang in northern Saskatchewan, and his volunteer legal-aid work in Yorkville. But he put these good works down to youthful noblesse oblige and said Peterson's leadership bid would be a "carriage-trade campaign".

To be sure, Peterson talked a lot about individual initiative in his leadership campaign. Announcing his candidacy, he used phrases with which Frank Miller would have been entirely comfortable: "My immediate priority is economic growth. . . . Liberals are committed to growth because we know that economic policy is social policy. . . . Growth – growth which provides new jobs and new revenues – is the only fiscally responsible way that Ontario can meet the social imperatives of the coming decade." But Peterson also described himself as a "reform Liberal", committed to environmental clean-up, pension reform, equal pay for women, and the right to universal day care.

The party rebounded to Peterson after the attempts of former leader Stuart Smith, a sharp-tongued psychiatrist, to impose a substantial swing to the left. After Smith, the party rejected the left-Liberalism of Smith's protégé, Sheila Copps, Peterson's runner-up, in favour of a safe, low-key, and moderate leader. The out-going Smith compared Peterson to Bill Davis. "There are two possible strategies for the Liberals," Smith said. "To be more like the NDP and try to build an anti-Davis coalition. Or to be like the Tories and figure that when people get fed up they'll turn to the closest similar party. Peterson will go for the latter strategy."

For some time, Peterson did attempt to out-bland Bland Bill. He became, difficult though it was, even fuzzier on the issues than the premier. One newspaper columnist described

Peterson's policy as drift. Another, Orland French of the *Globe and Mail*, waded through an interview in which he tried to discover why a Liberal wanted to censor free expression, in the form of hate literature and pornography, and came away pronouncing Peterson "a man of two minds". In September 1983, Prime Minister Trudeau paid a visit to Queen's Park and asked Davis to guarantee French-language rights in Ontario in the new Constitution as a sign of good faith to Quebecers. Asked for his comments as the Ontario Liberal leader, Peterson attempted to dodge the issue in a series of muddy and contradictory statements to the press, favouring the principle of official bilingualism but rejecting the idea of entrenching it in the Constitution. Instead, he wanted a single Ontario law embodying Francophone rights. For this stance Peterson was later scorched by the federal Conservatives, who called him an impediment to official bilingualism in Ontario, scolded by Quebec Liberal leader Robert Bourassa, and roundly condemned in the press. Peterson didn't have Davis's talent for saying nothing inoffensively, or the prestige to carry it off. He didn't change his mind on official bilingualism, but he learned from the reaction and decided to try harder on other issues to stake out clearer positions from the beginning.

Peterson was taught his second lesson in the value of clarity later that month after the federal Liberals launched the Canada Health Act to ban extra billing by doctors. Peterson at first talked lamely of the extra-billing right as a "safety valve" protecting the individuality of the medical profession. Gradually he moved from condoning extra billing to condemning it. After a fractious caucus meeting in early September 1983, he announced a change of policy, citing a case in his own riding that had convinced him that extra billing must be banned. He was late catching up to his federal cousins. Peterson's change of mind, compared to the unwavering fight staged by the provincial NDP against extra billing, made him look like what he was – a latecomer on a popular bandwagon.

However, the change of position on extra billing meant that something was quietly changing in the Liberal caucus. In 1982

Peterson had inherited a party so poorly organized that no one knew the size of the membership. The post-election debt was close to $1 million, fund-raising and organizing out of party headquarters were amateurish, and, worst, about half of the thirty-four elected MPPs were a conservative, rural rump group from southwestern Ontario. Liberals held only six seats in eastern Ontario, one in the north, and two in Metro Toronto. The federal Liberals were strong in Ontario, but that very fact often worked to the disadvantage of the provincial Liberal party. Federal Liberals drained away much of the talent and money. The "feds" also reached tacit deals with the provincial Conservatives not to contest some provincial seats too strongly, particularly in the north, if Davis's organizers would lie low in certain Metro ridings in federal elections.

As leader, Stuart Smith had made a good beginning at tackling all these problems. He had ordered an end to lie-down deals with the Tories, had begun recruiting attractive urban candidates, particularly in Metro, and had attempted to swing his party left on policy, achieving his greatest success by championing environmental issues and by promoting industrial strategy for a province whose manufacturing base was increasingly obsolescent. Smith was a powerful speaker and an impressive intellect, but he lacked the personal skills to meld together right and left in his caucus. Also, his harsh criticisms appeared negative compared to Davis's smiling self-confidence – even though Smith's industrial strategy was better thought out than Davis's hastily assembled BILD program. Ontarians rejected Smith just as they had already rejected the NDP's brilliant Stephen Lewis. The province seemed to prefer its politicians dull and inoffensive.

But, although Smith was defeated electorally, he gave Peterson a base on which to build, particularly in Metro, where he had increased the Liberal vote in 1981, even if he had not increased representation in the House. After 1981, the Liberals were in a better competitive position than they'd been for a long time: they'd come first or second in seventy-seven per cent of the province's 125 ridings. By comparison,

New Democrats were first or second in only thirty-three per cent of the ridings.

Peterson was not in Smith's intellectual league, but his political instincts were superior. The internal debate in the Liberal party over what to do about Davis's Suncor announcement is a good case in point. Smith shared the NDP view that the province should have purchased a controlling, rather than a partial, interest, and owned its own oil company. Peterson disagreed: he thought the Suncor purchase would be a financial disaster and would appal the business community. Smith deferred to Peterson's business expertise and subsequently led the fight against the Suncor purchase. Smith wasn't very comfortable philosophically with what he was doing, but he had to admit that the Liberals got headlines – and points – for being right on Suncor.

Peterson, a more ordinary leader, was also much better liked by his caucus-mates than Smith had ever been. Smith's caucus meetings had been tense affairs in which he often lectured resentful MPPs, then afterwards suffered migraines from the frustrations of trying to overcome their rural attitudes. Peterson, by contrast, ran loose, joking caucus meetings, in which rancor was rare. Because they liked him, because he was seen as more of a moderate than Smith, Peterson was able to accomplish what his predecessor could not.

The caucus was fractious and disjointed. The only thing uniting right-wingers like Jack Riddell, a farmer and auctioneer from Huron-Middlesex, and the leftish urban liberals, best represented by Sheila Copps, who eventually deserted Peterson to become a federal MP and leader of John Turner's "rat pack", were their seats at the same table. Peterson somehow cajoled them into at least a semblance of party discipline and then began the policy shift towards appropriately Liberal positions.

Agreement that extra billing should be banned, for instance, finally put the provincial party in line with the federal Liberal government's policy. For at least one important Liberal, Ian Scott, it was the litmus test that persuaded him to run again for the provincial party. Scott, a highly respected Toronto labour lawyer who had run unsuccessfully for Smith in 1981, hadn't been sure what he would do after Smith was pushed out and the rural right wing appeared to be in control. When Peterson persuaded the party to agree on the extra-billing ban, Scott saw it as proof that the Ontario Liberals were prepared, after all, to be a modern urban party. In 1985 he contested and won the downtown Toronto riding of St. David and became one of Peterson's most influential ministers.

Extra billing was an early sign of what was, in large part, still to come. Peterson did not move himself, and his caucus, to the strong left-Liberal platform that he ran on in the election until much later. But, in the meantime, he built a leader's team in his office that was capable of running a modern, progressive campaign when he finally gave them the freedom to do it. Peterson's staff represented his efforts to reach beyond the old Liberal base: Daphne Rutherford advised on women's issues; Mordechai Ben-Dat tempered the leader's businessman views on labour unions; Anitha Johns-Noddle, an East Asian radio reporter, worked with the ethnic press; and Vince Borg, of Italian and Maltese extraction, had strong connections with the west-end Italians, who were federal Liberals but switched to the NDP's Italian MPPs in provincial elections. Peterson's choice of talented staff, from whom he was willing to learn and to whom he gave responsibility, was crucial to his later success.

Some of those staffers had first been attracted by Smith. Tom Zizys, a quiet, straightforward young lawyer, originally from Sudbury, became Peterson's director of research. Zizys is so indifferent to partisan politics that he has only voted twice in his life – once for René Lévesque's Parti Québécois when he lived in Montreal, and once for the Liberals in the 1985 election when he became excited at the prospect of toppling the Tory dynasty. What interests Zizys is public-policy formation and here he quickly proved his value to Peterson. With the help of financial expert John Whitelaw, he investigated the trust-company scandal, delving into the series of financial manoeuvres behind the $500-million flip of 11,000 Toronto apartments by financier Bill Player, and coming up with enough each day to give Peterson the edge in the legislature. He excoriated the government for its failure to regulate the trust industry – until the government finally moved to a full-scale investigation and seizure of one firm. For a few months, Peterson, and not the articulate Bob Rae, dominated Question Period.

Zizys had found Smith, with his intellectual grasp and breadth, a joy to advise, but Smith's staff were a warring, often unhappy group. Peterson is a man who insists on short verbal briefings, because he doesn't like painstaking intellectual endeavour. But he created a staff with good mutual chemistry. Peterson kept reminding his researchers of the excellent team that had made Stephen Lewis look so good in the mid-1970s and declared, "I want that too." Peterson resisted his staff's attempts to place him always on the attack, saying he had to have positive policy alternatives as well. Task forces of Liberal MPPs, notably the Sheila Copps task force on health policy and John Sweeney's on youth unemployment, fanned out to Ontario communities to investigate, produce reports, and offer fresh approaches. But much of the real policy formation came from the work that Zizys and his team invested in what were euphemistically called "backgrounders". In a party that then had no formal policy apparatus for deciding its public platform but relied on caucus for direction, Zizys and his researchers provided the brains trust that came up with ideas and brought them to caucus. In the early days, caucus wasn't always receptive. But the research team kept plugging away on its backgrounders, waiting for the day when the ideas would be wanted. Zizys was the keeper of the Liberal flame.

Vince Borg, whose Italian mother and Maltese father operated a tropical-food import store in Kensington Market, was a young Liberal who went to work for Smith as a university student, driving his car and travelling with him on the road. Borg had a pleasant, gentle manner and good party connections. Smith chose him as chairman of candidate search, finding new faces to contest the 125 ridings in the 1981 election. Meanwhile, Borg and Peterson had become friends and Borg found himself acting as liaison in the tense atmosphere between Smith, the party leader, and his incipient challenger. When Smith resigned, Borg became Peterson's personal aide, handling relations with the party, smoothing out disputes, travelling with Peterson on the long drives to speak to small audiences, staying in hotels so crummy that Borg remembers using the drapes when there were no towels. As a result of the constant intimacy, Borg became the one staffer who always knew what Peterson was feeling or how he would react.

The pivotal addition to the Peterson team was Hershell Ezrin, a former Canadian diplomat who worked in the Canadian Unity Information Office during the constitutional talks, and afterwards started looking for more action. Ezrin, who combines rumpled personal charm, a flair for public relations, political savvy, and an intelligent understanding of public-policy issues, was just what Peterson needed. The problem was to convince Ezrin to leave his federal Liberal haven, where he had heavyweight friends in government, and take a flyer on the Ontario Liberals. Peterson called Ezrin in March 1982 and told him that together they could make history by toppling the Ontario Conservatives. It seemed a wild gamble to Ezrin. The Tory regime had been ruling Ontario since 1943, the year Peterson was born, and Ezrin is four years younger. Neither had ever known another government. But he met Peterson for lunch and decided the Liberal leader was not as right-wing as he'd been portrayed. Ezrin took the job as Peterson's chief of staff, with a free hand to use his talents to make Peterson a winner. Peterson must have suffered a certain personal humiliation as Ezrin went to work on him.

The Liberal leader was uncomfortable with the Opposition job of criticism and attack. He didn't know how to go for the throat and too often threw away good research with an ineffectual delivery. His staff despaired of developing the missing killer instinct. It seemed Peterson would never master the art of placing a question in a context that explained its public importance. So Ezrin and George Hutchison, a former

London Free Press columnist, who directed Peterson's communications, found a balance: Peterson stuck to the one-liners that made for good TV clips, but Liberal research put out the "backgrounders" that explained what it was all about. These issue explanations from Liberal research were a useful tool for harried press-gallery reporters, and they built Liberal credibility. Hutchison mailed them to newspapers and to radio and television stations across the province. On the major issues, editors would usually find they had a Liberal backgrounder in their file.

Ezrin also called in Gabor Apor, an independent television producer who had worked with Peterson during his 1982 leadership campaign, in an effort to improve his speaking style. The two went to work, videotaping Peterson's appearances and then making him watch to see what he was doing wrong. Apor dragged Peterson out to television studios, sat him in front of cameras, and coached him over and over until he began to acquire an easier manner. Hutchison helped Peterson produce a cable show, "David Peterson's Ontario", on which the Liberal leader played curious host, interviewing public personalities like singer Salome Bey, business magnate Conrad Black, broadcaster Gordon Sinclair, and labour leader Cliff Pilkey about their lives. Hutchison peddled tapes of the show – free. In some smaller communities, the Liberal leader became a Sunday-afternoon regular. At the same time he became increasingly confident on television.

Peterson's appearance also underwent a thorough renovation. His staff, with Apor's help, persuaded him to abandon his heavy glasses, telling him they were a barrier between him and his audience. He adopted soft contact lenses and a more mature, groomed hairstyle. Bob Rae, also horn-rimmed, was sceptical at first, vowing "I'd rather fight than switch," but when he saw how much better Peterson appeared, he adopted contacts occasionally himself. Peterson's garb varied endlessly: navy three-piece suits one day, tweed jackets and corduroys the next. Gabor Apor carried him off to the men's stores to choose a wardrobe that would give him a consistent style – suits that were socially easy but well cut, and in dark colours chosen with television in mind. Jogging three miles a day made Peterson's body and face lean, less pudgy. Just before the election, Apor persuaded him to adopt the red tie that has since become his trademark. It was a small trick, intended to make him immediately identifiable – a more tasteful tag than the garish tartan jackets that Frank Miller wore only a few times but could never escape thereafter.

Amusingly, that little red tie was the end product of a year's discussion in Peterson's backrooms. Hershell Ezrin and George Hutchison had had endless deliberations about an appropriate and memorable symbol for their leader. Finally, they felt they had it. Peterson was a jogger, and they intended to use lots of pictures of him in motion in an election – a man running into the future. What would be better than a campaign button featuring a pair of red running-shoes and the slogan "Running With Peterson"? However, Gabor Apor was not impressed. Instead, he came up with the simple trick of the red tie, and the others acclaimed his brilliance. None of them knew that the tie was an old idea. Mitchell Hepburn always wore red ties too when he appeared at major events. For one election, his tie was so bright that a biographer described it as "crimson". But that had been almost half a century before, and Peterson's Liberals didn't remember.

The Peterson team had decided to sell him as a caring, compassionate businessman. They wanted voters to feel he was competent and modern, and philosophically a man of the safe centre occupied for so long by the Tories. Peterson, they felt, was not uncaring. He was ready to be progressive and active on social issues, but his background as a businessman had not exposed him to a wide spectrum of society. They decided to groom his ideas as well. Peterson wouldn't sit still for written briefings, so the staff took him out to see for himself – to a day-care centre, to downtown Toronto flophouses for the indigent, to the low-income high-rises of the Jane/Finch corridor, to talk to labour leaders such as Robert White of the Autoworkers. A Women's Perspective Advisory Committee was formed to educate the leader on key women's issues.

Over a two-year period, Peterson's staff grew very pleased with themselves. They had good chemistry, liked working together, and felt they were the best leader's team at Queen's Park. Their good spirits were viewed sourly by experienced MPPs in the caucus who couldn't see reasons for optimism at that point in the party's fortunes.

Peterson had retired half of the party debt, leaving it about $700,000 in the hole. The ridings were in better shape financially. However, party headquarters was still so under-staffed and disorganized that supporters complained they weren't getting their receipts to allow them to claim tax deductions for their political contributions. The Conservatives and New Democrats both had five full-time paid organizers, one for each region of the province, while the Liberals had only one part-time official. The polls also showed that Peterson was making no impact on Ontarians. In the House, he was outshone by Bob Rae. It was Bicentennial year, and Bill Davis and his ministers were making the most of the celebrations as they travelled the province planting white pines and appearing with visiting dignitaries.

Peterson spent part of the summer of 1984 at his cottage, a time he remembers as "the worst holiday in my life". He was filling in as househusband to three small children, one in diapers, while his wife Shelley played in summer stock at the Huron Country Playhouse near Grand Bend. Mired in domesticity, he also faced serious political woes. He'd been leader for a little over two years, and the media were unkindly pointing out that the Liberals had lost all three by-elections held in that time. Earl McEwen, Liberal MPP for Frontenac-Addington, crossed the floor to the Tory benches, saying Peterson was going nowhere. Then, at the cottage, the tele-phone started ringing. Sheila Copps, the only woman in the Liberal caucus, was calling to say she had decided to run on John Turner's team in the federal election. So was Eric Cunningham, holder of a Hamilton-area seat that seemed likely to go Tory without him. Then Don Boudria and Albert Roy, the two Francophones in the caucus, checked in with the same news. It was awful, said Peterson. It got worse.

In September, John Turner was swept from office in Brian Mulroney's Tory tide, and commentators suggested that Canadian Liberalism was in its death throes. At Queen's Park, the MPPs began muttering about Peterson's leadership. He had failed to give his party a clear profile on the issues and didn't know how to mount a fighting opposition. Two of the most senior MPPs quit politics altogether. Patrick Reid, the Liberals' only member from Northern Ontario, left to become executive director of the Ontario Mining Association, and James Breithaupt of Kitchener took a Tory appointment as chairman of the Ontario Law Reform Commission.

Peterson kept up a bouncy public front, telling interviewers that his party was in good organizational shape, that he'd worked hard at getting strong candidates for the expected fall election, and – more tenuously – that the NDP was collapsing everywhere and Liberals would benefit. Then, suddenly, before his boasts could be put to the test, came the announcement that was to reverse his fortunes entirely. Instead of calling an election, Davis told the world on Thanksgiving Day that he was stepping down.

It took a while for the significance of the departure to sink in. All that fall, while the media were filled with the leadership race to choose Davis's successor, and Davis himself still sat reassuringly in the premier's chair, Ontarians continued to think Tory. Davis called five of the seven impending by-elections, attempting to tidy up for his successor. Four of the seats had been Liberal and only two stayed that way. The legislature then had 72 Conservatives, 28 Liberals, and 22 New Democrats. Bob Rae pointed to the by-elections, in which his party picked up two Liberal seats, while one went Conservative, as "proof the Liberals are in decline and we are on the move." Polling that fall by Decima Research gave the Conservatives a spectacular 53-per-cent lead, to 22 per cent for the Liberals and 25 per cent for the NDP.

In this crucible of humiliation after humiliation, Peterson began to show some steel. He had meant well, and had tried hard, and his instincts hadn't borne fruit. Now he began to ask his staff and his confidants in caucus, Sean Conway and Robert Nixon, "How do I make this thing work?"

They replied that he'd failed to define what he and his party stood for. His own people told him that, and so did some powerful federal backroom Liberals. John Turner's electoral defeat turned out to have a bright side for Peterson. Frightened by the tide of anti-Liberalism that had swept them from office, the federal Liberals now realized that if they were to rebuild, they had first to mend fences in Ontario. The provincial party, once a despised poor cousin, suddenly became the carrier of the torch. Peterson, however, had his own team, which he trusted, and was not about to allow Senator Keith Davey or federal Liberal pollster Martin Goldfarb to take over.

But, although it has been a carefully guarded secret, Peterson did get considerable help from "the feds". Davey was certainly in the picture. The week Bill Davis was contemplating his resignation, reporters keeping vigil at Davis's retreat in the Harbour Castle Hotel happened to notice Peterson and Davey heading into a strategy session together. Davey had been boosting Ontario Liberal spirits for some time. A year before that, when Robert Nixon considered giving up the battle – a potential mortal blow for Peterson, who needed the experienced former leader for his strength and advice – and lobbied for a Senate seat, Davey told him to hold on. The Grits would win the next Ontario election, Davey said – he could feel it in the political tremors – and then Nixon would want to be in Ontario. But Davey's role seems mostly to have been to provide long-distance advice. The Ontario Liberals didn't then, and don't now, want to be seen as puppets of the slick backroom boys who advised Pierre Trudeau when he was prime minister.

However, two federal Liberals did play major roles for Peterson, guiding his rehabilitation and laying some of the groundwork for his astonishing electoral win. The federal Liberal who the press knew in some hazy way was operating behind the scenes was Gordon Ashworth, a former federal campaign director who was known to Ezrin, to Borg, and to Peterson's sister-in-law Heather. Ashworth is a calm, cool, political mechanic who was campaign director for the Trudeau Liberals when they lost in 1979 and again in 1980 when they won. He was part of the salvage team that Keith Davey assembled part-way through the 1984 federal election in a desperate attempt to stop John Turner's slide out of the prime minister's seat. Afterwards, Ashworth formed a consulting company with former Trudeau aide Tom Axworthy, but Axworthy soon departed to teach at Harvard, leaving Ashworth at loose ends. Peterson hired Ashworth to be what he euphemistically called his campaign co-ordinator, a backroom assistant to the Liberal campaign chairman, Ross McGregor. But while they kept him hidden at party headquarters, and kept denying his importance, Ashworth was really the overall strategic planner for the spring election campaign.

Working under even deeper cover was Senator Michael Kirby, Ezrin's former mentor at the Canadian Unity Information Office. Kirby, former head of the policy unit in Trudeau's office and a man with experience running provincial campaigns in Nova Scotia, had recently become a partner in pollster Martin Goldfarb's firm of Goldfarb Associates. In February 1985, Kirby conducted a series of fourteen focus-group interviews in five Ontario cities on behalf of the Ontario Liberal party. Focus groups are less expensive than polls of a scientific size, but because they are conducted in person and at greater length, they are a useful guide to public attitudes. Peterson couldn't afford anything more. But, through Kirby – who naturally spent a lot of time talking to Goldfarb – Peterson tapped into the federal Liberal pollster's considerable information bank on the current state of public opinion. Kirby spelled out in detail for Peterson just how badly he was doing, and how much he needed to change.

Kirby's report told Peterson bluntly that if an election were called soon, the new Conservative leader Frank Miller, elected only a few weeks earlier, could expect to win with a reduced majority. The NDP would be the beneficiary of any Tory fallout and could expect to replace the Liberals as the Official

Opposition. The NDP's Bob Rae was seen as a dynamic young leader who stood up for working Ontarians, and therefore represented a constituency different from the Tories. But Peterson had a much weaker image; people were not very impressed by him, and felt that he represented the same well-to-do and middle-class constituency as the Conservatives. Kirby told Peterson that he had to become bold, caring, and noticeable. He recommended he adopt strong, clear positions on a few key issues, positioning his party in the left-centre of the Ontario political spectrum.

Kirby's advice coincided with the great lift in spirits that Peterson had felt as he watched the Conservative convention choose Frank Miller. Peterson had never known how to perform against Bill Davis's unflappable self-confidence. "Davis was a fearsome adversary," Peterson confessed after the former premier retired from the field. "He always had a style, a presence, that few politicians have." Peterson's worst fear had been that Davis would be replaced by Roy McMurtry, who he felt had a visceral teddy-bear appeal that would be hard to beat on television. But Miller was a small, mediocre-looking man whom Peterson rated as far less dangerous. Others in the Liberal caucus worried that Miller might be a threat in the rural, small-town ridings, but not Peterson. He felt Miller would be a disaster politically, and he felt able to deal with him. His caucus watched the lift in Peterson's confidence with some surprise, but his instincts turned out to be right.

Suddenly, with Miller as premier, Peterson knew what to do. He'd been unable until that moment to decide where to position his party. But Miller was a perceived right-winger. For the first time in forty-two years a vacuum was left in Ontario politics in the middle which Davis had straddled so effectively. Tom Zizys found his backgrounders in demand. Zizys had been appalled at the thought that Davis would call a fall election. He knew Peterson had his candidates ready, and the Liberal campaign bus was ready to roll, but the party platform lacked thrust. All Peterson had to offer, in a speech he gave the day after Davis resigned – a speech designed for an election kick-off – was "change from forty-one years of Tory rule" with its polls, patronage, and privilege. Peterson attacked, but failed to offer an alternative.

Now, with Miller in office, the Liberals were willing to move on all that pent-up policy Zizys had been pushing. Miller's Ontario was a small-businessman's world, which left a lot of people out. The Liberals moved to grab the social-conscience role from the NDP, and to appeal to the people Miller was turning off – urbanites, women, youth, and ethnic organizations. In the past, Zizys had taken policies on such subjects as rent review to caucus only to have doubters turn them back. Now he was taking three or four projects to caucus a week and coming out shaking his head over how easy it had been to persuade the members. Suddenly the Liberal MPPs were in favour of bringing buildings built after 1976 under rent controls, or in favour of first-contract arbitration to end bitter union-recognition battles such as the one going on at Eaton's. Peterson knew the only way he could win was to be bold, and he persuaded his mates to take the chance with him.

There was a rush to get the platform out to the public before the election call. Peterson began announcing Liberal policies on youth unemployment or health care in press conferences across the province. Some of the policies had been developed over the last couple of years and some were brand new. For each announcement, the researchers used Stephen Lewis's old trick of picking a carefully chosen illustrative locale – day-care policies unveiled at a day-care centre, for example, or youth-unemployment announcements repeated over and over in communities where Peterson could say just how his proposals would work locally and just what they would cost. The technique was a dry run for the election campaign. It produced lots of local headlines and became central to the strategy Peterson was to use in the election.

There was some zip now to the Ontario Liberals, a sign of momentum. For the Ontario Liberal party annual meeting, held February 16 at the Metro Convention Centre, organizers were expecting about eight hundred people. Instead, thirteen hundred showed up, and, in high spirits, Peterson outlined the new Liberal platform: a guarantee of a first job for every young person looking for work; increased hospital funding; a ban on extra billing; the abolishment of OHIP premiums so that medicare would be paid totally out of general revenue; equal pay for work of equal value; ten thousand new subsidized child-care spaces – the bones of a program that soon included denticare, environmental clean-up, a housing program, and, for pizzazz, a commitment to allow the sale of beer and wine in corner stores.

As the Liberals cheered, Peterson looped a tartan scarf around his neck and dared Miller to match his promises. "Frank Miller is going to help us win this election," he proclaimed. Then, casting off the scarf, he added: "The people of Ontario will quickly catch on to just how out of touch Frank Miller and the real Tory party have become."

4

A Fatal Complacency

The day after Frank Miller became premier-designate, his aide Michael Perik called for copies of the government advertising contracts held by Norman Atkins' firm of Camp Associates and Tom Scott's Foster Advertising. Perik felt that the delegates who'd voted for Frank Miller wanted change at the top of the party – and he, Perik, was ready to start with Norman Atkins.

To his frustration, Perik found that the tourism ministry had renewed its contract with Camp Associates during Davis's last weeks in office. There was a ninety-day cancellation clause, but Perik never found time to use it, or to implement his plan to bring in competitive bidding for advertising contracts. He soon became immersed in election preparations, and then it was too late: Miller lost twenty seats and fired Perik. The tourism account stayed with Camp until David Peterson came into office and exercised the cancellation prerogative.

Atkins, in fact, never learned Perik's precise intentions. But if he didn't know the details, he certainly sensed that the Miller mechanics wanted to dismantle the Big Blue Machine as quickly as possible. Within the ruling circles of the Conservative party, a turf war was under way.

Miller and Davis seem to have made genuine attempts to smooth over the differences, but the people around them were not to be reconciled. At his media conference on the Sunday after the leadership convention, a conciliatory Miller said that Segal and Atkins, in particular, would be invited to play important roles. "During the campaign the ideological differences in our party were made to seem worse than they are," Miller said. "They are not half as extreme as they've been painted."

Miller, of course, shared Perik's wish to put the Davis backroom boys out to pasture. But he knew that what was expected of him as premier was compromise. In public, at least, he was prepared to moderate both his right-wing philosophy and his personal grudges. Others on his team were less restrained. Lou Parsons, chairman of Miller's successful leadership campaign, gleefully told the media that there wouldn't be room on the tartan train for the Big Blue Machine – and in particular for Hugh Segal, who had worked so hard for Grossman. The whole Davis circle was annoyed, not just on Segal's account, but because Parsons had himself once been a charter member of the BBM. Global television caught up with Norman Atkins, who snapped: "If there is no room for Hugh Segal, there is no room for me!"

Next, the indiscreet Parsons angered Perik by publicly admitting that Timbrell might have triumphed over Miller at the convention. "We wouldn't have won it against Dennis," Parsons acknowledged. "Our winning strategy was always to be against Larry . . . and in the end we were lucky." For these lapses, Parsons was quickly "deep-sixed". He went off to Florida for a holiday and was seldom seen around Queen's Park thereafter.

Other Miller loyalists met the same fate, though they don't appear to have committed overt mistakes justifying their exclusion. John Balkwill, deputy chairman of Miller's leadership campaign, went back to his Ottawa dental practice, only to find that his leader wouldn't take his phone calls. The premier was busy, he was repeatedly told. Hugh Mackenzie, a friend who'd run Miller's Muskoka campaigns – and a former party vice-president – also felt himself shut out. The small and inexperienced group around Miller were creating an exclusive club, and within it tensions were rising.

In the leader's office, Michael Perik and David Melnik competed over who was going to wield most influence over Miller. The 28-year-old Perik shared as little information as possible, rousing Melnik's suspicions that Perik was trying to cut him out of the game. For his part, Perik felt Melnik had proved dangerously naive as Miller's negotiator during the leadership contest. He disliked the way Melnik now revelled in his role as adviser to the premier and swore that at the moment of Miller's victory he'd heard Melnik say under his breath, "My hour has come." The intense jealousy between the two men helped make the atmosphere around Miller jittery and devoid of the good spirits that usually follow political victory.

Miller found his stomach in knots. He was dismayed when Laird Saunderson, who'd handled Davis's scheduling and appointments for years, decided she would leave with Davis rather than endure the tensions of the new premier's office. Miller knew that the transition wasn't working, but there was no one to tell him just what was wrong. He was dangerously isolated.

Most of the old Davis crowd did little to mend the rift in their party. However, two of Davis's most faithful servants, his deputy, Ed Stewart, and his principal secretary, John Tory, stayed in their jobs to help with the transition. That was the way it had always been done in the Tory dynasty. Leslie Frost's staff had stayed to help John Robarts learn the ropes, and Frost himself was consulted on every major decision that Robarts made during his first year in office. A decade later, Robarts' staff remained with Davis, helping him through the first shaky months, until Davis established an election majority in his own right. Davis consulted Robarts before stopping the Spadina expressway and on several other policy issues. Therefore, Davis and his senior staff assumed that Miller would want them around and blinkered themselves to the awkward reality. Miller hadn't felt part of their inner circle in the last years, and he was not Davis's heir apparent, in the way that Davis had been Robarts'.

So Tory and Stewart prepared transition briefing books, and then sat in their offices waiting to be called. They didn't realize that to the Millerites it appeared that the Big Blue Machine, through Tory and Stewart, intended to go on running the government. Miller established a police-guarded suite of offices at the top of the Four Seasons Hotel in preparation for the handover of power on February 8, when he'd be sworn in along with his new cabinet. Davis didn't approve of Miller's temporary rival court, and his people were quick to take offence at real or imagined slights from what they called "the bunker". More than once Davis said he felt as if he was in the trenches with the Germans about to invade.

In turn, the Davis defenders had adopted their own siege mentality. When Joan Walters, who had been Davis's press secretary for a year, went up to the Four Seasons to join Miller as his media adviser, her former friends in the Big Blue Machine suddenly turned cold. The people down the street at Queen's Park treated her as a traitor, and Atkins cut off relations. Tom Campbell, chairman of Ontario Hydro and Miller's former deputy treasurer, also incurred the group's displeasure. Campbell had been on staff in Davis's office during the transition from Robarts, and, armed with that experience, he obtained Davis's approval before he went to help Miller. But Campbell, as it turned out, was not the efficient conduit for the Big Blue Machine's influence that its members expected. As a senior bureaucrat under Davis, he too felt that an unelected group of insiders had held undue sway over the government. So he began planning for a shake-up, both of personnel and of policy, which the Davis people rightly interpreted as a rejection of the old winning ways. To this day, Campbell hasn't been forgiven. Stewart, Segal, and Goodman blame him almost as much as they do Perik for destroying the dynasty by cutting out the old professionals who they think might have prevented Miller's mistakes.

The notion that the Davis pros could have benevolently guided Miller in his early days, however, overlooks the tensions that wracked the Conservative party in the aftermath of the leadership race. In particular it ignores Larry Grossman, who was determined that the Big Blue Machine would owe its first loyalty to him. Grossman expected to be Miller's chief lieutenant, a powerful influence with his own loyal and separate base in the party. Because he won forty-eight per cent of the convention vote, he felt he owned the progressive wing of the party, and had a claim to be second only to the premier. He didn't like the fact that Alan Pope was a regular in Miller's quarters at the Four Seasons, while he himself had to make an appointment and go there as a visitor.

Neither of the other two leadership candidates, Dennis Timbrell or Roy McMurtry, were in an immediate position to undermine Miller's leadership. Timbrell was stunned by his unanticipated defeat. He hung around only long enough to secure his own cabinet seat and then escaped to Florida to heal his wounds in the sun. Timbrell was to be minister of municipal affairs and housing as well as minister responsible for women's issues – a combination, the competitive Grossman noted, that would give him good contacts with municipal politicians across the province and a high profile handling women's issues. But Timbrell made the mistake of letting his team dissolve around him. He felt that he'd been robbed of victory not only by the convention-floor manoeuvres of his rivals, but by the failure of his own organizers to deliver. Before closing down Timbrell's campaign headquarters, Peter Weed, Paul's son, launched Operation Unity by asking Timbrell workers to climb aboard Miller's train. The gesture did the Weeds no good. Miller was annoyed at the suggestion people had to be persuaded to like him. Timbrell cut himself off from managers he now believed were bunglers.

Roy McMurtry was preparing to leave politics altogether. During the leadership campaign, when he had made himself the voice of Tory populism, McMurtry had promised he would stay and fight for more compassionate government. In defeat, however, an offer from his good friend Brian Mulroney seemed more attractive. Joan Walters and Tom Campbell, learning that McMurtry was holding a farewell party at the La Scala restaurant, cornered him there and argued that he should stay and fight for the things he had stood for in the leadership campaign. McMurtry said there was no use, because he was outnumbered by people who shared Miller's right-wing views. The next day, McMurtry and Miller held a joint news conference at the Four Seasons, at which McMurtry insisted his departure had nothing to do with Miller – it was just time to move on. "To everyone there is a season," McMurtry said. The former attorney general then flew off to Extapa, Mexico, to await Mulroney's formal announcement that would send him to London as Canadian High Commissioner. Miller was upset and hurt: Davis's closest friend in cabinet was saying, in effect, that Miller's Ontario wasn't worth staying around for.

Grossman, too, retreated for a few days' skiing in Collingwood, but was soon back making waves, protecting his own position and his people. He and Miller attempted a formal peace. Grossman demanded assurances that he was wanted, and Miller gave them. But they could not overcome a mutual antipathy going back many years. Friends trace it to the days when Miller was health minister and Grossman, as a newly elected backbencher, successfully fought his plans to close Doctors' Hospital in Grossman's riding. Over the years, the rivalry and dislike intensified. In private conversations, each said the other was not to be trusted; each assumed the other would destroy him, given an opportunity. Grossman threatened to leave, knowing that his resignation would weaken Miller's chances in Metro Toronto. It was a powerful weapon, and Miller agreed to reappoint him treasurer, and to keep Susan Fish, a Grossman loyalist, in cabinet. But he dropped George Taylor of Simcoe, the former solicitor general, and Grossman resented losing this ally.

Miller had his reasons for bitterness, too. The animosity his team displayed towards Segal came from their conviction that he'd associated them with those who engaged in anti-Semitic whisperings during the leadership campaign. Grossman and Segal, on the other hand, both believed that Miller organizers had played Grossman's Jewishness against him, although Grossman was always careful to say that he did not suspect Miller himself. David Melnik, Miller's business adviser and now head of his transition team, was a Jew who had lost family at Auschwitz and hated suggestions he'd work for an anti-Semite. One of Miller's first acts as leader was to arrange a meeting at the Four Seasons with leaders of the Canadian Jewish Congress to lay to rest any worries about his alleged anti-Semitism.

Melnik also still bore a grudge against Alan Schwartz, Grossman's fund-raiser and close friend, who had deceived him so thoroughly during the leadership. He wanted to strike Schwartz's name from Tom Campbell's list of those invited to join the transition team. Schwartz felt Melnik simply didn't understand why it had been necessary for him to lie, so he marched down to Melnik's office at Vanguard Trust one day for a confrontation. Schwartz argued that he'd been put in an impossible position when Melnik asked him straight out about the deal with Timbrell, and that a political pro doesn't put another in the position of having to lie to protect his candidate. It was an angry scene, which neither man enjoyed, and the patch-up was perfunctory.

By this time it was obvious to everyone that there would be no quick fixes of the division within the party. Miller had been strongly advised by Davis's people to hold a unity dinner, like the famous 1971 dinner where Davis won Atkins to his banner from his rival Allan Lawrence's camp. Senator William Kelly, Davis's fund-raiser, was asked by Miller to arrange the dinner at the Bradgate Arms hotel. Kelly made some calls, but soon reported back to Miller that a unity dinner wouldn't work – people were not in a receptive mood.

Miller was puzzled. He felt he had gone through the appropriate motions. He spent his first few days calling key people on the other campaign teams, telling John Laschinger and John Bitove and Brian Armstrong that he wanted them on board. He was leader now, and he had just assumed that they'd fall in behind him. He didn't seem to understand that he still had to prove himself by taking charge – firmly – and that being elected leader was only one step to becoming premier.

Miller's prolonged negotiations with Norman Atkins revealed the new premier's uncertainties. In the beginning, Miller and Perik were determined that Atkins would not continue to play the role he'd enjoyed with Davis. Instead, Miller would put his own stamp on things by appointing Patrick Kinsella as chairman of the election he intended to hold soon. Kinsella, they thought, would be a peace-offering to the whole party: he was the former executive director of the Ontario Progressive Conservatives, but had spent the last four years working in British Columbia and so hadn't been a partisan in the internal party war. He'd worked for Larry Grossman at the convention, but he was also an ally of Perik's from the days when Perik had worked for him at party headquarters. It seemed Kinsella could cross all the party's internal lines.

No sooner had Miller made his choice, however, than he began to waver. Roy McMurtry urged Miller to make Atkins campaign chairman, arguing that no one else could offer his combination of experience and immense prestige within the party. Miller consulted Joan Walters, who knew that Perik and others feared Atkins would expect future ad contracts in return for his services. Walters advised Miller to put aside such fears and choose Atkins on the basis of his previous electoral successes. With this advice in mind, and perhaps a little intimidated by the Atkins legend, the new premier ended up asking Atkins to be chairman when the two men met in the premier's hotel suite.

Having brought himself to that difficult point, Miller was nonplussed by the reply. Atkins is often described by his friends as a lovable teddy bear, but he can be blunt and steely-eyed when he wants. This was one of those occasions. Atkins urged Miller to put election planning to one side and concentrate instead on preparing a Throne Speech before going to the people. As for being campaign chairman, Atkins said, "I'll have to think about it." He wanted to be sure that Miller was handling things right, which meant keeping Ed Stewart and John Tory in their jobs. Finally, Atkins stressed that, if he were to be campaign chairman, he had to have complete authority to do it his way. Miller, a man who makes a point of pleasant courtesy, was taken aback by Atkins' aggressive manner toward an incoming premier. He didn't know Atkins well enough to understand that he always came on surly and tough until he'd made a commitment – and then spared no effort.

Understandably enough, Miller also felt he now was in charge and was entitled to do things his way – not the Davis way. He asked John Tory to come to see him at the Four Seasons, and he told Tory that Michael Perik would be taking over as principal secretary. Miller expected Tory to take his dismissal quietly, assuming he'd understand the leader's desire to give this key job to someone he trusted and liked. But Tory had been assured by Davis that he would be essential to the transition. He felt Miller owed him, because the premier-designate had asked him to be secretary of the election campaign, and Tory had agreed. He had his own political ambitions: he wanted to run as a candidate in the election and move quickly into cabinet. Miller wasn't encouraging about Tory's future in his administration. In dismay, Tory rushed down to Bill Davis's office, where the departing premier was having his picture taken with his staff, and reported he'd been fired.

A troubled Davis set out to see Miller, reaching his well-guarded Four Seasons suite by the freight elevator to avoid the ever-present media. He urged Miller, as strongly as Davis ever urges anything, to retain Atkins as campaign manager and to keep both Tory and Ed Stewart around for a while because he would need their experience of government. Miller threw up his hands, and the next day called Tory back to the Four Seasons and said he had been lobbied by Davis, Kelly, and Goodman to keep him on. He wanted Tory to understand that he was not fired and that he would have another job in the cabinet office. Miller had backed down under pressure – and he knew it. He told his speech-writer, Jim Anthony, "We looked weak on that one."

Pushed in two directions, Miller was unable to choose between them. His own team, particularly Perik, strongly urged him to bring his own people into all key positions and oust the old regime. Les Jones, of Research Spectrum, had polled for Miller to determine what Ontarians were expecting, and found a strong sentiment for change. Perik felt it was important to send messages that the Davis days were over and somebody new was in charge.

The other view, championed by Davis himself, stressed the importance of continuity. Davis felt Miller underestimated the difficulties of being premier and did not know how much he would need advice in the first few months from seasoned staff. Around Davis, as he moved into private life, there was an overwhelming conviction that Miller could succeed only if he listened carefully to the former premier's key advisers.

Miller might have chosen one or the other of these strategies – a clean break or continuity – with some hope of success. Instead, he responded to both impulses at once, and the result was confusion and muddle. Miller couldn't make up his mind about Norman Atkins, who was absolutely central to a strategy of reconciliation with the Davis Tories. Atkins was an old football pal of Roy McMurtry's, the brother-in-law of Dalton Camp, a frequent attender at Davis's famous Park Plaza Tuesday breakfast meetings, and the chairman of Davis's majority election win in 1981. In 1984, Atkins had orchestrated Brian Mulroney's smashing federal election win, following which Camp Associates took over the federal tourism account.

Atkins also represented Brian Mulroney's large debt to Davis. Davis had freed Atkins to run Mulroney's campaign and had himself hit the election trail hard on Mulroney's behalf. The election had brought the federal Conservatives sixty-seven seats in Ontario, formerly a mainstay of Pierre Trudeau's Liberal government. With Atkins at Miller's shoulder, Mulroney would have been unable to give Miller short shrift, as he later did.

To Michael Perik's fury, David Melnik used his clout as a trusted adviser who was outside party squabbles to urge Miller along the path of conciliation. Melnik suspected that Perik's wish to part from the Davis crowd did not serve Miller's best interests and was, in fact, part of Perik's attempt to foist his own right-wing agenda on the province. Among the premier's other staff, Melnik touted Tory as a better principal secretary.

Against Perik's advice, Miller met once more with Atkins, this time at the premier's office at Queen's Park, and asked him again to be campaign chairman. And once again Atkins held back. He suspected that Miller wanted him as a symbol of reconciliation but didn't really intend to put him in charge, and Atkins was not prepared to play a token role. He repeated his demand for full authority over the campaign, and Miller agreed, on condition that certain people be included on the campaign team. Atkins met at Camp Associates with Kinsella, Perik, Tory, and Melnik to see if they could work out a mutually acceptable organizational plan. They reached an agreement that Atkins would be chairman, but Perik and Kinsella told him that McKim Advertising, a firm both had worked with in the past, would do the campaign advertising. Atkins felt that no single agency should have the job – Davis had always used a consortium – and was annoyed that his authority to establish the campaign structure was already being challenged.

Atkins flew to Curtain Bluff, Antigua, to holiday and play tennis. While he was away, Miller was rethinking the appointment. He'd been told, although he later doubted the tale, that on his way out of the premier's office, Atkins had muttered, "That guy will never win." Key people from Miller's leadership campaign – Ted Matthews and Larry Steinman – were threatening to quit if Atkins were chairman. Miller called for videotapes of the recent convention, viewed Atkins' devastated expression when Grossman lost on the last ballot, and then called Perik and asked, "Can we do it without Norman?" Perik quickly talked to Kinsella, who agreed to be chairman. Then Miller called Atkins in Antigua and told him he'd decided not to have him as campaign chairman after all. "That is your right, and I wish you and Pat well," Atkins replied. Miller was a bit shaken, and as he put down the phone, he turned to Perik and said: "We'd better win this election, Michael!"

Miller was later to call this a key error. He'd been offended by Atkins' manner and was unwilling to go to extra lengths to secure his services. Kinsella simply wasn't Atkins' equal: he was a good tactician, but his manner was hard-nosed. He'd been away from Ontario for four years and didn't know the party as well as he once had. He'd learned, during rough years as Bill Bennett's political lieutenant, to distrust reporters, and he treated members of the media as adversaries to be avoided at all times. Kinsella, who called himself the best hack in Canada – although he declined when the campaign went badly to take any money – was not in the election out of devotion to the Miller cause. He felt he owed the Ontario Tories for his start in politics – and besides he wanted to rebuild his contacts and business in Ontario.

Atkins, on the other hand, was an ideal election chairman. He was the big-picture expert, who could assemble a team that worked together in good spirits and without hitches. By firing him, Miller had renounced the one person who might have melded the hostile factions of the party into an effective election machine. It is easy to exaggerate this point, but on election day a handful of seats made the difference – and these Atkins might have saved for the Tories.

The media followed Miller's split with Atkins with considerable interest, and adverse commentary. Meanwhile, unremarked, Miller suffered a second setback by losing the man he'd been counting on to be his top civil servant and deputy in the premier's office. As we've seen, Tom Campbell had moved up to the Four Seasons immediately to help Miller with the transition, and Miller assumed he was there to stay. But Campbell had come to love his job as Hydro chairman in the short months since Davis appointed him. He had a five-year contract at Hydro and a salary bigger than a deputy minister's – and he was boss of his own operation.

During the leadership race, Campbell had shuddered at Miller's speculations about introducing a flat tax. It was too reminiscent of the right-wing panaceas that Peter Pocklington had been flogging in the federal Conservative leadership. He was also horrified by Miller's remarks about gays and school boards. Arriving at the Four Seasons the day after Miller's leadership victory, Campbell had harsh words for Miller about the impropriety of his ad hoc policy-making and extracted a promise from him that as premier he would consult carefully before sounding off. The more Campbell saw of the tensions and bungling in the Miller camp, the less he wanted to stay. He was on loan from Hydro, and within a few weeks he informed the new premier that he intended to go back.

In his ministries, Miller had always depended heavily on his staff. Now, faced with his greatest challenge, he was left without a right-hand man. There was no choice but to turn to Stewart, who by this time was mightily offended by the way he'd been treated. Stewart had been affronted, when he visited Miller at the Four Seasons, to see that Campbell was there taking over his job as deputy to the premier. He believed Campbell was behaving improperly in agreeing, even temporarily, to play a dual role as Hydro chief and adviser to Miller.

Stewart also felt that the Miller people were running roughshod. They'd won their leadership victory, and a poll taken by Decima just after the convention showed the Conservatives at fifty-six per cent in popular opinion – enough for a strong majority. They obviously felt they could afford to bruise a few feelings in the old administration and do things their way. But Stewart, the chief functionary of the Davis years, thought the polls reflected the popularity of the Davis government rather than anything Miller had done, and he was resentful of Miller's evident desire to change everything.

Stewart was not the only one who was becoming nervous. The entire top echelon of the provincial bureaucracy was suffering severe jitters. Since Miller hadn't taken charge personally, or reassured senior civil servants that their jobs were secure, they wondered if their heads, too, were on the block. Miller had promised to promote women as deputy ministers during the leadership – and he now appointed three. It was a long-overdue move but it raised the hackles of some senior deputies who felt he should have made other – male – choices first.

The new cabinet, sworn in on February 8, was beset by confusion. One story among many that spread quickly through the bureaucracy involved Phil Gillies. The young MPP from Brantford had supported Grossman in the leadership, and then was appointed by Miller to be a junior minister with special responsibility for youth, reporting to the treasurer, Larry Grossman. Gillies was just settling in when, in March, Miller announced a new ministry of skills development under Ernie Eves, MPP for Parry Sound, with Gillies' secretariat reporting to Eves.

The problem was, nobody bothered to tell Gillies, or Grossman, or their deputies, before making the changes. Instead, Gillies was called to a meeting in the cabinet chamber, along with Eves. The deputy treasurer, Brock Smith, was there, wondering – as was Gillies – what was up. Jim Anthony, Miller's speech-writer and policy adviser, made a presentation about the new ministry. Part-way through, Gillies leaned to Smith and said, "I think I'm being fired." As it happened, he wasn't being fired. He was being demoted to a junior minister in front of others. Smith went to Bob Carman, secretary to cabinet, to complain, only to learn that Carman hadn't known either. Grossman was supposed to be at the meeting, but had missed it. He hadn't been consulted, and now he was furious.

From the first, Grossman had viewed Miller's administration as a rather tacky operation. Miller's 32-member cabinet, larger than the Davis cabinet by three, hadn't been able to fit their chairs around the cabinet table, so Miller had the old leather chairs removed – except for the premier's chair – and replaced with narrow new blue chairs. The names of the ministers were stuck on the backs on typed labels. Each time he entered cabinet, Grossman carefully pulled back his ugly blue chair and moved one of the old leather chairs into its place.

In early March, Grossman took off for a holiday in Florida, after letting Miller know he was unhappy and would be deciding on his return whether to stay on in cabinet or to take up offers to go into the private sector. Miller had made him chairman of the Metro caucus and had kept him as treasurer, but Grossman didn't like to see his friends Atkins, Stewart, and Tory on the sidelines. He was unhappy that his friend Tom Scott of Foster Advertising had been frozen out of the election commercials. He felt that the Miller operatives who were trying to run the government were incompetent amateurs.

On the other hand, as treasurer he was in the midst of budget preparations, and it wouldn't be easy for somebody new to step in. An election was pending, and his resignation would be a major blow to the party's Metro fortunes. While Grossman probably wouldn't have minded wounding Miller, it was another thing to wound the party. He hesitated, and while he did, Tom Campbell intervened. He called Grossman's friend Alan Schwartz and arranged through him for Miller to talk to Grossman in Florida. Miller later regretted placating Grossman, but at the time made the effort necessary to keep him on board. He agreed to put Schwartz on the patronage committee, where he could do favours for Grossman supporters. And he invited Schwartz to join his Thursday-morning breakfasts at Sutton Place – Miller's version of Davis's old Park Plaza breakfasts. The Thursday-morning breakfasts proved a bust. Eddie Goodman was among the invited, too, but found he had no real influence because he couldn't get his advice past Michael Perik's guard in the premier's office.

At the time, all these tensions were internal and had no public effect. Miller's primary focus was on an election. He was intent on rushing to the people to prove to all those Big Blue Machiners that they were wrong about him and that he was another winner for the dynasty. So he disregarded the tremors in the bureaucracy and his failure to build an enthusiastic team in the premier's office. He put aside Goodman's and Atkins' advice that he first allay concerns about his personal agenda by offering the public a Throne Speech in the party's progressive tradition.

Miller made these fatal mistakes despite a decade of experience as a senior Davis minister largely because he'd come into politics in middle age as a raw recruit. He hadn't been raised on Conservative pablum, like Davis or Grossman. He didn't know the history of the party, or the stories that illustrated how things should be done, nor did he fully comprehend that the Ontario Progressive Conservative party was a coalition of interest groups of all philosophic hues. He was leading a consensus party, without taking time to gain its consent.

Miller was intelligent, but he lacked the wide grasp of the public-policy agenda which a premier must have. In past years, he had mastered the immediate concerns of several ministries – health, natural resources, treasury, and industry and trade. But when his own portfolio wasn't affected, he often wasn't interested. He got bored in cabinet, and frequently made an excuse to leave when debate dragged on over an issue outside his immediate bailiwick. Perik had spotted that weakness early and had urged Miller to get a strong policy adviser and to immerse himself more in public issues. But he didn't, and now he was premier without a sound grounding in, for instance, the issues surrounding the decision to fund separate schools. He was thus inadequately attuned to the political environment in which he had to survive.

He was also uncertain of his own purposes. Ever since Miller had arrived at Queen's Park in 1971, people had been telling him he was wrong. He had come in a right-winger, and had applied his principles as health minister in an attempt to rationalize the hospital system, only to be forced to back off. When he was in Treasury, he objected violently to Suncor as a waste of money when he was trying to balance a budget, but swallowed his pride and didn't resign. In the end, he didn't know quite where he stood. He said he had learned to be a Davis-style pragmatist, but he kept on mourning publicly over his own ideological impurity, remarking, for instance, that he'd like to abolish the minimum wage, or rent controls, but he had to be practical and couldn't. For a politician he was curiously impolitic.

Even Miller's style didn't work for him in the premier's office. His handlers told him to get rid of his Muskoka tartan jacket – which he wore on budget day as a kind of loud defiance of Bay Street decorum – and his hand-knit socks, made for him by his wife, Ann. The media talked about Miller's tartan jackets as if he wore them all the time instead of once or twice a year. Reporters tagged him a folksy bumpkin, ignoring his more sophisticated tastes for classical music and serious literature. They referred to his past as a used-car salesman and seldom mentioned his degree in chemical engineering

or his years as a science teacher. Miller provoked the ste-
reotyping himself by selling raffle tickets for Muskoka charities
to members of the Press Gallery, or telling reporters he had
a good used car for them. He did it humorously, and was
dismayed when he got stung. He had been one of the most
available and forthright ministers with the press, but now
his handlers told him he had to keep away from the media.
As a result, Miller came to the premiership unsure of his
own instincts, ready to be guided by "the political experts".

Relying on good advice had worked for him in his ministries.
But now Miller's advisers were either politically naive like
Melnik, or abrasive young hotshots like Perik, plunged into
the vortex of power with insufficient wisdom to steer a steady
course. Campbell, the one strong guiding hand, was already
distancing himself, and as he did, Miller was cut off from
the voices of experience. Those remaining in Miller's circle
pressed him for a quick election. Once he had a mandate
from the people, they argued, he could shake off the endless
demands for compromise, and move firmly to establish a
business government that would get the engine of free enterprise roaring again.

The pro-election hawks reasoned this way: an election was
traditional in the fourth year of a government's five-year term,
which left only an immediate spring election, or an election
in the fall, as options; the federal finance minister, Michael
Wilson, was about to introduce a budget that could hit Ontario
hard and turn the voters against Conservatives; an Ontario
budget had to come soon and would not be pleasing to the
people either; the separate-school issue was starting to surface
in many communities, and would only get worse when the
new school terms started in the fall. A spring vote seemed
all the more desirable because the polls promised certain
victory. Decima Research had polled for the party right after
the leadership and found the Tories at 56 per cent, Liberals
at 18 per cent, and New Democrats at 20 per cent. An easy
win seemed assured, and a fatal complacency set in.

The Decima poll should have roused more apprehension
than it did in Miller's camp. Gregg reported in his accom-

panying memo that the support was – in a phrase that became famous once things started to go wrong – "a mile wide and an inch thick". He said that people didn't know Miller and weren't sure of his intentions, so the support, although still high, was soft. Miller had a serious problem among the suburban middle-class voters who had been so essential to the Tory coalition because they felt he reflected an older, rural, small-town set of values and didn't represent their interests. Miller was viewed as being out of touch with the needs of women and unsympathetic to the demand for a cleaner environment. In one significant sentence, to which nobody paid much attention until it was too late, Gregg warned that "the issue of the environment could pose a significant threat if allowed to become an issue in the campaign." Reading that sentence over in mid-election, after a spill of dangerous PCBs in Northern Ontario, John Tory, then campaign secretary, shuddered in hindsight over the blindness of Miller's managers.

On the one issue that was to prove so explosive – separate-school funding – Decima reported confusing results. Gregg and his vice-president, Ian McKinnon, said they couldn't really read the public mood following Davis's full-funding announcement. They recommended simply that Miller give the impression that the matter was under good management. Davis had urged Miller to immerse himself in the details of full funding, so that he would understand the issue emotionally and be able to defend it on the hustings. Warren Gerard, communications adviser to Bette Stephenson when she was education minister, wrote a careful speech for Miller explaining the history of separate-school funding and defending the principle on the basis of fairness and equity. Miller never gave the speech, preferring to pretend the issue would go away if left alone.

Ed Stewart, a staunch opponent of full funding, kept telling the new premier that funding for Catholic schools would not be a factor in the election. "Leave it alone and it will be fine," he said. In addition, Miller was himself not sold on full funding, and dubious of his ability to defend it. When questioned by reporters, he said he supported the government's decision but he hadn't been at the cabinet meeting that made it. He was to pay for that equivocal stance later in the election. Gregg's polling in the fall, after Davis resigned, had found that for the first time the Catholic community would vote strongly for the Tories, but after Miller replaced Davis and called an election without setting doubts about his position to rest, Catholics returned to their traditional support for the Liberals and the NDP.

One man knew that Miller was playing a dangerous game by plunging toward an election. Martin Goldfarb, the federal Liberal party pollster who also did regular issue polling for the Davis government, made an attempt at this point to get in touch with Miller. While Gregg had been doing political soundings, Goldfarb had also been back into the field, taking a more detailed look on behalf of the premier's office at people's attitudes to full funding for separate schools. What Goldfarb found was worrisome. As he had predicted earlier, respondents to his poll weren't particularly upset over the funding promise in itself. But they *were* furious over the arbitrary way Davis had simply announced his decision without consultation. Goldfarb reported to Davis's office that the issue now was "dangerous stuff and explosive. . . . people are feeling very upset about it."

The pollster did some strategic planning for Davis on future handling of the issue – but this advice had never been passed to Miller. Feeling he ought to know, Goldfarb called, and, when he couldn't get to Miller directly, expressed his concerns to Michael Perik. Goldfarb told Perik that Miller should wait before calling an election because the Catholic funding issue needed time to die down. In a quick election, the issue was explosive enough to sway a lot of votes, he warned. Miller clearly didn't heed Goldfarb's warnings; and the pollster never discovered whether or not his message had gotten through to the premier.

At any rate, Miller was depending on Decima Research, Allan Gregg's polling house, for his political strategy. At the new premier's request, Decima conducted a second poll shortly before the election call. This poll lacked the analytic depth of the first: it was a "quick and dirty", intended to make sure the general picture hadn't changed since the leadership convention. Apparently this rough survey failed to plumb the depths of feeling over the separate-school issue, so Miller didn't get a needed warning at this point. The purpose that the quick poll did serve, however, was to give a more realistic picture of overall party standings, putting the Conservatives at 47 per cent. Gregg and McKinnon weren't alarmed. They decided that 56 per cent had been an aberration and that 47 per cent still indicated a strong majority government. But the drop also suggested that support was not holding firm, and Gregg advised the Conservatives to go to an election while the party still had a healthy lead.

To overcome Miller's image as the hard-nosed minister who'd tried to close hospitals – the politician with the secret right-wing agenda – Gregg proposed he be sold as a Tory populist. Former leaders of the dynasty had been small-town aristocrats, but Miller was from the common folk. Gregg thought he could project a grandfatherly appeal to all the little guys, small-businessmen and farmers, who wanted to pull themselves up by their bootstraps, just as Miller had himself done. He thought the campaign strategy should focus on Miller's strength in economic policy, emphasizing his empathy with small business but also demonstrating that the new premier knew about the high-tech challenge. Gregg argued that Miller should flesh out his perceived weakness in social-policy areas by platform announcements that would demonstrate a continuing Conservative commitment to fairness and equity.

But Gregg, who had worked hard for Larry Grossman, didn't really have his heart in an election campaign led by Miller. The flashy pollster asked his quiet vice-president, Ian McKinnon, to be Miller's day-to-day strategist. McKinnon was leery of the social-policy initiatives being prepared for the campaign by Jim Anthony, Miller's speech-writer, and by Bob Carman, who was to be secretary of cabinet. They had called for ideas from the ministries and had come up with a strong social program, including a commitment to rent controls, a housing program, day-care announcements, initiatives for working women, and a pollution crackdown. Dennis Timbrell, responsible for women's issues, was champing to announce an omnibus of women's reforms: funding for private and public day-care spaces, passages of family-law reform to divide business assets equally after marriage breakdown, pay equity in the public service and subsequently in the private sector, and contract-compliance guidelines for companies wanting to do business with the government. Morley Kells, minister of the environment, was ready with a $100-million superfund to clean up old polluted dump-sites and a hit squad of tough environmental inspectors.

This version of an election platform stalled first at cabinet and then because of doubts cast by McKinnon. Only two social planks made it for the election kick-off. Gordon Walker, minister of consumer and commercial relations, accepted the inevitability of rent controls – reducing the control limit to four per cent from six per cent – at a news conference where reporters openly taunted him for the torture such a decision must have inflicted on his free-enterprise soul. Social services minister Robert Elgie announced 7,500 new subsidized day-care spaces to be provided over two years at a cost of $30 million. But at that point McKinnon's advice caused the premier's office to call a halt. The pollster feared that if Miller kicked off his campaign with a platform stressing women and the environment, the public would decide those must be the main issues – and on those issues the Liberals and the New Democrats had better records. With the polls looking so good, it was better to run a campaign that made no waves and not take any chances of disturbing the slumbering voters.

Miller was willing to compromise to win the election, but McKinnon knew he didn't really care for the social initiatives, with the exception of environmental protection. As the television ads were being made, and Miller attempted to talk about day care, his already wooden performance became totally unconvincing. The small test audiences broke into laughter. So McKinnon told the strategists to launch the campaign with an economic program, playing to Miller's strengths, not his weaknesses. He argued, rightly as it turned out, that people would not find Miller credible if he tried to play the progressive.

McKinnon convinced both Perik and Kinsella, and although Anthony continued to protest, none the less he sat down to write Enterprise Ontario, the election platform that Miller was to announce on March 22 at a media conference at Toronto's Convention Centre. Reporters immediately made comparisons with Davis's attempts to bribe voters in 1981 with his BILD program. BILD had promised expenditures of $1.5 billion over five years, while Miller's Enterprise Ontario spending would be $1.3 billion over three years. But while BILD promised roads, electrical projects, and technology centres, Enterprise Ontario was aimed specifically at small business.

Some $975 million of the $1.3 billion total was the cost to government of eliminating the corporate income tax on small businesses. Another $250 million was for an Enterprise Technology Fund to provide loans to install new technology in small and medium businesses. There was a skills-training program, but stripping away the initiatives on behalf of business left less than $400 million over three years for social programs, including $22 million set aside for workplace day care.

Despite its strong pro-business tilt, Miller regarded Enterprise Ontario as a compromise. He had faith in the tax holiday for small business and the initiatives on skills training – but not in any of the rest of it. He was opposed to the technology fund, just as he'd been opposed in the past to Larry Grossman's technology centres and the IDEA Corporation. Both, he believed, were better left to the private sector.

Miller told reporters: "The first priority of Enterprise Ontario is to clear the way for small business," and he set out "some fundamental principles for his government". Government itself would take less out of the economy in order to encourage private-sector growth, insist on the best value for its expenditures, and work in partnership with the private sector. Present social programs would be maintained to help individuals who couldn't help themselves. Women who suffered discrimination on the job would be provided equality of opportunity. The principles were pure Miller. On even the women's issue he was a free-enterpriser. He objected to legislation on pay equity as an unworkable form of heavy-handed government intervention, but he was in favour of changes that provided fair opportunity for women to fight their own way upward. He thought the voters would go for his economic laissez-faire prescriptions once he'd properly explained they would lead to economic recovery.

John Tory urged Miller's advisers to flesh out their platform with strong social programs. Jim Anthony mourned the large territory that Miller was leaving to the Liberals and the NDP. Tom Campbell shook his head and buried himself further in Hydro's affairs.

But almost nobody else was worried. Perik told John Balkwill in a telephone conversation the strategy was "Dullsville" – Miller just needed to go through the motions to win. The Tories were floating confidently on their 56 per cent in the polls – the lower figure of 47 per cent hadn't leaked to the media yet. So widespread was the assumption of majority that Conservatives who'd worked against Miller in the leadership were expecting their heads to roll once the new premier had his election mandate. In Sudbury, Jim Gordon, an MPP who had supported Grossman, calculated that his own prospects for future advancement were dim. He believed Miller was about to start another of the dynasty's ten-year terms and would never elevate a Grossman ally to a position in cabinet. Gordon called Grossman and told him he'd decided not to stand for re-election. Instead, he would run for mayor of Sudbury and enjoy the advantages of an office close to home.

But Grossman told Gordon to hold on, because politics was an unpredictable game. He was so convincing that Gordon agreed to stand once more. Later Grossman could not explain why he'd talked to Gordon that way: he was as sure as everyone else that the Tories could not lose. Perhaps he was remembering the dinner at the Albany Club shortly after the leadership contest when he and his pals – Alan Schwartz, Hugh Segal, John Laschinger, and Tom Scott – gathered to mourn their loss. As the others grieved, Laschinger pounded the table. "This thing is not over yet," he said.

5

The Big Blue Machine
Runs Down

As he issued his election call from Queen's Park on March 25, Frank Miller evoked the spirit of Bill Davis. "If a government ever wanted to run on its record, this would be the time to do it," he said. "My government will build on the foundations that were put in place by William Davis. There is no need for radical change or a sudden shift in direction, only a change in emphasis. Under my leadership, we will focus more on job creation and job security. . . . I am seeking a mandate to manage the affairs of this province through a period of economic change. A mandate to create jobs in the small-business sector. A mandate to maintain and improve our social services, in keeping with the principles of decency and equity which have characterized the government of William Davis."

The pitch came straight out of Decima's polling results. The Decima pollsters had told Miller to offer continuity with the Davis years, as well as change. They had said that the economy was the main issue on everyone's mind, and that Miller should play to his perceived strength as a former treasurer.

But Miller's economic prescriptions could hardly be called a vision. The media had already dismissed his Enterprise Ontario as election hokum, and at the news conference, reporters were much more interested in asking whether his heart could stand the pace of an election. "I've had a checkup and, yes, I'm in good shape," said Miller. He was also cross-examined about rushing to an election without a Throne

Speech. "I've been around eleven years. People have an image of me," the premier replied, erroneously.

Miller couldn't persuade the media to follow his agenda of explaining and defending Enterprise Ontario. He couldn't get the voters to pay attention to it either. Halfway through the campaign, an Environics poll for the *Globe and Mail* showed that voters still listed the economy as their top concern, and gave the Tories the best rating as economic managers. But that was a rating that sprang out of the government's past performance, and had little to do with Enterprise Ontario. Miller's economic prescription was neither big enough nor adventurous enough to catch the voters' imagination. In a period of burgeoning economic revival, Ontarians, however important they automatically rated the economy, turned their attention to social issues, and to the personalities of the leaders. Patrick Kinsella, the campaign chairman, started to worry when he saw the contest turning into a vote on Frank Miller, rather than the Tory legacy.

Decima's polling had shown that although the voters rated the Conservatives highly for their economic management, they also had a comfortable assumption that Ontario was a naturally richly endowed province that any government could run well. The Tories mistakenly assumed that only they would be trusted as guardians of the economy – a complacency that was to prove fatal. Miller and his election team were caught unprepared when separate-school funding, the environment, and to a lesser extent women's issues became the sleepers of the campaign. These were the very issues that the premier – taking Ian McKinnon's advice too literally – had chosen not to address. As the gaps and weaknesses in his platform were revealed, the Conservatives found the 37-day campaign left them without sufficient time to change course.

David Peterson came out of the gate fast, running – in the media's eyes, and in the fears of his worried handlers – from third place, but seeing a real opportunity in Miller's handicaps. This was the first election for all three – Miller, Peterson, and Rae – as leaders of their parties. With the popular and expe-

rienced Bill Davis in retirement, the Opposition leaders were
starting on a more equal footing.

The strategy devised by Michael Kirby, the Goldfarb Associates strategist, from his focus-group interviews called for
Peterson to be bold and caring on policy matters. Kirby warned
Peterson that he'd trail in third place if he continued be a
nice, but largely unknown, guy. Fortunately for the Liberal
leader, Kirby found that Miller, too, lacked a clear image.
This gave Peterson an opportunity to create one for him by
portraying Miller as pro-business and likely to cut back on
health and social services, just as he had once tried to close
hospitals.

Kirby advised Peterson to ignore Bob Rae, except for
occasional attempts to generate fear by suggesting the NDP
leader was the tool of union bosses. The idea was to hive
both Miller and Rae off as the representatives of the special
interests of right and left, leaving Peterson to inhabit the wide
middle ground which Davis had always cultivated.

Peterson adopted the strategy at his campaign kick-off
following fast on the heels of Miller's in the Queen's Park
media studio. He gave a quick outline of the Liberal platform:
open and accountable government, a ban on extra billing,
denticare, abolition of OHIP premiums, equal pay for work
of equal value, affordable child care, tax breaks for companies
that would give guarantees of job creation, and beer and wine
in the corner stores.

The beer-and-wine promise was injected because candidates such as Monte Kwinter in Wilson Heights thought it
would appeal to ethnic groups, and because it made Peterson
look more modern than Miller. But the issue also allowed
him to be different from the other parties. The Tories would
never agree to it, Peterson said, because that would upset
"the cozy relationship between the government and the
brewers", and the NDP would oppose freer sales because that
would upset the big union leaders whose members might lose
jobs in the brewery warehouses and retail stores if independent corner stores were allowed to steal their business.

Peterson amused Gallery reporters, who knew Miller for

Bill Davis wipes away a tear as he announces his resignation on Thanksgiving Day, 1984.   (TORONTO STAR)

Gagged candidates in a stifling debate. (Left to right) Frank Miller, Roy Mc-Murtry, Larry Grossman, and Dennis Timbrell on stage in Toronto in January 1985, as they vie to become Tory leader and, automatically, premier of Ontario. (TORONTO STAR)

Dennis Timbrell reacts on the second ballot, as he realizes he is six votes behind Larry Grossman and about to be eliminated as a contender in the January 26, 1985, Progressive Conservative leadership convention. (TORONTO STAR)

Honouring the Deal: Although he knows he is hurting his own future chances, Dennis Timbrell accepts a Larry Grossman button as he throws his support to his rival in the gang-up to keep Frank Miller from the leadership. MPP David Rotenberg, a Timbrell supporter, is between them. (TORONTO STAR)

Frank Miller (centre), with Alan Pope behind him, makes his way to the stage after being declared Conservative leader—and premier elect—in a victory that was sweet only for this moment. (TORONTO STAR)

Before and after the Grooming: David Peterson as a losing candidate in the 1976 contest for the Ontario Liberal party leadership (left), and (right) on his way to winning Ontario in February 1985, when he wound a tartan scarf around his neck in mockery of Frank Miller and challenged the Conservative leader in the forthcoming election. *(TORONTO STAR)*

David Peterson, a Liberal leader in trouble, takes a punch from former Canadian middleweight champion Joe Henry in a September 1983 charity bout—a stunt that showed the grit behind the loser's image. *(TORONTO STAR)*

The Business Leader: Frank Miller announces Enterprise Ontario, the Conservative election platform that pollsters said was right for him, but that flopped with voters. (TORONTO STAR)

(Left) Michael Perik, the young political buff with a computer brain who helped Frank Miller become Conservative leader and premier, and (right) Patrick Kinsella, who came back from British Columbia to be Miller's campaign chief in the Ontario election.

(Left: TORONTO STAR; right: CANAPRESS PHOTO SERVICE)

Frank Miller jokes with the press. When photographers
hoped to get a shot of his 1983 budget, they found
only a comic book inside. *(TORONTO STAR)*

Bill Davis, Frank Miller, and Brian Mulroney celebrate Tory hegemony on All-
Ontario Night, the televised rally that was to be the highlight of the election
campaign, but that turned into a fiasco. *(TORONTO STAR)*

Bob Rae, leader of the Ontario NDP, sings for reporters as he plays his lap piano aboard his campaign bus. Rae softened his reputation as an aloof intellectual, but was not a convincing contender for the premiership. (TORONTO STAR)

Shelley and David Peterson on the campaign bus.

(TORONTO STAR)

(Left) Frank and Ann Miller watch glumly at their Bracebridge home as the election results come in on May 2, 1985; (right) David and Shelley Peterson acknowledge the cheers on election night. Although he won 48 seats to 52 for Frank Miller, he was the real winner.

(TORONTO STAR)

an affable sort, by talking about the "darker side of Frank Miller's Ontario". The Liberal pitch was aimed directly at a public in whom Peterson wanted to rouse fears. Miller was folksy, he said, but "whistles an altogether different tune when it comes to getting tough with our hospitals, our poor, and our senior citizens." As premier he would weigh lives against dollars. He'd already tried to close community hospitals, stuck a sales tax on hamburgers and feminine-hygiene products, and mused aloud about the advantages of abolishing the minimum wage. "It will be a question of trust," said Peterson. "People will ask, 'Who is the real Frank Miller?'"

As soon as he had finished speaking, Peterson was out the door, climbing the steps of his campaign bus. It was ready to roll to his first campaign stop, his home town of London, Ontario. Some of his advisers had wanted a more traditional campaign, opening slowly and gathering momentum. But Peterson was fighting for his very political survival, and he'd decided there was no choice but to take risks and run flat out. The day the election was called, he was prepared with his platform, his one-liners, a red backdrop with the word Liberal in white under a rising sun – which his people installed in the media studio after Miller and his Tory blue had left – and a prepared text for reporters. It was a professional job – far more professional than Peterson had ever looked in the legislature as Opposition leader. He was to prove more effective on the hustings than in the House, taking nearly everyone by surprise.

Bob Rae, by contrast, performed below the standard expected of him from the start. He met the press armed only with a few handwritten notes and no apparent sense of direction. He talked about five huge issue areas: the half-million unemployed, wasteful government spending, air and water pollution, the problems of working women, and heavy taxes. He had a lot to say about Conservative bungling in those areas, but he wasn't yet ready, or willing, to spell out the NDP response.

Rae was tense, and a bit defensive, as he watched the Liberal team dismantle its election backdrop, which had to be removed before he could take his turn in the Queen's Park media studio. Nobody on the NDP election team had realized the importance of appearing in fighting trim on the first day. Bob Rae had been a star in the federal Parliament, and easily outshone Peterson in the Ontario legislature. As a result, the NDP failed to take Peterson seriously enough when he moved his party onto left-liberal ground and weren't ready for his swift appropriation of the progressive position that Rae had intended to occupy with his moderate NDP platform.

Also, although Rae himself denied it, the New Democrat election team assumed that the Tories were unbeatable. The New Democrats were aiming at winning more seats and making Rae the Official Opposition leader, but they had no idea of taking over the government. Rae was unhappy with the strategy his advisers had devised for him. "I've never run for second place in my life," he told reporters. But he was doing just that, and it was harder knowing that Peterson was already out there striving to be premier.

Miller, meanwhile, had suffered a setback at the hands of his supposed federal ally, Prime Minister Brian Mulroney. Reporter Bob Hepburn of the *Toronto Star* had been looking into details of Mulroney's recently announced western energy accord and discovered that a gasoline tax hike was on the way. On Miller's first day of campaigning, the headline story appeared, anticipating that the federal budget would impose an increase in gas prices of 3 to 5 cents a litre. (The increase later turned out to be 2.8 cents a litre.)

As he got off his bus in Kitchener-Waterloo for a breakfast meeting, Miller was surrounded by reporters demanding to know what he would do to protect Ontario's interests. The campaigning premier was taken completely off guard. For all the vaunted recent co-operation between the Conservative government in Ottawa and the Tory provinces, Mulroney's officials had not bothered to tell Queen's Park what was in the wind. Joan Walters, Miller's press secretary, called the prime minister's office to check the accuracy of the story, and learned nothing. Miller, surrounded by his staff and police guards, pushed past the reporters without comment, and by the end of the day was reduced to declaring that he would raise the matter when he went to Ottawa later that week for an aboriginal-rights conference.

When he arrived at the conference, Miller demanded and obtained an audience with Mulroney to discuss gasoline prices. Tom Campbell and Joan Walters had tried in prior conversations with Bernard Roy, Mulroney's principal secretary, to explain the political difficulties of a gas hike during an Ontario election. But, despite these efforts, Mulroney was not helpful to Miller – perhaps because he didn't like Miller's treatment of Norman Atkins. Or, he may have been influenced by his own political needs: Ontarians were more likely to vote Conservative federally if they didn't also have a Conservative provincial government. After a private chat, the two leaders told press secretaries Joan Walters and Bill Fox that they had agreed only to a seat for Miller on the team negotiating natural gas prices with the west. Walters asked that Mulroney at least take the lead in talking to reporters, but outside in the scrum, Mulroney said only that he'd had a good talk with Miller, and then turned and walked back into his office.

Miller was left to face combative members of the media, with very little to offer by way of good news for his voters. The prime minister's concession was extremely thin and not at all consistent with the respect Ottawa usually showed the Ontario dynasty. Miller was chagrined and wondered, not for the last time, whether he'd been sandbagged by the Big Blue Machine. David Peterson began telling audiences that Miller was turning Ontario into "a 97-pound weakling".

Miller's already strained relations with the media turned rapidly worse. Those first couple of days of pushing past reporters who'd been accustomed, before the leadership, to friendly exchanges with him had done irreparable harm. Bill Davis had campaigned in the same closed manner, but most of the reporters had joined the Gallery after 1981 and weren't familiar with this style on the hustings. They were accustomed to the jockeying for leadership, during which ambitious Tory politicians had endless time for them. Suddenly they were confronted – and affronted – by a general election in which the incumbent's plan was to avoid rousing the voters, a strategy Perik called "Dullsville".

Perik and Walters didn't want Miller subjected to a scrum every hour, nor did they want him exposing some of his real views. They tried hard to keep Miller to an agenda of planned statements. Miller wasn't happy with that approach. At the beginning, he told Perik and Kinsella that, since he was an inexperienced campaigner, he would leave the planning up to them and deliver the platform speeches when and where they told him. But in the first week, he started fighting the strategy. He told Perik he had won the leadership by being an unconventional candidate. Candour had been one of his strengths, not a weakness to be hidden from the public. Perik disagreed sharply: he said Miller had won the leadership on the strength of good organization, and that his unbridled tongue had diminished the early lead given him by his legmen. The first night on the trail, Miller blew the cover. He wandered back in the plane to where reporters were sitting and told *Globe* reporter John Cruickshank, "They won't let me talk to you."

The *Globe and Mail* put Miller's peekaboo campaign plan on the front page, likening Miller's new style to the closed election campaign that Mulroney adopted in 1984 when Kinsella was the "wagonmaster" in charge of his tour. Miller, stung by the criticism, blamed his principal secretary. Alone in the bus that weekend, Miller told Perik, "You have destroyed my relationship with the press and my confidence in myself, and you have done it all in four days."

Perik was appalled at Miller's inability to understand the error of his conversation with Cruickshank. The premier's gesture had been intended to win reporters' sympathy, but instead it had made media access a printable story. Pollster Ian McKinnon repeatedly warned that Miller's biggest liability in the campaign was the Opposition charge that he had a secret agenda, and now Miller had played to that weakness by telling the media that he was muzzled. The only conclusion that the public could draw was that those who knew Miller best feared the consequences of letting everyone else know what he was really like.

Walters felt that Miller had to bear his share of the blame, because she was finding he would not keep to agreed-upon media strategy. She'd tell reporters they had free time to file their stories, only to have Miller come out and start chatting to those who hadn't left. Reporters who missed the chat were angry with her. Walters tackled Miller in Thunder Bay that first week and stressed the importance of sticking to the plan, but the premier was only puzzled and hurt. "I won't be pushed around," he said. Walters replied that she was just trying to co-ordinate his campaign.

The tensions were never resolved. Perik didn't get the carefully controlled campaign that permitted no mistakes. Miller wasn't open and affable with his friends in the media. The result was the worst possible combination: Miller's pleasant personality wasn't coming across, but his goofs were.

Miller's next move – refusing to debate the other two leaders – compounded his problem. Inaccessible to the media, he now appeared inaccessible to the public, too. The television networks pressed hard for a leaders' debate, but all Miller's strategists agreed he should turn them down. The Big Blue Machine had kept Davis out of election debates in 1981, ostensibly because his great stature made it unnecessary to lend credibility to unworthy opponents. Privately, his advisers admitted Davis wasn't so hot on television: he was rambling and circumlocutious. This time the Tory strategists were afraid Miller might not come off as well as the Opposition leaders because he was smaller, older, and lacked depth on major social issues.

Miller himself didn't want to debate. He felt he'd be on the defensive against two sharp-tongued opponents, who would benefit more than he would from the television exposure. One lonely adviser disagreed. Larry Steinman, the deputy campaign-manager who was president of a television satellite company, argued that Miller needed to be better known and that television was a good vehicle for him. But Perik, suspecting by now that Miller was accident-prone, warned, "He could lose us the election in one night."

There was still the matter of how to avoid the debate. Hugh Segal advised Miller to use an old Davis trick of saying he would be happy to debate once arrangements were made – then making sure the details were never worked out with the networks. Miller said that approach was devious. He'd also been warned by Brian Armstrong, the Toronto lawyer who negotiated with the networks for the party, that this time the television people were determined not to be outmanoeuvred. So, on March 30, Miller told reporters point blank that he wouldn't debate. "I've never been afraid of the media," he said. "But my job is to decide the best way to win the election."

Bob Rae immediately accused Miller of putting his personal advantage ahead of the interests of the 5.8 million voters. In a democracy, Rae said, candidates are supposed to put forth their views and allow the electorate to make an informed choice. Miller later regretted not being evasive, as Segal had advised, because it would have permitted him the flexibility of agreeing to debate after it became obvious that his under-wraps style was hurting. The Tories thought the initial reaction was just a media storm that would blow over within days. "I doubt you will be interested in this for long," Miller told reporters. He was wrong: neither the media nor the electorate forgot a refusal which began to crystallize something that had been worrying Gregg in the polling – a widespread feeling among the public that a cocksure government was taking the voters for granted.

Despite the storm warnings, several Conservative candidates failed to sense the shifting winds and were punished accordingly. Local candidates, too, had been told by Conservative headquarters to keep a low profile, so Brampton's Jeff Rice, the 25-year-old who was nominated to succeed Bill Davis, dodged most of the all-candidates meetings. He left interested voters staring at an empty seat and lost a riding that had given Davis a strong vote for twenty-five years.

Miller's errors in communications wouldn't have mattered so much if he'd been leading a united, fighting party. Kinsella claimed the organization was in good shape, but one of the first things he discovered was that party staff had been exhausted by the federal leadership and election, by the repeated false starts for an Ontario election while Davis contemplated his resignation, and by the internecine warfare of the unofficial and finally official leadership race. As he realized how depleted party reserves had become, Kinsella was overheard saying to a Miller staffer: "You might as well blow up Dundas Street [party headquarters] and put a padlock on the door."

Kinsella himself was at sea in a party in which a bunch of outsiders had just come to power. When Hugh Mackenzie, Miller's friend and Muskoka-riding organizer, and a former vice-president of the party, offered to go on the bus with Miller as he had during the leadership race, Kinsella threw away the telephone message. "Who is Hugh Mackenzie?" he wondered aloud. Nobody called Mackenzie, and he sat in Muskoka in a huff – until Miller telephoned halfway through the campaign asking where he was. Mackenzie thought Perik was keeping them apart, and said so.

Kinsella and Perik had worked together in the past at party headquarters and were in touch by telephone nearly every day during the campaign. But Perik's relations with Miller were becoming increasingly strained, and in the growing formality between them, much may have been left unsaid. Experienced campaign organizers later expressed the opinion that lack of good communications between headquarters and Miller's bus was the most serious flaw in the Tory campaign. Brian Armstrong, the Tory lawyer who a year later was to get the job of putting the battered Big Blue Machine back together, was astonished when he got his first look at the election chart depicting Miller's campaign organization. The premier's bus was represented on the chart simply as a separate little box, with no connection to the rest of the organization. The bus appeared to be off in the blue, with no formal line of communication to anyone. "I can't believe this," Armstrong said as he stared at the organizational chart. "It tells you in a nutshell what went wrong."

Perik and Kinsella both reject this common wisdom in the party about where the breakdown came on the campaign trail. They knew they were in touch, Perik from the bus and Kinsella from headquarters, and that their daily communication didn't make any difference to the eventual outcome. The real communications breakdown appears to have been between the Miller team, including Kinsella, and nearly everyone else. John Tory, the campaign secretary, found himself the conduit for the frustrations of the Big Blue Machinists and the media. Tory was the official campaign spokesman because Kinsella refused – apparently after unpleasant experiences dealing with reporters when he was chief of the British Columbia premier's staff – to have anything to do with the media. Besieged with requests for interviews with Miller, Tory recommended that Miller counteract his new image of arrogant inaccessibility by doing hot-line shows and interviews. Kinsella said he approved, and passed on the requests to Perik, but nothing came of them. Tory listened in dismay as David Schatzky, host of CBC's "Radio Noon", interviewed Peterson and Rae and thereafter mentioned daily that Miller wouldn't come on his show. Finally, Bette Stephenson went on in Miller's place.

Election headquarters was a tense and unhappy place to work. Ted Matthews, the Miller loyalist who was director of organization for the election, said later that there were "two separate, distinct and not always related campaigns" being conducted out of the second and third floors at 20 Toronto Street, where Kinsella had set up Miller's campaign headquarters. Many Conservatives, particularly the urban Red Tories, just didn't have the heart to work hard for Miller. Some, like Atkins, Segal, and Tom Scott, were for practical purposes excluded from the campaign. They were, however, part of a campaign advisory group, including the public servants Ed Stewart and Tom Campbell, that met periodically at the Albany Club. The advisory group was, Atkins felt, a sop to those who were left out, but they weren't asked to provide the strategic advice that Miller so sorely needed. Stewart and Sally Barnes, Davis's former press secretary, tried to warn Miller's strategists that the campaign was falling apart. Barnes, who lived in the Kingston area, had several Tory friends who were planning to vote Liberal, and was alarmed. But Allan Gregg reported reassuringly from his polls that Tory support was not dropping but was still holding steady, "as flat as piss on a plate": tracking of key ridings was showing that incumbent Tories were holding strong despite Miller's central campaign.

By now, however, reporters were seeing past the sanitized information peddled by Tory. Conservatives who were unhappy with the Miller campaign let their discontent show. Grumblings from unnamed sources began appearing in the newspapers, causing Miller to wonder who was saying such nasty things about him. Then came a mortal blow. On Saturday, April 13, the *Globe* and the *Star* both reported that Tory support was slipping. The *Globe's* front-page article quoted well-informed Conservative sources as saying that Decima's polling had the Tories down to 47 per cent from 56, and that voters who normally vote Tory were losing their commitment.

In fact, Decima hadn't done a new province-wide survey at this point; what had actually happened was that disgruntled Conservative sources had finally leaked the results of Decima's "quick and dirty" pre-election poll. The belated leak had a remarkable psychological impact. At 47 per cent, Miller would still win a majority. But the newspaper accounts emphasized both the slip from the earlier unusually high level of public support and the growing doubt in Tory circles. The public suddenly was given the impression that the government was in trouble. Until then, both major houses polling this election, Decima and Environics, had found that most citizens simply assumed there was no chance of a change in the government. When they were told it was possible, pent-up resentment over the Tory assumption of its right to rule was released, and slippage was transformed into a landslide.

Even as the negative stories appeared, the campaign's inner collapse began to show on the hustings. Headquarters had planned, and advertised, an evening with Miller and Bill Davis in the Tory heartland of Mississauga, but the event turned into well-publicized disaster when only seventy-five people turned up in a 650-seat high-school auditorium. Miller at first blamed tour director George Stratton, an experienced Big Blue Machiner who had run smooth campaigns for Davis but seemed unable to deliver as well for Miller. This time, however, Stratton was trying to scramble together a tour when many ridings, particularly in Metro, felt a visit from the premier was no asset. He had, as well, to contend with chaotically contradictory messages from headquarters and from Miller's bus over just what Kinsella or Perik wanted done, and when.

After the Mississauga fiasco, Miller tried to bolster spirits by making his first visit to headquarters, where he walked around, followed by members of the media, shaking hands with the workers. Kinsella made a little speech from the middle of the floor, declaring, "We'll win it for you, Premier. We'll do our part." The pledge rang hollow even as he made it.

Already suffering intense strain from public speculation about his faltering campaign, Miller was stricken by the flu. By the time he reached Kingston on April 16, he was floundering badly. At an early-morning news conference at the Holiday Inn, reporters pressed the premier on women's issues because the equality-rights provisions of the Canadian Charter were coming into force that day. Perik and Anthony had briefed Miller carefully on their plan to announce the introduction of equal pay for work of equal value in the Ontario public sector, but Miller wasn't enthused over the policy. He approved of equal opportunity for women, but he thought legislated pay equity was unworkable. To the reporters, Miller stressed the complexities and difficulties of introducing pay equity. He wondered aloud how anyone could evaluate the relative worth of his secretary and his driver, saying, "My secretary can save my job, but my driver can save my life."

Perik and Anthony were appalled, wondering whether Miller hadn't listened to them or whether he had simply decided not to go along. Sitting in the bus that was taking the candidate and reporters to tour Ontario's Urban Transit Development

Corporation outside Kingston, Perik for the first time entertained the notion that Miller might lose the election. When they reached the UTDC facilities, Kinsella joined Miller's party, realized Miller's aides were upset, and asked why. Reminded of the announcement he was supposed to have made, Miller simply said that in his illness he'd forgotten. After lunch, when the tour stopped at Conservative candidate Keith Norton's headquarters, Miller made public his pledge that men and women civil servants would get the same pay for work of the same value. He wanted to explain to reporters that he'd been too ill to think clearly that morning, but his advisers insisted he must not reveal such weakness. Instead, the premier appeared, according to the news accounts, to have changed his mind on a major issue while at lunch.

In his briefcase, Kinsella had brought unsettling news. As they gathered in the privacy of the UTDC offices, he showed Miller the latest Decima poll of voter intentions, in which the Conservatives had dropped to 43 per cent. The Liberals were at 33 per cent and the NDP at 24 per cent. Kinsella was troubled by the drop (as he phrased it "one wheel had come off" the Tory campaign) but the figures were still good enough to bring in a Conservative majority government. "We can pull it through," he reassured Miller.

But the Tory campaign had already stumbled into yet another potential disaster. In Belleville, Queen's Park reporters picked up locally distributed announcements of "All-Ontario Night", a Toronto rally featuring Prime Minister Brian Mulroney, Premier Frank Miller, and former premier William Davis, which would be transmitted across the province on television via satellite. At the time the stories went out, Mulroney had not yet agreed to take part, and his staff were not amused by what appeared to be a blackmail tactic but was really just the amateurish enthusiasm of those staging the affair.

The television satellite hookup was the brainchild of Larry Steinman, president of Canadian Teleconference Network, a small company that designed satellite networks for special applications. Steinman had been a key floor organizer for

Miller at the leadership convention, and was deputy campaign leader for the election. Other Tories disapproved of the planned television event, which would rely on the question-and-answer format Steinman had staged for Miller during the leadership battle. Seasoned organizers suspected the night would be a fiasco: there was too much money and effort involved in staging the main event in Toronto and also ensuring that Conservative associations out in the boonies rented receiver dishes and attracted respectably sized audiences.

Mulroney's office hesitated to confirm the prime minister's participation. Norman Atkins advised Mulroney against getting involved in provincial election campaigns, and wise heads in the provincial party didn't want to draw attention to the Conservative majority in Ottawa. For once, an Ontario premier couldn't enjoy the luxury of blaming the province's woes on a Liberal prime minister, and already David Peterson was warning voters that Mulroney, Atkins, and Miller would run the province from the Albany Club. After some sharp scrapping between Tories in Toronto and Ottawa, Mulroney finally cancelled another date and agreed to turn out for Miller – but not before the media had begun laughing at what was intended to be the campaign's highlight.

Miller's early confident forecast that he would win eighty seats was beginning to look like pie-in-the-sky. In internal memos to his superiors at the CBC, commentator Larry Zolf, a man with experience of other election upsets, had begun predicting a minority government for the Conservatives. On Monday, April 22, the *Globe and Mail* published a poll by Michael Adams of Environics showing that Conservative strength had slumped to 41 per cent; the Liberals were still at 33 per cent and the NDP at 26 per cent. Environics said Miller would still squeak through with a majority government if the sag in the Tory vote stopped, but noted that Miller was delivering a disappointing performance as a new Conservative premier. Miller enjoyed only half the personal popularity of Davis at his height and was trailing in popularity behind his own party.

Adams also found that separate-school funding – the issue

Decima's McKinnon had been unable to read – was the most divisive issue in the campaign. Without Davis in the saddle, the full-funding pledge was not attracting new Catholic votes to the Tories because they were unsure of Miller's commitment to the promise, and was turning off the party's core support among older, middle-class Protestants. Canvassing in Eglinton, candidate David McFadden found the school question of overwhelming concern to the voters he met as he went door to door, but party headquarters told him he must be misreading the voters, because separate-school funding was not really an issue.

Throughout Metro, other canvassers found the biggest issue was Miller himself. Voters didn't like the premier's under-wraps campaign and his refusal to debate. The pollsters at Decima noted an unusual pattern: the public was turning hostile to Miller before turning off the party. Tory canvassers also began to report a negative "Mulroney factor" that was sapping support. In Ottawa, Mulroney was indulging in an orgy of patronage that took the gloss off his new government. Pollster Peter Regenstreif, sniffing the winds on behalf of Dennis Timbrell, met a disenchanted old Tory gentleman in St. David riding who'd worked for years against the Trudeau fat-cat Liberals. "But now we are no better than they are," he confided tearfully.

In the third week of April, pollsters for all parties reported the Tory vote had been "shaken loose". Michael Adams of Environics, in his *Globe* poll, had already found that more than half the voters felt the Conservative government had been in power in Ontario too long. As the Tory election bungles started to pile up, voters began actively to consider alternatives to another decade of Conservative rule.

At first it appeared that the New Democrats would attract the votes that were falling away from Miller. Both NDP polling by ABM Research and the Tory polling by Decima showed that the New Democrats for a short period in April were the main beneficiaries of the Tory slide. Rae was still the better-known Opposition leader and was perceived as a sincere champion of the workingman. His popularity was equal to that of his party, rather than trailing party support as both Peterson and Miller were doing. And Rae was benefiting, briefly, from a bizarre incident that highlighted his campaign criticism of the Tories' poor record in environmental protection. Near Kenora in northwestern Ontario, a truck leaked polychlorinated-biphenyls (PCBs), a toxic carcinogenic chemical, along a 250-kilometre strip of highway. The chemical sprayed vehicles that were following the truck, including a car carrying a pregnant woman. In Toronto, environment minister Morley Kells, cast in a defensive position because he had never been allowed to announce his pollution crackdown, uttered the foolish sentence that became symbolic of Tory indifference. "If you are a rat eating PCBs on the Trans-Canada highway, you might have some problem," said Kells. Bob Rae replied with a song he composed on his electric lap piano in the NDP bus. PCBs, he sang, stood for Progressive Conservative Bungling.

But the young NDP chief, hampered by inadequate staff and a second-rate strategy, was unable to seize the opportunity presented to him by the Tories. The NDP platform – a reduction in unemployment by two per cent; equal pay for work of equal value; tough controls on polluters; a fairer tax system; a reversal of cutbacks on health and education spending – was moderate enough to be mimicked and stolen by the other two parties. Rae was fighting from a much narrower base than the Liberals – in 1981 the New Democrats had lost their right to public reimbursement of their expenses in forty-eight ridings by gaining less than fifteen per cent of the vote, while the Liberals lost the reimbursements in only six ridings. All along, too, the pollsters had known that voters were alienated by the NDP's alliance with labour unions. When asked which party was the best alternative to govern Ontario, most voters said Liberal.

Rae's pollsters reported the NDP upsurge, but because the party was on a tight budget, they did not sample again. Rae thought he was about to make major gains, and on the day before the vote he forecast thirty-eight NDP seats. That expectation made it all the harder for New Democrats to accept the final results.

Within days, the vote abandoning the Tories had floated on from the NDP to the Liberals. The Liberal campaign was carefully designed to appeal to the groups they felt Miller was alienating – the large urban electorate in the Golden Horseshoe around Lake Ontario, younger people, women, and ethnics. Peterson expanded his electoral promises by including a guaranteed job for every young person looking for work, enforcement of the federal law to ensure equal access to abortion services in hospitals while closing the Toronto abortion clinic of Dr. Henry Morgentaler, a major housing program, and relief for hard-pressed farmers. When asked how he would pay for his promises, he turned to the populist appeal that once worked so well for Mitchell Hepburn. Peterson said he'd sell Suncor and the provincial land-banks at Pickering and Townsend, he'd save $50 million by ending extra billing, and he'd slap a minimum tax on the rich. Against what was increasingly perceived as Tory arrogance, this was potent stuff.

At Liberal headquarters, Gordon Ashworth, the campaign co-ordinator, concentrated the party's limited resources in two areas. Peterson had to look good on tour because that was where media attention would focus, and the ridings needed strong support from headquarters. Peterson's tour clicked smoothly along, carefully advanced by experienced pros from federal battles. The Liberal team was casual and friendly with reporters, who increasingly found the Peterson bus the best fun of the campaign. The leader's speeches were vigorous, interlaced with crackling one-liners from the pen of Alan Golombek, a former writer for the *Toronto Sun*. Peterson's inexpensively produced television advertising was lively and compelling, compared to Miller's preachy electronic sales pitches. Meanwhile, the care and feeding of the ridings was the responsibility of campaign chairman Ross McGregor, who distributed Peterson brochures into which local candidates' material could be inserted – delivering a more co-ordinated campaign than the ridings had experienced in the past. Liberal strategists had other creative tricks, such as the flyers designed by MacLaren Advertising extolling the advantages of beer and wine sales in corner stores. Liberal workers handed them out the weekend before the election at crowded Brewers' Retail stores.

The Liberals couldn't afford telephone banks to talk to voters, slick direct mailings, or the massive polling commissioned by the Conservatives. They had a small-time pollster, Michael Marzolini, who sampled in a dozen selected ridings and who produced some startlingly accurate results from a small data base. Marzolini's problem towards the end was that he couldn't get his clients to believe the happy findings pouring off his computer. Starting with the leaked Decima poll on April 13, Marzolini tracked voter reaction to published polls and found each bit of news about Tory slippage was followed by a surge to the Liberals. He'd trot his statistics downstairs at Liberal headquarters on St. Mary Street, only to have Ashworth and Ezrin pat him on the back and laugh. On April 25, Marzolini's numbers suddenly showed the Liberal popular vote surging ahead of the Tories, and he sent down the news on a silver platter that he kept for such congratulatory occasions. Ezrin and Ashworth by then believed there was a new volatility among the electors, because their workers were reporting strong voter sentiment against Miller, but instead of breaking into the wild cheers Marzolini anticipated, they grinned indulgently and sent him back to his computers.

Meanwhile, at Conservative headquarters, Tory and Kinsella knew they were in deep trouble. Before Marzolini had called a Liberal victory, Decima's polling had recorded a sudden drop in Conservative strength, and after that, Tory fortunes went into free fall. Eight days before the vote, Decima's figures, too, showed the Conservatives four percentage points behind the Liberals. Ridings that had been safe Tory bastions were crumbling. The Tory candidate had been thirty points ahead in Scarborough North, the riding of former cabinet minister Tom Wells, but it was now about to elect a Liberal. The old Davis coalition of rural small-c conservatives and suburban middle- and lower-middle-class voters was coming apart.

Urban newspaper editorialists were in full cry for a change in government. The Kingston *Whig Standard* printed a front-page editorial "100 reasons why you should not vote Conservative". The *Toronto Star*, on April 24, called for a Liberal government. The *Globe* followed the next day with "time for renewal".

Patrick Kinsella climbed into a red Corvette with Miller's aide Andrew Barnicke at the wheel and they drove to Hamilton, where the premier was campaigning, to share the bad news. He found Miller and his wife, Ann, at dinner in their hotel suite. Miller asked him to come back in half an hour, and when they sat down together Kinsella laid out the situation: the falling trend-line that he'd shown Miller in Kingston had not levelled out but was continuing to drop. "What does it mean?" Miller asked, and Kinsella replied that if the trend did not turn around, the vote on May 2 would bring a minority government. Kinsella did not believe the blip in the polls that showed the Liberals temporarily ahead. He and Allan Gregg at this point thought the Conservatives would win somewhere between 60 seats, a minority, and 63 seats, a bare majority. Miller looked at his watch – he was due for a speech – then at Kinsella, and asked, "Can you stay around for a while?" He also asked for the written figures, so Kinsella handed over the mass of data from Decima. The premier glanced at it and quickly handed the papers back. "I don't need this," he said.

Perik felt afterwards that Miller had not absorbed the full implications of what he was shown. The premier continued to put the best face on the polling. Decima's overall projection of party standings was showing Tory support falling fast. But the tracking of key ridings still indicated, incorrectly, that many incumbents would hold their seats. Allan Gregg had never seen that kind of divergence before, and wasn't sure what it meant. Later, he found that the bad overall impression of Miller's campaign became more important on voting day than the popularity of incumbent Tory MPPs.

Miller admitted after the election that he may have shut his eyes to reality. To the end, he believed that enough Tory-held ridings would remain firm to save his government. That evening in Hamilton, Kinsella told Miller to "get out and fight". And Perik later tried to pump his leader up for a strong attack on the opposition. Miller was uncomfortable with the script, and came off spiteful rather than tough when he delivered speech-writer Jim Anthony's lines about Liberal irresponsibility and the NDP's "dumb socialist ideas".

After the speech, Kinsella hung around the hotel with Perik until late in the evening. But Miller didn't send for him again.

In Toronto, John Tory decided that if the voters didn't trust Miller, they should be given firm written promises from the Conservative government. By now, Tory and party executive-director Bob Harris were anxious to abandon the original campaign strategy with its concentration on economic issues. The two men gathered up the latest poll results and tapes of the commercials and carried them up to a special meeting at Camp Associates, seeking help from the old Davis pros gathered there – Hugh Segal, Norman Atkins, Tom Scott, and Allan Gregg.

With Segal scribbling out paragraphs and Tory taking notes, they roughed out a platform for Miller to announce on All-Ontario Night. They concentrated on eleven points: removal of tax loopholes favouring the rich, including a minimum tax which every taxpayer would have to pay; equal pay for work of equal value in the public service; broadened government services to multicultural communities; equal access for all teachers and students to Catholic schools after full funding; a new ministry for the elderly; a reiteration of Miller's promise of more extended-care beds and northern-travel subsidies for the sick; introduction of the long-awaited family-reform act; low-interest credit for farmers; measures to encourage the auto industry; incentives for construction of rental accommodation; new measures to control transportation of hazardous materials, a clean-up of landfill sites, and a war on acid rain. Just the day before, Inco Limited had issued a politically timed announcement, promising to cut its emissions of sulphur dioxide in half – an about-face which the company knew would take steam out of Rae's anti-pollution campaign.

Tory typed out the eleven points and showed them that night to Perik and Kinsella as they came off the bus into the Four Seasons Hotel. Tory told them: "We have to do something or the party is going down the drain."

The next morning Tory presented the new program to Miller's "transition group" of David Melnik, Tom Campbell, Bob Carman, Lynn McDonald (executive director of the premier's office), Perik, and Anthony. Melnik, Carman, and McDonald had been cozily at work at the hotel on plans for Miller's post-election cabinet and were shocked almost speechless when Allan Gregg and Ian McKinnon backed the need for a program of written promises with polling data. Melnik protested that he hated the idea of reacting so late in the campaign. Someone else wondered aloud whether the policies were consistent with Miller's image. But Gregg flattened the protests with a stark ultimatum. "If Miller doesn't like these NDP ideas, Bob Rae will be premier," he said.

Perik carried the program to Miller in his suite. At that point the program still included a promise of a minimum tax that could not be avoided through tax loopholes. But Miller interrupted when he heard the words "minimum" tax and struck them out. "I would rather lose," he said. Anthony then took the remaining points and wrote "People Working Together", the speech Miller gave on All-Ontario Night.

The new promises couldn't save All-Ontario Night – or Miller's campaign. The evening turned into a fiasco. At headquarters, there had been bitter fights following the premature announcement of the event. Tour director George Stratton feared another small crowd and asked his workers to hand out tickets at subway stations or to friends. This infuriated the night's sponsors, Steinman and Matthews, who saw it as a vote of no-confidence and were embittered at the idea of free tickets for some when they'd been selling them at $50 a head to others.

On the night of April 25, the hall was dangerously crowded. Angry Tories jostled one another and craned for a view, while the overly long program dragged on and on. Mulroney, Davis, and Miller were paraded in late, to much fanfare. Miller's speech was larded with pretentious phrases about how the Conservatives were, and deserved always to be, the party of Ontario. Then Miller worked his way through a long question-and-answer, with Tory supporters phoning in carefully pre-screened questions. It was tedious. In some centres the satellite transmission was garbled and people switched their television sets to regular programming.

Whether or not the more progressive campaign platform announced that night made a difference is a matter of contention. Its authors think so. There was an improvement in the polls, pulling the Tories even with the Liberals once again. Other experienced Conservatives think that what happened was that the Tory core rallied in the face of impending disaster. Many Conservative supporters didn't like Miller, but they suppressed their dislike and voted to prevent the loss of government.

The Liberal campaign faltered a little at the unexpected taste of success. Marzolini's polling margins had continued to hold up, and experienced professionals like Michael Kirby could tell from the activity around Miller that the Tories were panicking. But Ashworth and Ezrin feared the consequences of signalling what they knew to the public. They worried that if they said the Liberals would win, disaffected Tories who were planning to stay home would get out to vote. They feared the Tories would pour money into a final barrage of advertising that would blow Peterson out of the water. The Liberal campaign went quiet in the last days. Peterson might have gone over the top with bold moves in the last week, but he feared to take the chance.

The real drama in the last days of the election was created by Anglican Archbishop Lewis Garnsworthy of Toronto, who suddenly entered the fray on April 25, charging that Davis had behaved like Hitler when he announced separate-school funding. "This is the way Hitler changed education in Germany . . . by decree," Garnsworthy said, making headlines across the province. The effect of his accusation on the election is a matter of debate between pollsters and politicians. Liberal and Conservative pollsters alike argue that the result of

Garnsworthy's remarks was not the arousing of religious passions. Had that been so, the Conservatives would have lost most in the Old Orange rural areas of eastern Ontario; instead, the major drop in support came in urban areas. The pollsters say the real effect of Garnsworthy's outburst was to confirm a perception that the Conservatives were no longer the smooth managers, able to conciliate and prevent confrontation.

Politicians who faced the issue on their doorsteps believe otherwise. Miller later said that people had hidden their real feelings from the pollsters because they were ashamed to sound prejudiced. In the aftermath of the election, he received hundreds of letters expressing passionate opposition to more money for Catholic schools. Miller was convinced that Davis's promise was a major cause of his defeat.

There is evidence in the polls, however, that the immediate effect of the archbishop's remarks was not that great. Garnsworthy's charge preceded the actual vote by only seven days, and two days after he made it, Conservative fortunes actually picked up. The Tories had been four percentage points behind the Liberals and then they drew ahead again.

The weekend before the election, Decima's tracking showed the Conservatives headed for minority government. Perik and Kinsella decided not to tell Miller immediately, waiting until April 30 when the premier was in the Northern Ontario town of Kapuskasing. Kinsella flew north and found Miller speaking to a luncheon group at the town's old hotel. The campaign chairman stood around feeling awkward until the electioneering was over, and then went to Miller's room to tell him the government was in trouble. At this point, Decima was forecasting somewhere between 55 and 60 Conservative seats, and perhaps 40 for the Liberals and 25 for the New Democrats. Miller took the news with dignity, asking Kinsella if there were anything they could have done differently. The two agreed the basic strategy had appeared sound, and there was no way they could have known what to expect. Miller later talked himself back into a more hopeful state, but for the moment he was upset. In his speech he lashed out at the

New Democrats as the party "of misery and hate", an insult he was to regret when the election was over and he needed Bob Rae's help.

On Wednesday, May 1, the day before the Thursday election, Decima's pollsters foresaw 53 seats for the Conservatives, 47 for the Liberals, and 25 for the New Democrats. Miller wasn't shown that data. No one went to him and warned: "Look, we could lose the government." He never saw polling that would have told him that the Liberals would be in a competitive position – all the information he was given indicated that, at worst, he would head a minority administration against two Opposition parties which both were without enough seats to claim the government.

Miller kept his faith, and hours before the election rashly told reporters he would win 73 seats. His forecast appears ridiculous in hindsight, but at the time he wasn't alone in thinking the Tories would continue to rule Ontario for the foreseeable future. Very few – outside the tiny circle who knew the final poll results – anticipated what was to come. The *Toronto Star*'s Queen's Park columnist, for one, forecast 65 Conservative seats in a front-page column in the *Star*, and was left red-faced the next day.

Then, on the night of May 2 the stunning results poured in. Cabinet ministers fell: Gordon Walker in London, Keith Norton in Kingston, Russell Ramsay in Sault Ste. Marie, John Williams and Morley Kells in Metro. For a while, the television commentators were forecasting a Liberal minority government. Hearing that, Elinor Caplan, the newly elected member for Toronto-Oriole, reported feeling "sheer terror in the pit of my stomach" at the idea that her Liberal party would have to take over in a totally unprepared state. But it was not an upset – not yet. Miller clung to government with a minority of 52 seats.

Watching with his family and a few friends at home in Bracebridge, Miller felt faint and suffered chest pains. He wondered whether he would survive the shock. "Frank got hit blind-sided," his friend Hugh Mackenzie said bitterly later. A decade earlier, Bill Davis had watched similar results – in

fact in 1975 he got one seat less than Miller. But that first
Conservative minority was different. This time the opposition
vote was not evenly divided. This time the Liberals had won
48 seats, stood higher in the popular vote, and were in a
position to challenge for power.

On CFTO television later, Davis appeared on a split television
screen with Miller. The former premier was an election
commentator – a task he said on screen he would not have
accepted had he anticipated the result. Davis reminded Miller
that after 1975 he had survived minority government and had
gone on seven years later to majority success. "You'll be
premier for a long time to come," he reassured the grey-faced
premier.

A disappointed Bob Rae was the first of the three leaders
to talk to his supporters. Already the commentators were
calling Rae a potential kingmaker. But that kind of third-party
clout was not what he'd been anticipating. He'd envisioned
becoming Leader of the Opposition, chief of an NDP that was
growing and could reasonably expect to take power in the
future. Instead, in an election in which the voters had clearly
expressed a desire for change, the NDP had managed to pull
only twenty-five seats. Still, Rae told his people he took heart
in the "interesting discussions" his caucus would have over
the next few days about what to do with the balance of power.

Miller spoke to his supporters in the Bracebridge Arena
after the results were clear, saying he was proud that his party
still formed the government. He also let his wounded pride
show, saying that with time maybe Ontarians would get used
to the idea that a good premier could come from Muskoka.
The Conservative vote had held strong for him in Northern
Ontario, fallen off in the rural ridings of eastern and western
Ontario, and plunged a spectacular fourteen percentage points
in Metro Toronto. "We'll try to make it work," Miller said,
but his dejection was obvious. Television viewers that night
saw a beaten man.

David Peterson, surrounded by family, spoke of "this mag-
nificent moment" to gleeful supporters in London. Although
he had four seats fewer than Miller, his Liberals had actually

garnered 35,000 more votes. The Liberals took 37.9 per cent of the 3.6 million votes cast, the Conservatives 37 per cent, and the NDP 23.8 per cent. Peterson was careful not to assume he'd become premier, but just to be confident. "The next legislature can only work if we work in a spirit of goodwill, generosity, and co-operation," he said. "The people of this province want forward-looking and compassionate government." He quickly outlined his party's agenda, and said he looked forward to working with both Miller and Rae. In stark contrast to a dejected Miller in his tartan tie, Peterson was jubilant and sleek in a dark-blue suit and red tie. The television viewers saw a winner.

6

Bob Rae Tries Something New

Suddenly, attention focussed on 36-year-old Bob Rae, the sandy-haired, bespectacled leader of the smallest party in the legislature. Rae had had previous experience with toppling a Conservative government. It was he who, on December 14, 1979, moved the motion in the Parliament of Canada that defeated the short-lived minority government of Joe Clark and paved the way for Pierre Trudeau's return to power. Rae hadn't enjoyed that plunge into the second national election within a year.

Now Rae was faced once again with a "hung Parliament", the dissolution of which would force his broken and dispirited party back onto the hustings. To avoid an early disaster for the New Democrats, he had to encourage the creation of a stable government. But whose? And how?

Rae, the son of a Canadian diplomat, was a rising political star whose lustre dimmed a little in the harsh personal politics of Ontario. He was a former Rhodes Scholar, Oxford debater, Toronto labour lawyer, an elected MP for Broadview-Greenwood. He'd been a media darling as the New Democrats' articulate finance critic in Ottawa. Senior New Democrats had hoped to transplant that high profile to their faltering Ontario wing when they persuaded Rae in early 1982 to take on the leadership of the Ontario New Democratic Party.

Rae won the leadership convention easily, but soon found that his new job offered less public recognition than life as a federal MP – and a lot of tedious party-building work. He was having less fun, and bearing the enormous weight of responsibility created by the belief that he was the saviour on whose coat-tails everyone else could coast. In fact, Rae had difficulty adapting to provincial politics, where leaders' careers are built on painstaking research that breaks news, not on after-the-fact television commentary, which had been Rae's forte in Ottawa. Most members of Stephen Lewis's highly effective research group were long gone from the leader's office. The party no longer had vigorous riding associations or a strong sense of purpose. The Ontario NDP had made important inroads into the west-end ethnic communities in Metro Toronto, but it was shut out of the political struggle in vast rural reaches of the province.

Rae had attempted to bury some of the old socialist policies that he felt made the NDP unattractive to voters and to place his emphasis on progressive reforms. He wanted to control Inco Limited's acid rain rather than nationalize the big resource company, for instance. But, as he discovered during the election, he staked out ground that could easily be inhabited by David Peterson and his Liberals. Rae ran a principled but uninspired and badly organized campaign at a moment when the province was finally ready to consider real change. His party carried twenty-five seats, only slightly more than it had in the Tory landslide of 1981. Rae, exhausted and disappointed, was confronted by a situation that, no matter which choice he made, appeared perilous for his party.

The morning after the election, both Peterson and Miller called early to sound out Rae's intentions. From the conversations, Rae concluded that neither leader really yet grasped the possibilities – that Miller with 52 seats could lose the government, or that Peterson with 48 could assume office. Miller talked of 1975 and 1977 when the Conservatives had governed under similar circumstances by winning the support of the NDP on some issues and the Liberals on others. He was blithely confident that he and Rae could work together and wanted an early assurance that Rae agreed. Miller said he wanted to establish a direct and personal relationship with Rae.

Rae felt there was no basis for it. He'd heard of Miller's

boast that he'd been friends with Stephen Lewis. But, on checking it out, Rae found that, while the socialist Lewis family had indeed spent a weekend with the Millers at their Bracebridge lodge, they had come away feeling little affinity with their Muskoka hosts. Rae was even less inclined to consort. He had a personal distaste for Conservatives, growing out of his experiences in Britain, where he had come to despise the Tories as the party of privilege. All his life, Ontario had been governed by Conservatives, and Rae didn't want to go down in history as the man who had extended the life of the dynasty beyond its 42-year hegemony. Rae had also been disturbed by Miller's peekaboo election performance, by his repeated assertions that he was being gagged. Rae wondered what Miller's real agenda was.

The NDP leader had more in common with Peterson. While at law school, Peterson had roomed with Colin Coolican, son of an old Conservative family known to the Raes. Rae first met Peterson at the Rae cottage on the Rideau Lakes in the 1960s. Rae and Peterson's brother, Jim, had served on the same finance committee in Ottawa. They were friendly acquaintances, out of a similar milieu.

Rae felt close to Hershell Ezrin, whom he'd known at the University of Toronto, and was appalled when Ezrin hired on with Peterson. By then, Rae and Peterson were serious rivals, both having been chosen in 1982 to lead two constantly warring parties. Rae regarded Peterson as an ineffectual Opposition leader, soft on the issues, particularly during the flip-flop on extra billing. But he liked him personally.

When Peterson called, he chatted about how well the Liberals had done and wondered aloud whether he and Rae should be putting their heads together. Rae agreed they should, but not until he'd consulted his party and his caucus, which would take a few days. Peterson asked whether he and Rae could meet after that and shake hands on an agreement to defeat the government. Rae felt that it wouldn't happen that easily and that this was not a matter to be settled by two leaders in a private meeting.

In that private conversation, Rae's views were very different from those he'd expressed in the recent election. Five days before the vote, host Bill Walker of CFRB's "Let's Discuss It" asked if Rae would work with the Liberals to topple a Tory minority government and form a coalition government to replace it. Rae replied that a coalition was "absolutely not on the agenda". He said he had watched the Ottawa Liberals in their last years and found them lacking in feeling for what the people wanted. The federal Liberals had been right-wing at the end, and he said the provincial Liberals were "even more right-wing on many issues".

At that point Rae still thought his New Democrats were going to inherit much of the sliding Tory vote, and he was busy undercutting Peterson's progressive image. More than that, he was voicing the long-standing hostility in Ontario between the New Democrats and the Liberals. Both Opposition parties were embittered by their 42-year struggle to provide the "real" alternative to the Conservatives. New Democrats viewed the provincial Liberals as rural troglodytes, remnants of the past. NDP theory held that politics was polarizing in Canada between the Conservatives and the New Democrats, and that Liberals would eventually fade away. In the wake of federal Liberal John Turner's defeat, that hope seemed real. The social democrats prayed earnestly for the defeat of Liberalism.

To the dismay of NDP theorists, David Peterson snatched the dream from their grasp. Liberals across the country saw Ontario leading a party resurgence that gave cause for celebration. On the night of the election, former Liberal leader Bob Nixon turned to his wife, Dorothy, as the final results came in and said, "This means the government changes." Nixon called Peterson, and Peterson jubilantly agreed. But Peterson was careful not to assume anything with Rae, or to make public remarks that would either sound opportunistic or risk offending his potential allies in the socialist party. He told the media that Miller would have to move in a progressive direction and he called for immediate negotiations with the doctors to ban extra billing, tougher environmental controls, and legislation for equal pay for work of equal value.

He spoke modestly of his own constructive role: "Nobody got a clear mandate. It's not my intention to overplay our hand."

While Peterson waited calmly, Rae was inundated with advice. Most of the callers who kept his lines ringing that weekend – caucus-mates, trade-union leaders, party executives, and local New Democrats – favoured support of the Liberals. Michael Cassidy, Rae's predecessor as Ontario NDP leader and now a federal MP, said on the air on election night that Rae's duty was clearly to topple the Tories. Others wanted to go further. Ross McClellan, MPP for Bellwoods, urged Rae to use the NDP's leverage to make the Liberals accept a coalition government.

So did Elie Martel, a hawk-faced veteran New Democrat from Sudbury, who, after many frustrating years venting workers' concerns in the legislature, was eager for real power. Martel was already having dreams of being labour minister in a coalition government. On the day after the election, Bob Nixon called up Martel in Sudbury to find out how New Democrats were feeling, and broke into laughter when Martel's son answered the telephone, found out who it was, and, dropping the phone, ran through the house calling out, "Dad, Dad, it's coalition." After his conversation with Nixon, Martel felt that if the New Democrats moved very swiftly to demand a share in power, the Liberals might agree. But it was not to be.

There were few Canadian precedents for coalition governments. The only recent coalition in Ontario had been between 1919 and 1923 when the Independent Labour Party helped the United Farmers to form a government in exchange for two cabinet positions. But McClellan was looking to southern European and not Canadian experience for inspiration. His mother and many of his constituents came from an Italian socialist tradition. There, and elsewhere in Europe, social democratic parties have often joined in coalition governments as junior or senior partners. McClellan believed that the three-party system had become a permanent feature of Ontario politics, and the NDP could usefully borrow from European patterns.

Others in the party were leery of the Liberals and favoured support for Miller's government. Former leader Stephen Lewis said in a radio interview that Rae should not rush his New Democrats into siding with the Liberals but should use his voting power on an issue-by-issue basis. Lewis later came to believe that the NDP should support a Liberal government, but without guarantees. He was death on coalition with a capitalist party. So were many in the left wing of the party who feared co-option and destruction of the NDP in an election because voters would see no difference between them and the Liberals. On the right wing of the party, many of the older members, who remembered the long struggle with the Liberals for second place, argued that Peterson could not be trusted. The right-wingers recalled the labour legislation passed, under pressure, by the Conservatives during Davis's minority years, and wanted to repeat those successes.

Rae's heart was with those caucus members who spoke bitterly of the electoral defeat their party had suffered in 1981 after six years of propping up Conservative minorities. They'd won no credit for the accomplishments, and, after the election, they'd watched promises dissolve as William Davis rubbed home a new reality – that he now had a majority and didn't need to listen.

Rae liked the idea of coalition. He flirted briefly with the idea of being attorney general or, like Martel, labour minister, or even deputy premier – but his party was having none of it. On Sunday, May 5, Rae met with Ed Broadbent in Toronto, and found that the federal leader was disturbed by the talk of alliance with the Liberals. "If you put Peterson in, you are looking at another election in three to six months – he'll cook up something," Broadbent warned Rae. But Broadbent also said he understood why Rae was getting conflicting advice; he'd gone through the same thing when the NDP supported Pierre Trudeau on the Constitution. Rae would have Broadbent's support, whatever he did.

Rae agreed with Martel and McClellan that there could be no coalition unless he hit Peterson with the idea fast, before the Liberals began to sense they could have the support of most New Democrats anyway. Rae couldn't know that Nixon and Peterson had quickly realized the NDP was in the bag and had no intention, once convinced of that, of sharing power. The NDP leader realized, however, that there was no time to debate the fateful coalition idea properly within the party and get majority consent, in time to dicker with Peterson for cabinet seats.

Rae began casting for alternatives, trying to achieve two things: avoidance of an election and assurance that the NDP would get credit for reforms introduced by a Liberal government. Rae had heard too many federal New Democrats mourn the 1972-74 period, when their party supported Trudeau's minority government against the Conservatives under Robert Stanfield but got little recognition for even such a clearly socialist initiative as Petro-Canada. The germ of an idea came to Rae from remarks he'd once heard from federal New Democrat MP Stuart Leggatt. Broadbent and Leggatt discussed the strain on human relations caused by the constant uncertainty of minority government. "It's a crazy way to operate," Leggatt said. "If we do it again, we should ask for a promise of no election for two years and an agreed-on list of legislation."

Rae decided to make a two-year pact, signed by Peterson, the price of support. But first he had to canvass his party and find the appropriate negotiating vehicle. Both he and Peterson were keenly aware of time constraints. Constitutional expert Senator Eugene Forsey was saying publicly that if the government were defeated quickly, precedent would require the Lieutenant-Governor to ask Peterson to form a government, but it was not clear how quickly the defeat had to come. The most obvious precedent was the 1926 King-Byng affair in which Liberal Prime Minister Mackenzie King asked Governor General Lord Byng, eight months after an election, to dissolve Parliament. Byng refused, and the Tories took over. Three months later a parliamentary crisis forced an election, which King won, largely by attacking Byng as a remnant of colonialism. No one could be sure how Lieutenant-Governor John Black Aird would react if Miller imitated King and asked for dissolution of the legislature. Rae and Peterson both believed that Miller would gain credibility as premier the longer he remained in office. To avoid an election that no party wanted, they had to act fast.

Frank Miller awakened too late to the gathering storm. Like many in the media, he was assuming that, although his grip had weakened, power was still his. "At this moment, the Progressive Conservative party is still the government, and I'm proud of that," he had said on election night. Miller mistakenly felt that disappointed Conservatives were more of a threat to him than the Opposition parties. He was absorbed by internal Conservative difficulties, and paid too little attention to the effects of his post-election actions on the Liberals – and particularly on the New Democrats.

The Conservative premier, perhaps still in shock, made his single greatest error at a news conference in Bracebridge the morning after the election. Asked about separate-school funding, Miller said it was the issue that was the main cause of the loss of Tory seats. Tory voters had stayed home to protest the reversal of long-held policy, and he would have to consider the message that the electorate had sent him. Pressed as to whether separate-school funding would go ahead that fall as planned, Miller said he could no longer guarantee anything. "Look, last night all the rules changed, didn't they?" he replied.

The idea that Miller's Conservatives might renege on a solemn commitment because it had cost some votes outraged the Roman Catholic community. Catholic educators foresaw turmoil if the money weren't available that fall. Cardinal Carter noted that the other two parties had given full support to Davis's funding announcement, so there was no reason to delay. Anglican Archbishop Garnsworthy, however, said delay and consultation were needed, and John Tolton, director of the Metropolitan Toronto School Board, called on the government to "immediately suspend" implementation plans. Miller's faltering reopened debate on the Davis decision, and the result was even more controversy and uncertainty.

In his own party the news broke with stunning effect. Veterans like Eddie Goodman were appalled not only by the appearance of panicky vacillation, but also by the political

ineptness of Miller's comments. In a legislature where the two
Opposition parties now far outnumbered the Conservatives,
such provocation could lead to the government's quick defeat.
Goodman heard the news at his downtown Toronto law office,
and he was soon burning up the telephone wires to others
in the Davis Old Guard. Miller was quickly made aware of
his mistake, and issued a clarification. He said his doubts
had been exaggerated, and the legislation would go ahead
as planned.

Miller's remarks helped drive the Liberals and New Democrats into one another's arms. For both Opposition parties,
the Miller wobble raised a horrid spectre. What if he intended
to force an early defeat of the government by proposing to
defer separate-school funding? The Opposition parties would
have to combine to stop such a move in the House. Miller
could call that a vote of non-confidence in his government,
and go to the people in an election which would divide
communities and rouse religious passions. Who could safely
predict the result? The fear that the Conservatives would use
separate-school funding again, as Davis had in 1971, caused
the Opposition parties to draw together. Rae told fellow MPPs
that Miller was "an unguided missile". He felt that if Miller
wanted to make a major policy change, he was obliged, in
a minority legislature, to talk first with the Opposition
leaders – not just to spit it out in public. To New Democrats,
whose support was vital to the survival of Miller's administration, the premier appeared increasingly unattractive as
a partner.

There was more to the aura of instability around Miller
than his waffling on separate schools. In the aftermath of
an election that endangered a recently secure government,
the Conservatives were a wounded and angry lot, and Miller
was the focus of much of the fury. It appeared possible that
his own party might finish the job that the public had begun,
so New Democrats had to calculate as well that alliance with
Miller might not last more than a few months.

In an attempt to protect Miller, David Melnik helped him
issue invitations for a Tory summit to the men who used to

run the Ontario Conservative party. It must have been galling for Miller. Three months before, he'd been sworn in as premier, triumphantly looking forward to a comfortable decade in power. Now, only two days after bringing the 42-year-old dynasty to the brink of oblivion, he had to face the last steward of the legend – his former boss, Bill Davis. The only comfort for Miller was the remembrance that Davis too had known the fall into minority. The premier arranged for a government plane to fly Bill Davis, Eddie Goodman, Hugh Segal, Ed Stewart, and John Tory to Muskoka Airport, where they were met by a van that took them to the Miller family's Patterson-Kaye lodge near Bracebridge. Miller had also invited his old friend Hugh Mackenzie, the Muskoka newspaperman and former riding organizer, whose advice he'd missed since becoming premier; Robert Carman, the secretary of cabinet; and David Melnik, his lawyer and adviser.

Michael Perik, his principal secretary, was conspicuously absent. Perik knew the party blamed him for mishandling Miller's election tour and was howling for his blood. Perik told Miller he would absent himself from the meeting to make it easier for the others to talk about him, and he offered to leave Miller's employ at once, taking up his deferred plans to go to Harvard graduate school. Perik's fate indeed was a major topic of conversation at the meeting, which was held in a comfortable cottage on the lodge grounds.

Miller wanted advice from people who had steered the Conservatives successfully during minority in the past, but he also wanted to discuss what had happened to him in the election. Miller still saw himself largely as a victim. He felt that he had been savaged by a press corps that would give him no quarter, and – although he couldn't go on about it much in this company – that he had been saddled with the separate-school decision. The Davis crowd gave him some sympathy as a nice man who had been terribly mishandled, and blamed the amateurs who had brought him to the premiership in the first place. Miller's guests were thunderstruck when Tory asked the dejected premier if he had known that, days before the vote, the Conservatives had been four points behind the Liberals, and Miller replied that he hadn't.

Hugh Mackenzie, sitting in on the meeting as Miller's ally, was furious at the revelation that Tory and Segal had known things that Miller hadn't. He looked Tory in the eye and demanded: "If you guessed that Frank was not getting the information, why didn't you break down the door and tell him yourself?" It was a home question that brought an embarrassed silence, and went unanswered both then and now.

Davis and his friends advised Miller to make changes in his staff and appointed themselves as a steering committee to handle the tricky days ahead. Back in Toronto, Miller's ally Bette Stephenson was added to the group, and they started meeting twice a week at the Bristol Place Hotel to talk strategy. In the media, stories appeared saying Miller was on trial, with ninety days to prove he could make the changes that might save the party. Miller himself said that he was given no deadline, and that Goodman and Davis both urged him not to quit precipitously but to give himself a little time to see how well he could pull the party together.

When the discussion turned to Perik, Miller described him as "the guy who got me here" – whose encyclopedic command of organizational details was responsible for his leadership victory. He also acknowledged that Perik was hard on people, and that he'd "had to count the bodies he leaves in his wake." Miller made it clear he would sacrifice Perik, and Davis then urged him to accept Tory as principal secretary for his experience of government and his knowledge of the party. Stewart was to be the real deputy to the premier again, running the government for the month or so before he was entitled to full pension and would be free to go to work for the private sector. Miller also agreed to bring his leadership rivals, Grossman and Timbrell, into his inner councils.

While Miller was making peace with the Conservative Old Guard, and preparing himself emotionally for the break with Perik, the Liberals and the New Democrats were courting. Sean Conway, Liberal MPP for Renfrew North, had been intrigued by the possibility of an alliance with the NDP from the moment he sensed the Tory election weakness. Conway had smarted under Conservative barbs during Davis's last four majority years and had struck up casual friendships with New Democrats Ross McClellan and Richard Johnston. He'd taken note in March when George Samis, former NDP MPP from Cornwall, said the only hope for toppling the Tories was alliance with the Liberals, and listened with amazement when Nixon, asked by reporters for his reaction, also talked of the advantages of coalition. The time had come, Nixon said, when a deal with the NDP was possible and desirable.

Nixon had long believed privately that the two Opposition parties needed to combine forces, but for a former Liberal leader to say so just before an election struck Conway as highly significant. Conway approached Dave Cooke, NDP member from Windsor-Riverside, and found he was willing to consider some sort of NDP/Liberal arrangement for an alternative government. So, well before election day, there had been a growing understanding breaking down the old antipathies between the Opposition parties. The election results were barely in when Conway called Richard Johnston and the two chatted casually, with Johnston stressing the NDP's strong desire to avoid another election. Conway passed back the message to the Liberals that the NDP's first concern was stability. Conway began canvassing Liberal party opinion. One of his calls was to Elinor Caplan, one of the new group of rookie Liberals. "What do you think, Elinor?" Conway asked. "Can we form a government?" Caplan had by now gotten over her election-night terror and replied, "Yes we can!"

Bob Rae knew his party's morale, organization, and finances were in no shape for a quick election. Even more, he needed time to prove to the electorate that a vote for the third party is not a throw-away vote. Although in Canada the public likes the benefits of minority governments, the party that does the propping up is usually punished at the polls. Rae wanted to prove that minority governments can be stable, and that the third party can play a significant role during minorities. His theory, which he outlined later in speeches and in the winter 1985-86 issue of the *Canadian Parliamentary Review*, was that parliamentary government had become executive government, with excessive power concentrated in the office of the prime minister. His hope was to use NDP leverage to return some of that power to the ordinary members.

On Monday, May 6, Rae called a special session of the party caucus, executive, members of the election-planning committee, and key staff members – about sixty New Democrats in all – to decide how to handle their 25-seat balance of power. The leader had been hammered by contradictory advice all weekend, and he knew that the decision he now faced was potentially fatal to party unity.

His first job was to win over a strong party minority that disliked and distrusted Peterson. Peterson's repetition during the election of the charge that the NDP was the tool of big union bosses had been an unpleasant reminder of years of Ontario Liberal union-bashing at NDP expense. At the same time, MPPs in the caucus with strong union connections, such as steelworker Bob MacKenzie of Hamilton, thought that more gains for labour might be won from the Tories. They felt that the Red Tories, with their urban connections, understood working people better than the rural Liberals.

On the other hand, there was Frank Miller. Under his leadership, the Conservatives now appeared the more right-wing, rural party. By contrast, Peterson's Liberals shared many major policies with the NDP. Indeed, NDPers felt Peterson had stolen their platform. There was a new urban contingency of MPPs in the Liberal caucus, led by left-leaning labour lawyer Ian Scott, who spoke a common language with the New Democrats. This had its dangers of course: the Conservatives argued that the New Democrats would sign their death warrant by allying with the Liberals because they'd be competing for the same urban turf in the next election. But Rae said the greatest danger was for the NDP to be seen to be standing in the way of progressive change. By propping up Miller they'd be perpetuating a decaying regime when the people wanted something new.

Rae told his caucus to abandon its dream that the Liberals would disappear and leave the NDP as the alternative to the

Conservatives. He argued that within a mature Ontario three-party system the NDP could be a force for progressive change and for stability. Rae scouted the possibility of a formal coalition with the Liberals to give the NDP an up-front role in a new government. He suggested that New Democrats could hold as many as three portfolios in a coalition government with the Liberals, rather than simply providing twenty-five supporting votes to keep a minority government in power.

This was too sudden for some New Democrats, such as Paul Forder, a labour member of the executive. Forder favoured an alliance with the Liberals, but exploded at the suggestion of coalition. He voiced the strong opposition of influential New Democrats, including provincial secretary Michael Lewis, brother of Stephen Lewis, who said a socialist party could not join with a capitalist party and preserve its identity.

Rae realized that taking a lengthy debate on coalition to the party membership would give Frank Miller extra weeks – perhaps months – in office. He declared the coalition idea was off, to the intense disappointment of Ross McClellan, Oshawa MPP Michael Breaugh, Richard Johnston, and Elie Martel – the group that had pushed him to demand a coalition government at once. Weeks later, McClellan complained that constituents of Italian origin kept coming up and greeting him as if he were a cabinet minister and expressing great confusion when he said it wasn't so. How could he be supporting the government and not be a minister? they wanted to know.

Still, Rae won from the caucus a majority agreement to field a team of negotiators. Its mission was to wring from Peterson, or from Miller, a solid deal specifying a guaranteed length of time before another election. The New Democrats agreed they wanted a signed document spelling out mutually agreed reforms which they could wave at their constituents and say, "See, this is what we won for you." Most of the caucus favoured a deal with Peterson, but a significant minority still preferred the Tories. Besides, Rae would have lost all bargaining leverage if he'd let on at this stage that he was ready to jump in the Liberal pocket. For both these reasons, the

New Democrats decided to invite the blandishments of both major parties. Rae announced that he would be naming his negotiators and asked the other two parties to do the same. Rae knew that both Peterson and Miller would be unhappy at the idea of formal negotiations: they would both have preferred gentlemen's handshakes. But he wanted room to manoeuvre and time to continue to take soundings within his own party.

Rae was correct in believing his announcement would upset the other parties. Miller remarked to reporters that he didn't remember the NDP's demanding formal pacts as the price of support in the past. In a similar vein, Bob Nixon spoke angrily to Liberal caucus mates about Rae's putting his party up for auction. Nixon felt that the many informal contacts between the Liberals and the New Democrats, and the large areas of policy agreement – extra billing, minimum tax, equal pay, proclamation of the spills bill – ought to have led to an immediate decision by the NDP to support the Liberals. Liberal strategists fretted at the delay, which tended to legitimize Miller's tenure. Nixon, a more hot-tempered and impatient character than his leader, even suggested that the Liberals should ignore Rae's invitation to field negotiators.

Peterson rejected this hawkish view and argued that the Liberals should move slowly and not seem too hungry for power. People might start to sympathize with Miller and his tattered party if the Liberals appeared too eager to trample them while they were down. Peterson told the caucus to leave the next moves up to him, and called Rae to discuss his understanding of their common interest.

In Tory ranks, a few ministers, among them Larry Grossman, were beginning to twig to the danger of a Liberal/NDP alliance. But the Conservatives lacked the informal contacts with the NDP from which the Liberals were benefiting. Shortly after the election, Dennis Timbrell had telephoned Rae's office, in what was intended to be a friendly, informal gesture, and learned only that the NDP wanted to try something new. The Big Blue Machiners, when they found out about Timbrell's initiative, shut such contacts down. They feared Rae would get different messages from several Tory factions and use that as evidence of Miller's lack of control of his party. Shortly after this, John Tory called Rae's aide Hugh Mackenzie (not Miller's friend of the same name, but a Rae staffer) to offer patronage posts. At a meeting of the Premier's Appointments Committee, Tory advanced the proposition that, in the new situation, the committee should consult outside its own ranks. He asked Mackenzie for some NDP nominees for certain government boards, but Mackenzie didn't call back. At the time, Tory didn't make much of it.

When the Conservative cabinet held its first post-election meeting on May 8, internal warfare still topped the agenda, snapping the government's capacity to respond to the Opposition threat. The gathering included defeated ministers, who'd lost their portfolios after holding them only three months, and survivors badly shaken at the drop in Tory support. Talking to reporters, they offered many explanations for the May 2 result. Environment minister Morley Kells, who had gone down in Humber and was attending his last cabinet, said media sensationalizing of the PCB spill had hurt him badly. David Rotenberg, defeated in Wilson Heights, said Archbishop Garnsworthy's remarks had crystallized religious intolerance and hurt the Tories. "I think he would probably get the Ian Paisley award of the year, because his speech made it respectable to be anti-Catholic," Rotenberg said bitterly. Inside caucus, Miller listened quietly and took notes. Bette Stephenson expressed some of his bitterness by suggesting the election disaster was partly the fault of leadership rivals who'd failed to get behind their new leader. Grossman replied angrily to the thinly veiled rebuke. The biggest danger to his chances of succeeding Miller was the spreading rumour that he'd been part of a fifth column undermining the Miller campaign. Grossman told cabinet he didn't want to read or hear any more stories about disloyal Tories. No Grossman person had been involved in any attempt to harm Miller, he said. Grossman's outburst apparently convinced everyone and the accusations of sabotage died out, although Miller and his people continued to say that some parts of the party hadn't had their hearts in the campaign.

While the Tory cabinet met, Rae was closeted with about twenty labour leaders at NDP headquarters on Main Street in east-end Toronto, engaged in a discussion the Conservatives would have found distressing. Davis's Tories, among them former labour minister Robert Elgie, were convinced the union chiefs would advise Rae to stick by the old ad hoc system of supporting the government in return for legislative favours and some appointments to government agencies. However, Rae found, by his count, a bare majority of labour leaders were already in favour of supporting the Liberals. Later that day, Robert White, head of the Canadian Autoworkers and the most respected labour leader in Ontario, said that trying to win legislative changes from Miller on issues such as extra billing would be "like extracting a death-bed repentance". White said labour support for the Tories would thwart the popular will. "The people of Ontario voted for change and rejected the Frank Miller Tories, " White said. "After nearly forty-two years of one-party government a change would be good." Labour opposition to negotiations with the Liberals went underground after White's pronouncement.

About this time, Richard Johnston and Sean Conway, after taping a morning CBC show together, retreated to a local greasy spoon on Parliament Street for a serious talk. Until then, Conway and other senior Liberals had imagined they might cement a deal with a few high-profile NDP appointments. The Liberals, for example, could appoint Jack Stokes, the former NDP member and Speaker of the legislature, to investigate rule changes to increase the effectiveness of Opposition members. Perhaps Donald MacDonald, former NDP leader and former head of the select committee on Ontario Hydro, might like to be chairman of the huge Crown corporation? Johnston, taking the high road, quickly made it clear that the NDP would not settle for perks. It wanted a guarantee of stable government and a reform package. Conway in return assured Johnston the Liberals would not doublecross and call a snap election to win a quick majority. His party, he pointed out, would have to pass the separate-school funding legislation and wanted time to let the electorate absorb the change and cool down.

While Johnston and Conway were enjoying their meeting of minds, Frank Miller had finally brought himself to do what he'd promised Davis in Muskoka and was engaged in the hurtful task of telling Michael Perik he was finished as principal secretary. Perik, an obsessively private young man, had never dealt diplomatically with the bureaucracy or the party. His mission had been to free the Conservative party from the domination of the Big Blue Machine. He'd offended many, and now the party made him the official scapegoat for the election failure. As Miller's closest adviser on the tour bus, Perik was held responsible for the premier's performance. Miller and Perik, the former distressed and the latter disappointed and angry, agreed that from then on Perik would play a lesser role in the cabinet office, and in the fall would depart to the John F. Kennedy School of Government at Harvard. His replacement as principal secretary was John Tory, who flew up to Muskoka on business with Miller that afternoon.

People who had put Miller at the helm to humble and banish the Big Blue Machiners were appalled and frustrated. Miller was cut off now from his own loyal team and surrounded by the very crew that had run the province for Bill Davis. David Melnik, Perik's rival for Miller's favour, was also a casualty. He had offended the BBM circle by speaking for the record about the summit at Bracebridge. His usefulness to Miller was destroyed when the others said they couldn't trust him to be discreet.

Stripped of his loyalists, Miller was isolated and only barely in control of his own office, but he felt that he'd had little choice. He had no chance of remaining in office without creating at least a semblance of peace in his own party. He still felt misunderstood, and hoped that Davis and the other guys from the old golden days might get him some decent press. Watching from the sidelines, Sean Conway remarked that Miller had become "a regent premier".

As they left cabinet the following week, Larry Grossman and Dennis Timbrell – the former outspoken and the latter quiet and watchful – compared their concerns about the way Miller was handling things. The brief alliance they'd developed after the leadership now broke down. Grossman felt that if Miller stayed in office, the Tories would keep falling in the polls. He wanted to inherit a government, not a tattered Opposition party, and felt his own and the Conservatives' best interests would be served if Miller could be pushed to resign quickly. Timbrell, however, had dismantled the leadership organization that he felt had served him poorly. An early leadership convention promised to be no contest for Grossman. When Grossman asked what the two of them might do together, Timbrell therefore offered no encouragement. He said he would not raise the issue of Miller's leadership in cabinet or in public. The rivalry was back on.

Grossman scored points early. Miller, choosing a team to win NDP hearts and knowing Dennis Timbrell felt he had contacts in Rae's office, named him a negotiator. Grossman baulked. Perhaps he felt only those known as Red Tories had any chance of succeeding with the socialists. Perhaps he wanted to keep Timbrell off the television cameras. In any event, Timbrell's name disappeared from the list and the Tories put forward Robert Elgie, the former labour minister, Larry Grossman, and John Tory, who replaced Timbrell on the pretext that the NDP had chosen two MPPs and one staff member for its negotiating team.

Miller's Red Tory choices were his best chance, but one look at the teams selected by Peterson and Rae made it clear where the real accord lay. Both leaders chose MPPs who were most eager for an alliance and sympathetic to the other side. Rae, in fact, deliberately denied a spot to Elie Martel, who expected as House leader to lead the NDP team. It wasn't that Martel didn't favour the Liberals – he did – but he was a long-time fishing buddy of Robert Elgie's and Rae wanted to be certain that friendship wouldn't cause Martel to pay too much attention to his old Tory friend.

As chief negotiator, Rae selected Ross McClellan, who got along well with two key Liberal negotiators, Nixon and Conway. McClellan was dedicated to a deal with the Liberals and the job of ensuring it came off suited his keen backroom intelligence. He quickly became the mastermind of the negotiations, ensuring smooth understandings with the Liberals while stalling the Tories. McClellan was supported by Michael Breaugh, an Oshawa MPP who had grown disillusioned with supporting the Conservatives during the Davis minorities, and by Rae staffer Hugh Mackenzie.

Peterson chose Nixon, Conway, Ian Scott, and Hershell Ezrin from his own office. Scott was a new member, a labour lawyer and an experienced negotiator whose first law partnership was with New Democrat MP Andrew Brewin. Left-wing and urban, Scott was dispatched to remind the New Democrats of a new Liberal reality in Ontario.

When the Liberal and NDP negotiating teams met for the first time at a downtown Toronto hotel on May 13, McClellan had a lengthy shopping-list in his hand. Between their first caucus and the negotiations, Rae and other NDP brass had worked out with the negotiators all the details of what was eventually to become the accord. On the list were legislative items that the Liberals and NDP had in common during their campaign – the ban on extra billing, equal pay for work of equal value, proclamation of the spills bill, extension of rent review to cover previously exempted buildings built after 1976, separate-school funding, OHIP coverage of medically necessary northern travel, 10,000 new housing units, and job programs for young people.

The list also contained many more items that fell by the wayside because they originated only with the NDP. Peterson had instructed his negotiators not to accept anything that he couldn't fairly claim he had promised during the election. Some essentially NDP concerns made the common program – such as first-contract arbitration of labour disputes, job-security legislation, workers'-compensation reform, and an audit of the northern forests – but Peterson, however belatedly, had endorsed them all. They were legitimate parts of an NDP/ Liberal agenda. Scott, on whom the niceties of party copyright were lost, stared at the list lying on the table before him and said, "My God, this is the reform agenda of a whole generation."

The NDP also proposed a series of reforms of the legislative process and found common ground with the Liberals, who had also developed strong opinions about the need to open up the governing process during the long years in opposition. These were what McClellan and Rae called "sunshine reforms", intended to let fresh air into Ontario democracy. Included were electoral-financing reform to put limits on amounts spent at the riding level, a strengthening and broadening of the role of the individual MPPs and legislative committees, a select committee to review the patronage system and recommend changes, expanded rights of public servants to engage in political activity, and freedom-of-information legislation. The importance of these items was not obvious to the public, but they meant a great deal to the New Democrats, who pursued them with relish. The Liberals were about to attain power, but they knew too well the humiliations of opposition. Both teams entertained themselves at times, too, chuckling over the changes that would be made in the bureaucracy, and picturing the anxiety felt by senior civil servants who had allied themselves too openly with the Conservatives.

The difficult question, as Scott pointed out at the first Liberal/NDP meeting, was how to achieve stability for a new government while the agreed-on program went ahead. The Liberals were interested in any proposal that would give them a guaranteed period in office to prove themselves. McClellan explained that the NDP would agree not to vote non-confidence in the government if the Liberals would guarantee not to call an election for two years. That meant the government could not be forced to an election by a defeat in the House on a matter of confidence. The New Democrats would be free, however, to join with the Tories to defeat measures, including money bills, so the Liberals would have to move carefully to ensure that their socialist partners were always on side.

Robert Nixon was concerned about the veto of money bills. He knew he would likely be appointed treasurer by Peterson, and he didn't relish the prospect of the NDP combining with the Conservatives to rewrite financial bills. He didn't like the possibility of proposing a sales-tax increase to, say, ten per cent, and having the other two vote to reduce that to zero. So a clause was inserted in the growing agreement saying that the legislation would be implemented "within a framework of financial responsibility". That put an onus on the NDP not to demand things the government felt it couldn't afford, and gave the Liberals an out if their partners acted irresponsibly.

As the negotiations with the NDP proceeded, Nixon, Conway and Scott, all "progressive" Liberals, became increasingly enamoured with the development of a written pact. They knew that the Liberal commitment to progressive reform had been born of pre-election desperation, and that Peterson's friends in the financial community would exert heavy pressure on him to renounce his socialist allies. A written pact would commit the Liberals to reform and override the objections of the party's rural right wing. Above all, the pact gave the Liberals a clear legislative agenda and a timetable for implementing it. That lessened the danger that the Liberal minority would be stalemated by powerful and monied interest-groups such as doctors, employers, and landlords the way the Tories had been in their last years. This would be active government.

The day after the Liberal/NDP meeting, the Conservative negotiators met the NDP team in a cabinet meeting-room at Queen's Park, and as they sat around the huge oak table, the Tories for the first time felt the intensity of NDP resentment at the way Davis had treated them once he'd regained the majority. McClellan reminded the Tories of how reforms like the spills bill had flown out the window after March 19, 1981. "The weight of opinion in our caucus and our party is with the Liberals," he told the dismayed Conservatives, but he added that no final decision had been taken, so he was ready to negotiate. McClellan said that this time the NDP would no longer settle for the loophole-ridden reform laws offered up during the Davis minority years. The NDP negotiators wanted two years' stability in the legislature, an agenda of solid reform legislation, and reforms of the process at Queen's Park. McClellan deliberately kept the outline vague; he didn't want to give the Tories a chance to catch up too fast to the pace of the talks with the Liberals.

On his side, Grossman replied that Frank Miller understood "there is a new reality" and that he could not expect to return to the old ad hoc way of doing things during the Davis minority years of 1975 to 1981. Grossman said that he was "not about to be left out on a limb" by Miller and that everything would have to be approved first by the premier. The Conservative negotiators had talked over their stance with Miller, and were there to listen and take notes of what it was that the NDP wanted. Grossman listened to McClellan's outline of how legislative stability would work and remarked that "none of this is any problem." He was willing to shake hands on a guarantee of two years' stability, and he offered as well to give the NDP the right to review the progress of reform every six months with the government and opt out of the deal if it wasn't working. "It would be your option, not ours," he said.

Grossman next attempted to frighten the NDP negotiators about the Liberals' real intentions. He warned that the Liberals, unlike the Conservatives, had voter momentum and would want an election soon – an election in which the NDP would be wiped out. Peterson's word couldn't be trusted, he said, because he wasn't really in charge. Senator Keith Davey and Jim Coutts, the old Trudeau backroom boys, were calling the shots for the provincial Liberals, and those two were jaded old pros who would find a way to trigger an election as soon as the polls were good enough.

After that, the meeting broke up, with the Conservatives promising to consider the NDP program. McClellan told friends later that Grossman and Elgie were like two guys who had just come from a painful funeral and didn't really have their minds on what was happening. The New Democrat negotiators, on the other hand, believed that, in their hurt and confusion, the Tories would do whatever was asked of them to stay in power. "It's a candy store," Breaugh reported back to Rae, but the NDP leader was not impressed by the Tories' new-found progressivism. He felt the Conservatives were oppor-tunists and he likened the scene to "the last days of Pompeii".

The Conservatives, meanwhile, were uneasy. In the meeting, Elgie had straightforwardly asked the NDP for support, and had been dismayed by the lack of response. He requested a date for the next Conservative/NDP negotiation, but McClellan dodged, saying the NDP first wanted to see the results of Miller's impending cabinet shuffle. Elgie warned Miller later that he didn't think an agreement was possible. But the next morning Miller, apparently not realizing yet how great was his danger, told reporters he wasn't interested in a written deal.

McClellan threw that in Grossman's face two days later when the Tory negotiator called. Didn't Miller know what was going on, or was he opposed to things Grossman had agreed to? he asked. Grossman, for his part, was annoyed by the smiles he'd seen on television after a second Liberal/NDP negotiating meeting, and asked what all the grinning was about. In fact, the Liberal and NDP teams had worked out an outline of a deal to be presented to their respective caucuses. But McClel-lan didn't want to reveal that secret yet. He countered by asking why Miller had rejected the concept of a written deal. Grossman thought this was nitpicking, but he promised to clear up the misunderstanding before the next meeting. He and Elgie went to Miller and told him that the New Democrats were watching every word to support their view that the Tories were hopelessly divided. They asked Miller to guard his tongue more carefully, and they sent off a letter, signed by Grossman, Elgie, and Tory, and approved by Miller, which said "the Premier has authorized us to establish a written agenda and timetable with respect to legislative priorities. It is our intention that such an agenda, and our negotiations, will deal with both procedural and policy matters, and will specifically ensure stability." The letter was to become a matter of controversy later when Miller accused the Liberals and NDP of making a deal that contravened parliamentary practice.

McClellan made the letter public, saying the Conservatives had been willing to make such a deal themselves, but Miller and Grossman denied they had ever agreed to a system in which the Opposition would not vote non-confidence for two years.

In the interim before the next meeting, Miller shuffled his cabinet, partly to fill portfolios left vacant by the election, partly to respond to the new political situation. He shifted Grossman into the education portfolio, where he spent the next weeks avoiding decisions related to separate-school funding. Bette Stephenson replaced Grossman in treasury, Robert Elgie once again became labour minister, a portfolio where he'd earlier won the approval of the union movement, in a clear signal that the Conservatives would agree to labour reforms. But Bette Stephenson's appointment did not go down well with the New Democrats, who said it was more evidence of Miller's real right-wing agenda. Miller said she'd been chosen for her experience and intellect. He said he knew by now that there was little he could do to find favour with the NDP and there were "clear signals" that Rae was going to the Liberals. The premier hoped that the NDP would come to its senses and recognize that "if their interest is survival, they are in much more danger of being swallowed up by the Liberals than by us."

Miller's warnings had little impact. The New Democrat caucus and executive met a second time to debate its direction, and sentiment this time was even more strongly in favour of the Liberals. But, although Peterson's team waited anxiously all day on the understanding that the NDP might announce its support that night, nothing happened. The NDPers were once again locked in debate over the question of a formal coalition. By now most MPPs were inclined to view coalition favourably, but the majority of the party executive was still adamantly opposed. The New Democrats' basic decision to support the Liberals was firmly in place, but because of their internal division over coalition, the Liberals and the public weren't to know it for several days.

During the hiatus, Miller sent Rae a four-page letter promising a Throne Speech that would reflect not only Conservative principles and priorities, but the degree of support Ontarians had given the NDP and Liberals in the election as well. He said his party, too, wanted a lengthy period of stability, but he would not ask the NDP to give any undertakings that would limit its ability to vote non-confidence in the House.

The premier said he regretted he hadn't yet had time to develop a relationship of trust and understanding with Rae, but he reminded him of the mutual respect between Bill Davis and Stephen Lewis during the previous period of minority. "While we may have disagreed in the past as parties on certain issues, we have done so on a position of principle that indicated a far deeper commitment to policy consistency and integrity than any review of recent or historical Liberal performance would suggest." The letter was hand-delivered to Rae on May 21, the day before the New Democrats met for the last time with the Tory negotiators.

At that final meeting, McClellan stated bluntly that the instability of Miller's leadership and the voters' desire for change were the real issues for New Democrats. He said the NDP's concern was that the Tory regime had major fissures and was still in free fall. The NDP negotiators wanted to deal with one team, but felt the Conservatives were internally divided. McClellan asked provocatively whether he was ne-gotiating with Miller's "fifth column" – bait that Grossman declined to take. Instead, he in turn asked McClellan about continuing rumours that what the NDP really wanted was coalition. "If coalition is what you are really talking about, tell us, so I can go to Miller and say 'What now?'" Grossman declared. McClellan took this as an indication that the Tories would consider even coalition. But he shut the discussion off, saying that the caucus had not ruled the idea of coalition out, but it was not being pursued "either with them or with you".

Most of the meeting was spent on the NDP's request for stability. Grossman wanted to know whether the NDP proposal on votes of confidence would allow the Opposition parties to combine to change a budget bill, for example, lowering sales taxes and reducing government revenue, without defeating the government. McClellan said yes, and Grossman wondered aloud whether a government could govern that way. McClellan said the NDP would act responsibly. McClellan has insisted since that Grossman agreed to his terms on nonconfidence, but Grossman denies it, and is supported by notes taken by Tory at the time. They show Grossman agreeing to a term of stability, but asking time to check with Miller on the non-confidence issue before another meeting with the NDP.

When Grossman proposed commencing discussion on a reform agenda, McClellan looked at his watch and said there was only twenty minutes left. The Conservatives deduced from this that they had lost. Nevertheless, Grossman went through the list. He said the Conservative government would oppose the free-trade proposals of Prime Minister Brian Mulroney. This was not a real departure – Miller had talked of something he called "secure trade", as opposed to free trade, and Hugh Segal had been giving speeches warning that free trade would cost Ontario jobs. Grossman also proffered a $500-million jobs program; $2.4 billion worth of accelerated capital-works projects; an end to extra billing by doctors; tax reform with a minimum tax likely; action to reduce acid rain from Inco Limited and Ontario Hydro plants; equal pay for work of equal value, but with no implementation date; reforms to OHIP premium assistance; enactment of the spills bill by September 1; first-contract arbitration; a housing program; and tenant-reform legislation by July 10, although he wasn't sure the Tories would go for NDP demands to apply rent controls to buildings built after 1976.

McClellan took these as firm offers, and claims Grossman once told him on the telephone he was willing to match the Liberals policy for policy. The Tories say, however, that they'd made it clear that any of these offers would still have to go to cabinet for final approval. Afterwards, Rae met the crowd of reporters that hung around the negotiating meetings and expressed public pleasure about the meeting with the Tories. This was the first time, he said, that the Conservatives had been willing to talk turkey, and they'd have his answer in two days' time, after the NDP caucus meeting on Friday.

Grossman informed Miller that the NDP was very unlikely to come their way. The premier's problems were by then almost overwhelming, and he sat in his office nearly paralysed by the difficulties he faced inside and outside his party. On Thursday, the premier roused himself in a final attempt to save his pride – but even that came hours too late.

In the lonely days after the election, Miller had sent for Sally Barnes, saying he needed one person in his office whom he could trust to tell him the unvarnished truth. She was ensconced in the old government vault across the hall from the premier's office, with a private mandate to guard against the encircling sharks and help him regain at least a semblance of control. Barnes was Bill Davis's former press secretary during minority years and had declared her support for Miller late in the leadership convention. A plain-talking ex-journalist, unimpressed by pretension of any kind, she had a flair for managing the news. Barnes felt badly for Miller and believed that if Perik hadn't excluded her, she could have showed the Miller team how to market him. She now had a last-minute opportunity to help him show a little fight. Her concern was that the Big Blue Machine crowd was so anxious to hold on to power – and its perquisites – that it would force Miller to make concessions destructive to his credibility, and to his base in the party.

Barnes advised Miller to put his trust in Eddie Goodman, the adviser to three preceding Tory premiers, whom she felt was sufficiently independent after all his years in Tory backrooms to give disinterested counsel. Miller talked to Goodman by telephone Thursday morning and took to heart his advice: that he couldn't in conscience accept all the NDP was asking. Miller knew Barnes had doubts too, and asked her to join him for lunch. In the modest basement dining-room at Queen's Park, the premier told Barnes that he wanted to end the charade of negotiations with the NDP. She agreed he had been sacrificing all he was supposed to stand for and undertook to write a statement announcing the Conservative withdrawal.

Barnes finished at 4 a.m. and dropped the text off at Miller's Sutton Place apartment. But before the scheduled 10 a.m. news conference at which he was to deliver the statement, Miller kept a prior appointment with Bob Rae in the premier's office. Without mentioning his doubts about the NDP agenda, Miller made a final pitch for a personal understanding that would allow the Conservatives to remain in power, and repeated his warning about Liberal treachery. Rae replied simply that the NDP wanted to try something new. At that point, Miller knew the jig was up, but instead of going on to his press conference, he summoned his policy-and-priority group to chew over the decision to stop bargaining. Elgie approved. He too had grave reservations about the NDP proposal for non-confidence votes, and he was ready with a written statement denouncing the NDP scheme for stability.

Dennis Timbrell argued that Miller was capitulating to an NDP/Liberal alliance that would put them out of office. Barnes said the premier preferred that to paying the NDP's price. Ed Stewart then told Miller he should be ready to give his soul to remain premier, and that once opportunity slipped away, it would be a long time returning. Once again Miller bowed to pressure and let the group go to work softening Barnes's statement. The original draft denounced both the stability mechanism and the NDP legislative agenda. "It would be less than honest for my party and its leader to advocate in the Legislature various programs the NDP believes to be right but which my party and I believe to be wrong," it said. ". . . I have no right to govern on behalf of Mr. Rae and the platform of the NDP." The sanitized version said that Miller was still open to compromise on the issues.

During the discussion, Larry Grossman was unusually quiet, probably sensing that whatever Miller did made little difference. As the others gathered around the typewriter, Barnes said to Grossman, "Larry, he can't buy that stuff." Grossman replied, "Sally, he would have bought anything." Barnes told

Grossman he had never understood Miller, and took herself off for a cooling walk.

The real effect of all the hurried rewriting was to deny Miller his last chance to save face. Liberal and NDP negotiators had met the day before to finalize their understanding on paper, and Rae decided to make one last try for a coalition. He didn't have the approval of his party, but he had persuaded the executive and caucus to allow him to explore the possibility. McClellan warned Nixon by phone of what was coming, but the Liberals were still taken aback. By then, they knew that they had the NDP anyway, so Nixon patiently explained that the party with forty-eight seats would form the government. "We assumed coalition was not high on your agenda after the first meeting," Nixon said. "Coalition wasn't raised very seriously with us then, so we haven't discussed it."

Not only were the Liberals unprepared to discuss coalition, they were, by now, hopeful of an easier deal than the NDP had asked for in the earlier meetings. Nixon, in some embarrassment because it went against his own personal conviction of what was good for his party, now informed the NDP negotiators that Peterson didn't want a written and signed list of agreed-upon reforms. The Liberal leader was prepared to sign the cornerstone document guaranteeing no election for two years, but that was all. McClellan was first stunned and then furious. For a few heated minutes there was a lot of yelling, and then the NDP negotiators left the room to cool off. "No deal," McClellan shouted as he went out. In their absence, Hershell Ezrin called Peterson to tell him that the NDP negotiators would not make a pact unless they had a written list of reform measures. Others in the room could hear Peterson swearing, but at last he agreed. Nixon called the New Democrats back and said, "Okay, there will be a list." It had been the most crucial, and most difficult, of the meetings between the two Opposition parties plotting Miller's overthrow.

The NDP caucus decided on Friday morning – while Miller's statement was being rewritten – to go ahead with the accord, and announce support for the Liberals at 2:30 that afternoon. McClellan informed Grossman of the NDP decision about noon, and word spread quickly to reporters. When Miller hustled into the media studio at 1 p.m., still trying to pre-empt Rae, he looked like a man who had discovered his principles only after being spurned.

Miller told the news conference he couldn't agree to the NDP demand for two years of stability with few opportunities for non-confidence votes. He was not willing to obtain peace by sacrificing the essence of parliamentary democracy. A written guarantee of no election would limit clashes of principle which otherwise would be decided by the electorate. Such a pact violated centuries of parliamentary tradition, and, in Miller's opinion, would lead to a congressional form of government. "It is more important to stand up for something than to say that all that matters is that I survive," he said in a voice rough with emotion. "I decided that if this spelled my death knell, that was better than spelling the death knell to a form of government I think very important." Later, Miller told reporters he'd felt at peace since deciding to oppose the NDP demand. There were worse things, he said, than being Leader of the Opposition. Luckily, he had never been one of those who believed the Tories ruled by divine right.

At 2:30 p.m., Rae announced publicly that his party would support a Peterson government. "Our meetings with the Liberals have not yet produced a final agreement," he said. "But we have reached a point where we are satisfied we can negotiate with the Liberal Party a joint written agreement, which will set out an agenda for reform, as well as a cornerstone document on process and stability in a minority parliament, and a commitment to reform on freedom of information and other 'sunshine' measures.

"Our caucus and party have made this decision knowing full well its significance.

"Ontario is unique in Canada because its three-party system has been matched by one-party Conservative government for forty-two years. The Miller Conservatives ran an election campaign in which their support plummeted, and in which many thousands of voters clearly lost confidence in a party and a leader that had lost touch, and that appeared to take victory for granted. We heard Conservative negotiators indicate a desire to respond to the mood for change, but in our view this promise to change is too late and too uncertain, and we are still profoundly sceptical about Mr. Miller's economic and political agenda.

"In short, we believe the Conservatives simply cannot be credible instruments for the changes that put people first. We have no blind faith in Mr. Peterson's Liberals; hence the detailed and tough negotiations for the framework and terms of an agreement. . . . We can help make history in Ontario."

Rae said that he'd be informing Lieutenant-Governor John Black Aird of his party's decision, and that the NDP would join the Liberals to defeat the government as soon as possible when the legislature resumed.

Shortly afterwards, Peterson told the crowd of reporters outside his office that he didn't want a snap election and wanted to see minority government work. "It is my intention, if called upon, to govern well with the advice of the other party," he said. Peterson called Miller's arguments about confidence votes specious and irrelevant. But, in fact, he wasn't taking them so lightly.

On the weekend, Liberals and New Democrats sat down to complete their agreement. For the first time, Liberal negotiators raised Peterson's concern that Miller might be right about confidence votes. Rae swore loudly at the hint of retreat from a central element of the bargain. He and his researchers had examined the precedents and found that, apart from explicitly worded motions of confidence – such as adoption of the Speech from the Throne and the Budget – confidence was whatever governments said it was. In many countries with parliamentary traditions, governments had been defeated on bills of importance, even budget bills, without admitting defeat and proceeding to an election. Even the Ontario Conservatives, as recently as 1976, had accepted defeat on a farm-income stabilization bill, and later on the attorney general's bill for a Metro Toronto police force complaints bureau. Rae said there was nothing unparliamentary in his party's agreement not to defeat the Liberals' program, or their overall budget plan. The possibility that other government proposals, even budget bills, could be defeated was a positive development. The Liberals would simply have to work hard to get the co-operation of the House – and ordinary MPPs would have more clout than in the past.

Rae had consulted constitutional experts Paul Fox, Peter Russell, and Eugene Forsey, and felt certain he was right. Still, Peterson proposed that a lawyer for the Liberals, a lawyer for the NDP, and an impartial person be invited to examine the accord and judge whether the potential defeat of budget bills without an election was constitutional. On Sunday, Nixon flew to Ottawa to see Forsey for reassurance. On the morning of May 28 – the day on which Peterson and Rae were to make history by signing the accord – Hershell Ezrin and Sean Conway came to Rae's office to say that Peterson still had reservations. Rae and McClellan marched down to Peterson's office, where the Liberal leader explained that he wasn't satisfied on the question of constitutionality. "Look, it is this or nothing," Rae told him and walked away. Soon after that blunt talk, Peterson called and confirmed that he would sign.

Shortly after the signing, Rae called a news conference and released copies of a four-page document entitled "An Agenda for Reform: Proposals for Minority Parliament" that he and Peterson had signed. It said that the two leaders had agreed on a period of stability, during which the government would undertake an agreed-upon program of public policy and legislative reform. Peterson would not call for an election for two years after becoming premier (he took office on June 26, 1985), and during that time the New Democratic Party would not move or vote non-confidence in the government. What it all meant, said Rae, was that MPPs would have a new freedom to debate and vote without fearing that their actions would plunge them into an election. "It is an important step forward. We'll have a government which in a minority Parliament will negotiate and persuade but won't be able to say vote with us or we'll call an election."

The document outlined reforms of the legislature including: a freedom-of-information bill; establishment of committees to reform the patronage system, investigate the commercialization of health services, act as a watchdog on Ontario Hydro, and report on environmental issues; a broadening of the powers of the provincial auditor; election-financing reform to put limits on spending at the riding level; the right of public servants to participate in political activity; and, finally, the introduction of television into the legislature.

The third section sketched the agenda for the first legislative session: legislation on separate-school funding; employment programs for young people; a ban on extra billing; proclamation of the spills bill; reform of tenant laws, including the extension of rent review to post-1976 buildings; introduction of equal pay for work of equal value in the public and private sectors; a first-contract law, providing arbitration to assist weak new labour unions; right-to-know rules for disclosure of workplace chemical hazards; an end to the years-old royal commission on the northern environment; and full OHIP coverage of medically necessary travel by northern residents.

Finally, the agreement set out an action program for the second year: an Ontario housing program; private pension reform; workers'-compensation reform; an independent audit of Ontario's forest resources and on-going regeneration of the forests; recognition of day care as a basic public service; reform of services for the elderly; low-interest loans for farmers; job-security legislation; and new and enforceable mechanisms for the control of pollution.

Rae told the news conference that the NDP wanted more, but that everything in the document was pleasing to his party. "The Liberals borrowed our programs for the election, so we felt it only decent to ask the Liberals to introduce them in the first session," Rae joked. He added that he couldn't quite explain how Liberals had done so much better in the election with the NDP's programs than he had. Instead, he offered a happier thought: the NDP's next job would be to define the new reform agenda for the province.

Rae was proud of the accomplishments of May. He felt he'd

recouped ground lost in the election and taken a bold stab at bringing more democracy to the parliamentary system. But he knew the popular judgement at the next election might be different. Having held the political spotlight for nearly a month, Rae now slipped into the background as Peterson prepared to assume government.

After Rae finished his statement, Peterson, still sticking to his low-key style, took his turn with reporters. As he entered, Hershell Ezrin jokingly called out, "Make way for the premier." Standing at the side, Ross McClellan suddenly realized that the signing about to take place would make David Peterson the new premier. "My God, what have we done?" he said to himself as he watched the Liberal leader walk by. It was a half-humorous rhetorical question that was to ring through the New Democratic Party for many months after.

Earlier in the day, an NDP staffer had proposed a joint press conference so that Rae and Peterson could sound the praises of their pact together. Hershell Ezrin scotched the notion, telling Peterson that the lasting image in the public mind would be of him and Rae side by side. Already, Miller was saying Peterson would be a "puppet premier with Bob Rae pulling the strings".

Peterson was frank with reporters about why he'd turned down a joint signing session: "I don't want to give you or anyone else the idea that we've formed a coalition," he said. "If I am called upon, I will form a Liberal government."

7

The Fall from Power

On June 18, the day the Conservatives were defeated in the legislature and fell from power, former Liberal leader Robert Nixon gave a masterly speech in the House. For him it was an exquisite moment, a sweet, long-awaited reversal of the day forty-two years earlier when his father, Harry Nixon, was driven from office only three months after being chosen the Liberal leader to replace Mitch Hepburn. The humiliation suffered by Nixon's father, and the long eclipse of the Liberal party of Ontario, were finally at an end. From the depths of his family experience, Nixon spoke of how difficult Frank Miller would find it to accept what was about to happen. But he was scornful of the extent to which Miller had been willing to compromise in his Throne Speech attempt to cling to power. Said Nixon: "As the Tory political corpse twisted in the wind, there was something unnatural, something shocking. It was like looking at a corpse that winks."

In his very last moments in office, Frank Miller behaved gracefully, visiting the Lieutenant-Governor as tradition required to tender his resignation and advise that Peterson be asked to form a government. But up to that point his behaviour had been so erratic and at times so threatening to the Opposition parties that they gave him a rough ride on his final day as premier. What Nixon described as Miller's unnatural aspect was the result of the terrific whipsawing pressures to which he'd been subjected. To save his party he'd reluctantly put himself in the hands of the Big Blue Machine, but in doing so he had alienated his own group of supporters.

Now, isolated, Miller was under assault from within and

without his party. Two days after Bob Rae announced his support for the Liberals, Bruce McCaffrey, Conservative MPP for Armourdale and a supporter of Larry Grossman, publicly called on Miller to step down as party leader. Beleaguered by reporters who pounced on him every time he stepped outside his office, Miller replied, "I am not a person who quits."

Grossman insisted that McCaffrey had spoken on his own, not for the Grossman forces. Grossman had told his people to lie low and avoid any appearance of disloyalty. All the same, there were telltale signs that both Grossman and Timbrell were quietly putting together teams for a second try at the leadership. Miller had only the slimmest chance of retaining his grip on government, and within the party he was supported only by the old hands who had met with him in Bracebridge and now accepted him on sufferance because they believed an immediate leadership contest would be harmful to the party.

In his desperation, Miller considered, but finally rejected, a wild scheme for saving his administration. The scheme was hatched after he, and his two most trusted friends, Tony Brebner and Hugh Mackenzie, had thrashed out all the alternatives to defeat in the House, and then decided they needed expert insights. They no longer trusted Decima's pollsters or anyone in Ontario Conservative circles to put aside vested interests and do what was best for Miller. So they hired Arthur Finkelstein of New York, one of Ronald Reagan's pollsters, who had worked previously in Ontario for another Tory right-winger, Gordon Walker, and they asked him to sound public opinion in Ontario and find room for Miller to manoeuvre. Finkelstein sent his bills through Research Spectrum, the Toronto polling-house which served Miller during the leadership, in case anyone suspected an American was surveying for Miller.

The pollster asked thirty questions and found that separate-school funding was the issue hurting Miller most because the public who were opposed blamed the Tories for it, even though all three political parties supported Davis's full-funding announcement. Among Protestants, the constituency of the Conservative party, opposition to full funding was as high as eighty-five per cent, while among Catholics opinion was more evenly split.

Finkelstein said Miller had a long-shot chance of saving his skin if he played the issue just right. He suggested that the desperate premier should call a news conference, say he had reserved network time for the day before he was to be defeated in the House, and then disappear. With suspense mounting, Miller could then announce that the election had made it clear that the people didn't want full funding thrust down their throats and that the Conservatives wanted to put the policy on hold. Miller would then argue that the election had given no party a mandate to govern, so he was going to the lieutenant-governor to ask for dissolution of the legislature and an election. Legal counsel had advised Miller that the lieutenant-governor would be hard put to resist advice given by a premier who had not yet suffered a defeat in the House.

Miller was tempted, for it might have worked – and there were many in his caucus who wanted to go out fighting. But he didn't like the idea that he would have to attack Bill Davis. Davis was an institution in the party, and was also a friend who had been giving Miller advice ever since the election disaster. In addition, the pollster had warned that Miller would be taking a huge risk. If the tactic didn't work, he might so divide the Conservative party that it would be destroyed.

Miller rejected the anti-Catholic gamble and then settled down to watch the old Davis guard write a Throne Speech that embarrassed him acutely. The Throne Speech Miller wanted – basically the Enterprise Ontario program with the election promises tagged on – had died with the voting results. Instead, Davis's former policy-writer, Les Horswill, was brought back with instructions to produce a Speech that would give the Tories a shot at winning the confidence of the House. At first the negotiations with the NDP set the agenda for what would be in the Throne Speech. An end to extra billing by doctors was high on the NDP list, so Horswill wrote a section saying that because of the Canada Health Act – the federal law imposing financial penalties on provinces that permitted extra billing – doctors would no longer be allowed to bill over the Ontario Health Insurance Plan rates. Miller okayed this draft, agreeing that this was a move necessary in minority government, although he wasn't personally for banning extra billing.

However, once Rae announced for the Liberals, the Speech was changed. Goodman and Segal read the prepared text on May 29, the day after Rae and Peterson signed the accord, and called for a rewrite. They argued that the Speech now needed to be a more conservative document. It should still contain a wide spectrum of promises, in the hope that the Opposition would be embarrassed to defeat a program that offered the people so much. But it should also be a platform that the Conservatives could run upon if an election came that year. The party had to position itself back on the middle ground that Miller had abandoned, but with some differences from the more progressive Liberal/NDP agenda. Segal proposed fudging on the separate-school issue, but he was overruled, and the commitment was maintained for the time being.

That afternoon, key cabinet ministers tackled the extra-billing question, while Miller attended to other business. In his absence, Grossman argued that the extra-billing section should be dropped from the Throne Speech. He said the Tories would need this issue in Opposition to attract the support of the doctors of the province. Timbrell wondered aloud whether the negotiators hadn't already agreed to end extra billing in their talks with the NDP, but Grossman said no commitments had been made. Miller was consulted and said that the promise to end extra billing should be taken out.

Most of the other promises in the Speech were approved by the policy-and-priorities board of cabinet, the key cabinet committee, but now there was a problem with cost. A ban on extra billing would have saved the province $50 million a year in federal penalty payments to the government, but by removing the extra-billing ban, they forfeited this. For the first year alone, the Throne Speech promises amounted to

$450 million, excluding the cost of full funding for separate schools.

Grossman wanted the Speech to include a commitment that all the new promises could be paid for without raising taxes and without jeopardizing the province's Triple-A credit rating. He must have known that that was highly unlikely. The new treasurer, Bette Stephenson, had been briefed by Treasury staff after the cabinet swearing-in on May 17 and had been told Ontario was likely to lose the credit rating unless the deficit could be reduced to $1.2 billion in the 1985/86 budget. This was a cut of $1 billion from the previous year and was possible only with a careful paring of programs – certainly not after a flood of new promises. Grossman had fought when he was treasurer against Miller's Enterprise Ontario promise of a $975-million tax holiday for small business. Now he tackled Miller again. Miller didn't want to give up this key promise – one that he felt was an important stimulus to the economy – but neither did he want the media to say his Throne Speech jeopardized the province's credit rating. In the end, he accepted vague wording that left it unclear whether the tax holiday would actually be put in place.

Miller was sickened by what he was becoming. His right-wing loyalists would be outraged at the Speech, and he couldn't blame them. He'd come into the premier's office planning to break the power of the Red Tories and turn the province to a more conservative agenda. Now, after losing twenty seats, he was being dragged to what he felt was left-of-centre and still had to smile, puppet-like, and tell reporters he was proud of the proposals. Reporters questioned him sharply in the locked room where they read the document before it was presented to the legislature. This was draft nine, he had to admit, and the result of "a consensus of opinions". His tax rebate to small business probably would be amended. The Speech still had an "entrepreneurial spirit", he insisted, but when pressed he conceded it was a "middle-of-the-road document because Ontario's been a middle-of-the-road province." But what was a right-winger doing making all those promises to the NDP negotiators and then presenting this

Throne Speech? "If you drive right, then left, you are in the centre," Miller explained. Peterson later dubbed this "philosophic harlotry".

The legislature galleries were crowded on June 4 by curious spectators attracted to the continuing drama at Queen's Park. Miller was flanked by Bette Stephenson and Larry Grossman. All his caucus wore blue-dyed carnations, as they had so often during the Davis majority. Peterson's Liberals sported red carnations. The lieutenant-governor then read the Speech Miller should have prepared before the election, but wouldn't. During the long strike by Eaton's workers at six stores earlier in the year, Miller had turned down Rae's personal appeal for a law to provide for arbitration of difficult first-contract labour disputes. Now the Throne Speech promised first-contract arbitration. Miller had delayed former attorney general Roy McMurtry's family-law reform bill because of doubts about the fairness of equal splitting of assets. Now it was to be Bill One of the new session. The spills bill, passed by the legislature five years earlier and never proclaimed because polluters who would potentially be liable complained, now was promised at once. Miller guaranteed equal pay for work of equal value in the Ontario public sector, pro-rated benefits for all part-time workers, the right to know of toxic hazards in the workplace, portable pensions, adoption disclosure, freedom of information, environmental clean-up, including a tax on dangerous toxic substances and a $100-million environmental-protection fund, improved forest management, a beefed-up northern-development fund, cheaper credit for farmers, an increase in the province's share of school funding, a freeze on OHIP premiums, a $400-million fund to stimulate rental supply. These were ninety new measures in all – and a promise of no major tax increases.

With this remarkable Speech, the political tenor of the province shifted radically from the small-c conservative, restraint-minded agenda that had swept Miller into the premier's office. Now all three parties were vying to promise progressive change. The newspapers ran charts comparing the Tory Throne Speech with the promises of the NDP/Liberal accord and found only small differences: the Throne Speech was silent on extra billing and on extending rent controls to post-1976 buildings, both of which were promises in the accord. The policy log-jam of the last Davis years had been broken, and the only question now was who would hold office while the changes promised by all three parties were made.

That night Miller held the traditional government reception at Ontario Place and said his government's new initiatives would be considered on their merits were it not for the "lust for power" of the Liberal party and the NDP's "blood chilling fear" of an election.

Three days later, Peterson moved the amendment that was to end the Tory dynasty: "It is our duty to respectfully submit to Your Honour that Your Honour's present government does not have the confidence of this House." Rae added a further amendment, saying the Miller government was failing to meet the challenges facing the province "even while borrowing frantically from the policies of other parties" and that the legislature must reflect the democratic will of the people as expressed on May 2.

The noose was now around Miller's neck – the non-confidence vote would take place in eleven days. He had publicly threatened a legal challenge to the constitutionality of the non-confidence-vote section of the Liberal/NDP accord. But the weekend before the vote, Donald Smiley, the York University expert he'd asked for an opinion, sent Miller his advice that the accord was legal.

His only remaining options were to ask Lieutenant-Governor John Black Aird to dissolve the legislature and call an election, or to submit his resignation and watch Aird call on Peterson to form a government. The election alternative was considered seriously in the inner circles of the Tory regime. Unlike most politicians, the Ontario Conservative cabinet ministers had never contemplated the possibility of defeat – and had difficulty accepting reality now. Conservative MPPs told Miller bitterly that it was his fault they were going into Opposition.

After the May 17 cabinet swearing-in, some ministers had had their new offices painted and had made staff changes, just as if they expected to be there for a while. To the end, ministers went on grimly presenting bills to the House, and reporters' mailboxes in the Gallery groaned under a deluge of announcements of studies and grants. The patronage committee went on handing out jobs – the most controversial being a membership on the Ontario Municipal Board for former cabinet minister Frank Drea. Thousands of square kilometres of forest-cutting rights were awarded to the big logging companies. One of Miller's last acts was his announcement in Huntsville of a $5-million loan and grant to the Deerhurst Inn, a luxury resort in his riding. Ministers' speech-writers were told always to say in speeches that the Liberals would lose the Triple-A credit rating, causing the ministerial aides to mutter angrily to one another about propaganda. By the end, senior aides were saying that they just wanted to see the Tories go.

Miller's speeches during these weeks were full of resentment. He talked of the NDP/Liberal "hijackers", of his loathing of the prospect of a Liberal government, of the "unholy alliance" and the anti-democratic deal-making. He would have made a deal with the NDP himself, but, like many sharing the cabinet benches, he could not now accept that others had a right to combine to upset the province's natural rulers.

Miller tried to prepare the ground for another election, but such thoughts soon died in face of cold reality. A Decima Research post-election poll showed Conservative support dropping drastically. On June 1, the *Star* published a poll by Goldfarb Consultants showing that 43 per cent of voters would now vote Liberal in an election, 33 per cent Conservative, and 24 per cent NDP. An election would give Peterson a majority. When asked whom they'd prefer for premier, 61 per cent said Peterson and only 30 per cent Miller. The premier had asked Hugh Macaulay, Davis's old organizer, to get the party in readiness for an election, and Macaulay had enlisted Segal and Brian Armstrong to help him. They now told Miller that if he forced an election, the party would not march with him. Key candidates would not stand for office again if Miller led them into an election. Why, for instance, would Larry

Grossman run again in St. Andrew-St. Patrick if he had to campaign under Miller's banner? And if he would not, how could the Tories hope to hold this downtown Toronto riding?

Miller kept up the dance of speculation with reporters, but in his speeches to the party he began talking of walking across the floor to the Opposition benches with his dignity intact. He had also quietly issued instructions to Stewart to prepare for transition, and Stewart held meetings with Peterson and other Liberals to discuss the transfer of power. Tory flew to Ottawa to talk to federal Conservatives who had the experience of transition which their Ontario counterparts had never before faced. Still, Miller wasn't reconciled to the change-over. In the final days, he even claimed that business would flee the province – as corporate head offices had fled when a separatist government had been elected in Quebec.

When the vote finally came on June 18, the Opposition parties were in no mood to let the government fall gently. Liberal and NDP MPPs had been enraged by Grossman's refusal, as education minister, to bring in separate-school-funding legislation. Grossman said that, although it had been months in preparation, he was not satisfied that the bill protected the right of non-Catholics to attend Roman Catholic schools or of displaced non-Catholic teachers to transfer to the separate system. The Opposition interpreted the delay simply as Grossman's attempt to avoid association with the controversial policy, and to leave it hanging around Liberal necks. They felt Miller was contemptuous, and Grossman scheming, and so they drove home the final blows with relish.

Speaking for the New Democrats, Ross McClellan declared that the fresh air of democratic change was about to blow through the halls of Queen's Park after forty-two years of one-party rule. McClellan also revealed the Opposition resentment over the way that promises made in the minority years disappeared when arrogant Conservatives were in majority. "After March 19, 1981, we had a government of studious inactivity and lassitude that did nothing session after session. . . . There was do-nothing session after do-nothing session, culminating finally in the announcement on October 8, 1984, by the premier that he was retiring and retreating to his office for the next four months. We never saw him again." McClellan advised the Liberals to avoid the arrogance and gloating of the Tories and restore a legislative atmosphere of mutual respect. The NDP, he boasted, was no longer on the fringe of Ontario politics, but "right at the centre writing the agenda". Nixon followed, talking of the "cold hand on my heart" when Grossman had announced he would not introduce separate-school-funding legislation.

Then came Miller's last speech as premier, a speech that illustrated well Nixon's earlier point about the final "twistings" of the dying government. Miller began with a statesmanlike survey of the reforms in his Throne Speech, but when he started talking of the political deal that was to bring him down, his language turned unpleasantly sexual. There was the usual talk of hijackers, of the Liberal and NDP lynch mob, of a puppet Liberal premier with the NDP pulling the strings, and of the Opposition's "frenzied fit for power", and the warning that the NDP was signing its own death warrant. But interspersed were references to unnatural acts in the back-rooms, compromising positions, pleas to the other parties to legitimize their relationship, and suggestions that Peterson and Rae would not "respect each other in the morning". Miller voiced his party's conviction that the Liberals would behave as his own party had in March, and rush to an election while the polls were favourable. "We know that at the first opportunity they will engineer an excuse to run back to the polls so they can get the socialist monkey off their back," he said. "We do not fear an election. We will be ready. We have already begun our comeback. We will return – to repair the damage and to pick up where our predecessors in our party left off – building, not destroying what has been created by the men and women who went before us." Minutes afterward, the legislature voted 72-52 to tell the lieutenant-governor that the government had lost the confidence of the House.

Barnes's strategy in writing the speech had been to switch Miller halfway through from premier to Opposition leader. There would be no more Mr. Nice Guy, but a fighter who looked just as competent to lead the Tories in Opposition as Grossman. Rae called the speech "cheesy" and full of cheap shots. And once again the Conservative club made Miller look an outsider. In Ottawa, reporters approached Bill Davis asking for his thoughts on the fall of the government he had led for fourteen years. But Davis declined any comment. He was one of the guests at a $500-a-ticket fund-raiser to defray the leadership campaign debts of his old friend Roy McMurtry, and he hadn't even watched the television coverage of the vote in his hotel room before joining the black-tie crowd. In Baie Comeau, Prime Minister Brian Mulroney called Miller "an honourable gentleman", but disagreed with the premier's warnings that Ontario was in for a period of instability and an exodus of head offices. "I don't see why," Mulroney said. "I've known Mr. Peterson for fifteen years, and as far as I know, there is nothing in his behaviour that would inspire such a fear." A couple of days later, McMurtry, in a CTV interview taped during his Ottawa visit, said that Miller indulged in unrealistic rhetoric. There was nothing unholy about the NDP/Liberal alliance, McMurtry said, and nothing contrary to the democratic process.

Lieutenant-Governor John Black Aird agreed. Rae had already been to see him to inform him that the NDP would support the Liberals and give him a copy of the accord. The day after the vote, Miller walked down the corridor to Aird's suite, informed him he'd lost the confidence of the House, recommended he call on Peterson, and drank a quiet brandy.

Aird summoned Peterson, who said later he was there in two seconds flat, and they had a second brandy. Aird then ended speculation about whether he'd find the accord unparliamentary and dissolve the House for an election. He issued a two-paragraph press release:

> In my capacity as Lieutenant-Governor of Ontario and as the representative of Her Majesty The Queen in Ontario, I have this day asked Mr. David Peterson to form a government, he having assured me that he can form a government which will have the confidence of the

Legislative Assembly for a reasonable length of time.

On the advice of counsel with whose opinion I agree, I have advised Mr. Peterson that the agreement between the Liberal Party and the New Democratic Party, a copy of which had been delivered to me, has no legal force or effect and that it should be considered solely as a joint political statement of intent and that the agreement cannot affect or impair the powers or privileges of the Lieutenant-Governor of Ontario nor the members of the Legislative Assembly.

A week later, Aird issued a second statement, bordered in black, which simply noted that he had accepted the resignations of Miller and his executive council. The names of twenty-eight fallen Tory cabinet ministers, carefully listed in order of precedence, ran down two funereal pages, starting with Miller, Stephenson, and Grossman and ending with Noble Villeneuve, minister without portfolio, first elected in a by-election only a year earlier.

Outside, in the sun, the lieutenant-governor was busy swearing in the new Liberal cabinet.

8

A Cautious Liberal Courtship

At a finance ministers' conference in Halifax that fall, federal minister Michael Wilson remarked teasingly to Robert Nixon, Ontario's new Liberal treasurer, that his presentation was very like the position taken by Larry Grossman a year earlier.

"That's not so surprising, Mike," said Nixon. "Larry was a Red Tory."

"What does that make you, a Blue Grit?" asked Wilson.

"That's why I'm here," Nixon replied with a grin.

David Peterson, Nixon, and the new Liberal cabinet were barely in office before commentators began suggesting that they, and not the Miller Tories, were the true heirs of the Bill Davis legacy. Peterson took to the premier's office as if born to it. His personality had been poorly suited to the tasks of Opposition leader. He was ineffective on attack and usually lacked the detailed command of subject matter needed to make criticism formidable. But suddenly his years of being dismissed as a nonentity were over, and he was bounding up the steps through the East Door of the legislature in the morning, telling reporters he was "having a ball".

Peterson loved being in charge again, managing the province as he'd once managed his family's electronics firm. He liked to be personally involved, to use his office to wheel and deal, making bargains and cooling crises. Within weeks of becoming premier he plunged into negotiations to bring a Toyota plant to Canada and "played hardball" with the Toronto Transit Commission to avert a threatened strike by streetcar and subway drivers.

Like Davis, Peterson was able to project an air of calm command. And, while Frank Miller, in his few months as premier, had acted like a short-term tenant and put no personal imprint on even his own inner sanctum, Peterson immediately made Davis's old office his own, displaying bold, bright paintings by London artists, a revolving gallery which he periodically opened to small receptions for the arts crowd. The Liberal premier was quickly visible on the old Davis circuit, attending dinners for Cardinal Carter and addressing the Canadian Italian businessmen's association. Reporters soon found, to their frustration, that Peterson could spend more time with them than Davis ever had, and be just as elusive. He habitually talked in vaguely comforting generalities and even, on at least one occasion, used Davis's favorite dodge: "I have no plans to have any plans."

But, despite his adoption of the Davis style, Peterson's fragile government *was* different. Ruling with only 48 of 125 legislative seats, Peterson could not permit himself the luxury of Tory complacency. He and his ministers had yet to win the trust and liking of Ontarians. They had to prove two things at once: that they were as capable and prudent as managers as the Tories had been; and that the change in government was worth while because they would do things differently. The government set out to be more progressive on the issues, and more open in style.

In this they were aided by the great good fortune of a predetermined political agenda – although the premier didn't like anyone to dwell on his debt to his New Democratic partners. He was so touchy on the subject that a senior cabinet minister joked that if you wanted to see Peterson really lose his temper, you just whispered the word "accord" in his ear.

Whether he liked it or not, Peterson was the main beneficiary of the negotiations with the NDP, not only because the deal put him into power, but because it saved him from the floundering indecision he'd displayed in the past. The accord gave his government a legislative program and a timetable of reforms to keep things humming for the first two years of Liberal administration. It put starch in spines that might have bent under the pressures of vigorous business lobbying against the promise of equal pay for work of equal value and other reform items. The accord ensured that the Ontario Liberal party would be liberal.

But while the government owed its agenda and its determination to its New Democratic partners, much of its immediate popularity was due to Peterson's personal skills. The new premier soon proved surprisingly sure-footed in his handling of the bureaucracy, the media, and the public.

Compared to the rocky Davis/Miller transition, Peterson's take-over of government was marvellously smooth. During the election, he had talked of shaving the "blue fuzz" around Queen's Park, by which he meant senior bureaucrats who at times seemed more conservative than their former political masters. As the responsibility of office loomed close, however, Peterson talked soothingly about how he'd judge civil servants only by competence and their willingness to work for change. "I'm not looking for blood. I won't go in with a broadaxe," he said.

Top civil servants soon were saying that they had felt more threatened by the advent of Miller than by Peterson's arrival in the premier's office. Where Miller had been tense and formal, Peterson was casual, good-natured, and enthusiastic. His transition team was made up of businessmen and other lay members of Liberal hue, rather than of internal advisers motivated by revenge for old slights. Peterson hadn't set up a bunker at another location, but remained in his own Opposition office in shirtsleeves making plans. Then, when the move came, he simply walked down the hall, trailed by staff pulling a cart with his half-written speech for the swearing-in on top. He went through the premier's office saying, "Hi, I'm David Peterson" to secretaries and staff, telling them they were doing a good job and that he wanted them to stay.

Peterson knew very well that the long-time bureaucrats were in a position to scuttle his novice government if he made enemies of them. Ian Scott, appointed attorney general only weeks after winning his seat, was greeted on his first day by a suggestion that he embark immediately on a media-grabbing tour of the province, including a swing through far-northern native communities. This came from the same advisers who had won for Roy McMurtry his sobriquet of Roy McHeadlines, and they assured Scott that if he put himself in their hands, they'd do the same for him. Scott, suspicious that this was an attempt to get him out of the way so the bureaucrats could go on running things their way, replied firmly that he intended to stay put and learn the ropes.

The Liberals had anticipated attempts by the bureaucrats to "bodysnatch" ministers – to get the novice ministers under their control rather than having to obey new political masters. If they hadn't already been suspicious themselves, their New Democrat partners were uttering loud warnings about the dangers of co-option by a civil service recruited through decades of Tory rule. Peterson felt his first task was to persuade the bureaucracy to make love, not war. In an important gesture, he asked Ed Stewart, Davis's former deputy, to postpone his plans to go to a private-sector job until the government had weathered the transition. Stewart, the powerful head of the bureaucracy, had been snubbed by Miller and left twiddling his thumbs, but now a Liberal premier asked for his help.

With Miller's permission, Peterson met with Stewart before the actual reins of government were handed over, and in the course of covering a range of topics asked the deputy over and over, "How would Bill Davis have handled this?" Stewart was charmed: he liked Peterson's easy friendliness, the loyalty he saw in the Liberal leader's staff, and their willingness to take advice. Peterson was not encumbered, as Miller had been, by personal debts to people who had supported him and in return expected cabinet seats or appointments. No one had seriously expected Peterson to win, so no one had asked him for anything. Stewart was impressed, and worked hard for Peterson, giving him the firm control at the centre of government that Miller had lacked.

Less tangible, but more important, was the signal sent to the rest of the bureaucracy by Peterson's willingness to rely on Stewart. If Davis's most political bureaucrat was welcome, then so were others. Peterson moved swiftly once in office to woo the deputies whose co-operation was vital if the Liberals were to achieve control of the government apparatus. The day after the cabinet was sworn in, Peterson and his ministers met with the deputies at the Harbour Castle Hilton in a get-acquainted and briefing session. The deputies soon discovered the new premier meant it when he said he wanted their ideas. He met with them individually at Queen's Park in the premier's office, and was shocked when one deputy said he'd never been there before. He also asked for their opinions at meetings of the cabinet's policy-and-priorities committee.

It was typical of Peterson that, when labour minister William Wrye and his deputy, Tim Armstrong, locked in dispute over first-contract arbitration for labour disputes, a promise in the accord, Peterson called both to his office and told them to put their different cases. Afterwards Peterson sided with Armstrong's more conservative version of the draft bill. Wrye must have felt some chagrin, but Peterson insisted that this was the way he would govern, without regard for official lines of authority or ministers' egos. They could work out their personal differences afterward: he wanted to hear the debate and make up his mind himself.

In Peterson's office, his aides called this the "spokes-of-the-wheel" theory of governing. The premier didn't want to be presented with consensus decisions arrived at by the "group think" of his advisers, they said. Instead, he wanted separate lines of communication and authority running out from his office into the government – and bringing back different sets of information. When Stewart left at the end of the summer, Peterson did not replace him, because he did not want one all-powerful bureaucrat running the civil service. Instead, Stewart's functions were divided among Hershell Ezrin, the premier's principal secretary, Gordon Ashworth, executive director of the premier's office, and Bob Carman, secretary to cabinet.

Stewart's departure, to become vice-president of Labatt's Limited, gave Peterson an opportunity to display the camaraderie by which he was fast winning the bureaucracy's fealty. Peterson, and not the Conservatives, threw Stewart's November goodbye party, charged all the loyal Tories and other guests $50 a head, and then proceeded to cover an embarrassed but pleased Stewart with effusive praise in front of his old pals. At one table, Hershell Ezrin sat with Davis's one-time aides Sally Barnes and Les Horswill, and all three chortled as the new and the old premier exchanged jibes. Peterson read out the congratulatory telegrams, some of them from Conservatives who'd been appointed by Davis to public jobs, such as former cabinet minister Tom Wells, whom Peterson described as Ontario's agent-general in London "for the time being", and Eddie Goodman, chairman of the Royal Ontario Museum "for the time being". Davis, unable to let that pass, rose and addressed Peterson as "Mr. Premier, for a little while".

The new Liberal premier asked advice from Clare Westcott, Davis's executive assistant for many years, who had been rewarded with an appointment to the Metro Police Commission. On several occasions, Westcott dropped by Queen's Park to advise on the handling of staff problems. Next, Peterson took Tom Campbell, chairman of Ontario Hydro, out to dinner for a three-hour discussion of energy policy and to offer reassurance that even so visible a Tory appointee would keep his job. Peterson reaffirmed Campbell's five-year contract at Hydro, and in doing so won Campbell to the ranks of Peterson boosters. The premier also persuaded Campbell McDonald, the civil servant through whom advertising contracts had been channelled to Tory firms, to devise a system of fair competition. When Elinor Caplan, chairman of management board, announced a watchdog review panel to oversee the new rules a few weeks later, McDonald sat by her side saying he had enjoyed the challenge of cleaning up the old ways.

Stories began appearing in the media saying how well Peterson was doing as he assumed government. Members of the Press Gallery were benefiting from the new informality in the premier's office, for it allowed them to impress news editors by reporting the news before it was officially announced. The premier, and his senior ministers, stood around the lobbies after Question Period, willing to answer questions almost as long as reporters wanted to ask them, and their accessibility was rewarded with an extended media honeymoon.

For the time being at least, the Liberal ministers were acutely conscious of their origins in Opposition. Peterson had promised a new openness in government and free access to information that his researchers had so often demanded and never got from the Tories. On the day of the swearing-in, the premier had invited the public into his office to see the inner places of government, but there were limits to his offer.

During cabinet the next day, Peterson noticed a middle-aged woman whom he didn't know. There were lots of new faces around these days, however. He'd supplied cabinet with a seating plan so newcomers could identify who was speaking. Peterson leaned back in his chair between treasurer Bob Nixon and education minister Sean Conway and inquired quietly behind his hand just who the woman was. Conway replied that she was probably with the cabinet office. So Peterson signalled Ed Stewart and asked him to make the introduction. "I thought she was with you," Stewart said in surprise. He then asked her business and was told: "I came to see the open government." She was politely, but firmly, ushered out.

Open government, it seems, was not to be taken that literally. But, while members of the public were not invited to share in the sworn secrets of cabinet, Peterson and his attorney general, Ian Scott, were committed to freedom of information. They soon realized they had to act fast. Liberals who'd argued for many years in defence of freedom-of-information legislation were changing their minds with the first taste of power. Scott found his cabinet-mates suddenly anxious to exclude their particular bailiwicks from public examination, so a freedom-of-information bill was introduced as one of the first pieces of proposed Liberal legislation, getting the promise into the mill before cabinet could scuttle it.

For most of the brief first session of the legislature, however, Peterson moved with caution. His plan, when the legislature resumed on July 2, was to do a few pressing tasks as quickly

as possible and then whisk his inexperienced ministers out
of the public eye before they could make serious blunders.
Miller had already given the Throne Speech, so Peterson
introduced his new government with a "statement on the
resumption of the sitting", a general outline of good intentions
with little substance.

There were promises of future action on day care, acid
rain, extra billing by doctors, and an announcement – infu-
riating to the impatient New Democrats – of yet another study,
this time a green paper, on ways to introduce equal pay for
work of equal value in the private sector. A few things were
to be done immediately: rent review was extended to all rental
dwellings; a freeze was placed on government advertising;
the spills bill was proclaimed; John Kruger, former executive
director of Metro Toronto, was appointed to consider ways
to sell off the Crown corporations; and there was to be a
reappraisal of the $181 million in special payments – extra
spending on provincial programs approved by Order-in-
Council by the Conservative cabinet after the May 2 election.

The Conservatives howled. They'd spent that money on
business left over at the end of their regime so that the Liberals
wouldn't get the credit. Included was some $43 million in
payments to the province's hospitals. Frank Miller walked out
on the last day of the sitting, leading his Conservatives in
protest while the bells rang. Unless the Liberals acquiesced,
the House could not adjourn and everyone's summer holidays
would be cut short. Peterson baulked at first. He wasn't really
intending to take back the hospitals' money, of course. But
he did want to make a little populist hay out of rescinding
items like Miller's $5-million grant and loan to the Deerhurst
resort in Muskoka riding. "Can we afford $5 million for golf
courses at Deerhurst?" Peterson asked. It wasn't long, however,
before the ringing bells forced Peterson to compromise by
repeating his promise that the $43 million would not be
touched. Miller enjoyed one of the few triumphs in his brief
tenure as Opposition leader.

The first session with Liberals on the cabinet benches lasted
only ten days. Miller denounced the Liberal resumption

program as mean-spirited, because he'd promised ninety reforms in his last-ditch Throne Speech, while the Liberals had come up with only forty promises. In a neat reversal of roles, Peterson gave the former restraint-minded treasurer a little discourse upon the importance of frugality in government. "The taxpayers trust us to put their money to the best possible use," he told the House. "We will not let them down. Any policy or program that is outside a framework of fiscal responsibility is nothing less than a boomerang that will turn around and smash social progress."

Bob Nixon, the new Liberal treasurer, adopted the same thrifty tone when he rose on July 11 to report the results of his investigations into the affairs of the previous government. Compared with the federal Liberal legacy after the Trudeau years, the Ontario Liberals had inherited a well-run Treasury, and Nixon knew it. But he and Peterson believed the balancing had been achieved at the cost of under-funded universities and schools and a polluted environment. To correct those serious social deficiencies, the Liberals needed to spend money, but they also wanted to persuade the public that they, too, were good managers. Nothing would have been more fatal to the new government than the impression it was squandering public money.

In pursuit of this difficult double agenda, Nixon, the 57-year-old former Liberal leader, was Peterson's most potent propagandist. With twenty-three years' experience in the legislature, and a convincing speaking style, the treasurer was superbly fitted for the role that now fell to him – that of the fiscally responsible progressive. From his father he had inherited the Clear Grit tradition of southwestern Ontario and the Progressive party politics Harry Nixon had espoused before joining Mitchell Hepburn's Liberal administration. Bob Nixon was a progressive on essential social programs, believing that investment in health and education mattered more than keeping the province's credit rating. He was also the big, ham-fisted farmer from Brant County, who still planted corn and soybeans on the land acquired by his great-grandfather – a descendant of Loyalists – in 1854. He shared with the hard-hit farmers of his riding a suspicion of the free-spending ways of the politicians in Ottawa and Toronto. As a member of the legislature's Board of Internal Economy, which regulates members' spending, Nixon had built a reputation for sabotaging fellow MPPs' junkets to sunny southern climes and questioning their hospitality accounts.

In the legislature, Nixon firmly suppressed the joyful smile he had been wearing since May 2, and became an outraged housekeeper who'd found cobwebs behind the couch. The provincial finances were in much worse shape than the Conservatives had led people to believe, he announced. As his immediate predecessor, Bette Stephenson, bristled in outrage, Nixon cast doubt on her contention that Miller could have honoured all his Throne Speech promises without raising taxes or losing the province's Triple-A credit rating. On the contrary, Nixon said, the Tory Throne Speech would have cost at least $400 million more than was projected, bringing the deficit to a total of $2.6 billion for 1985-86, far above the $1.2-billion benchmark that Treasury officials felt was the maximum acceptable to Standard and Poor's rating house. On top of that there was the spending of $141 million authorized by the Tories after May 2, when their government was already falling.

Larry Grossman denounced Nixon for creating an atmosphere of fear and instability, which was reflected later in the day by Standard and Poor's announcement that Ontario was on "credit watch". But Nixon won the battle of public perceptions anyway, successfully foisting the blame for the province's credit difficulties on the Tory record. When Standard and Poor's announced in October, after Nixon introduced his first budget, that the credit rating was reduced to Double A plus, there was a minimum of furor and little political damage to the Liberals. The public may have understood the truth – that the provincial debt was now so high that either party would have lost the credit rating after the May 2 election. If the Conservatives had managed to cling to power, they too would have been governing by minority. The spending cuts Davis promised during that New York trip a year earlier would not have been possible for a government needing the consent of the Opposition parties. A majority government might have felt secure enough to refuse demands for spending on the environment, housing, and women's programs, but no minority could do so and hope to remain in office.

When Nixon introduced his budget on October 24, 1985, it was the first since Larry Grossman's in March 1984. The legislature had been on hold for six months – from December 14, 1984, to July 2, 1985 – while the Conservatives took time to pick Miller, call an election, and suffer defeat in the House. After the brief session in July, Peterson had adjourned until early October to give his ministers time to learn the ropes.

By that late date, Nixon could do little more than tidy up loose ends. He put his emphasis on improved and dependable funding levels for hospitals, schools, universities, and municipalities and, to pay for it, raised the provincial personal income tax by two percentage points, with a surcharge on those making more than $50,000 a year. Nixon cleared the provincial books of the province's losses in Suncor and other "bad deals", adding $518 million to the provincial deficit – but winning Standard and Poor's commendation for "prudent accounting changes". Nixon said Ontario's Suncor shares would be sold off, BILD would be wound down, three provincial policy secretariats would be eliminated, the IDEA Corporation would be scrapped, and the land banks would be sold. In a swoop, the dubious interventions of the Davis era were thrown out as Nixon opted instead for old-fashioned service government – the tradition of good schools and hospitals established by Leslie Frost and John Robarts.

The budget created the image the new Liberal government sought, progressive but prudent. Some said unkindly that David Peterson and his treasurer were progressive whenever it didn't cost money, but immediately became cautious conservatives when big spending was in prospect. In fact, the amount of public progress or restraint Ontario would get depended on the strength of the economic recovery. Nixon would spend if boom times returned.

Peterson's closest advisers in the inner circle of cabinet –

Bob Nixon, Ian Scott, Sean Conway, and Elinor Caplan – were all of this stamp. As a group they were more left-liberal in philosophy than the majority of the 48-member caucus, but in action they were cautious reformers. Ian Scott, the trendy left-winger in the Peterson circle, moved at a snail's pace, missing deadline after deadline on the accord promise to introduce pay equity in the private sector. Naturally, that made Scott a focus of NDP criticism, and he became quite irritable about the barbs from the left. At one point he told a scrum of reporters that Bob Rae should have had a lawyer with him during the writing of the accord to dot the i's and cross the t's. Ross McClellan intervened, telling him Rae already had enough trouble from critics of the accord without hearing remarks from a Liberal who'd helped negotiate the pact. Shortly thereafter, Scott met Rae in private to apologize and promise to curb his acid tongue.

Rae was harassed incessantly by reporters wanting to know whether the accord had been broken and whether he would force an election over Liberal dilatoriness. Over and over he was obliged to repeat that he had anticipated the way the Liberals would behave, and signed the pact anyway. "We knew that when the Liberals became the government they would tend to become more conservative. But change was still necessary for the province," he said. The Liberal/NDP pact was really in no danger. A Liberal liaison team of Nixon, Scott, and Conway met regularly for lunch or breakfast with New Democrats Ross McClellan and Michael Breaugh to smooth the path of mutual understanding. None of the supposed breaches of the accord that agitated the media mattered a whit for the Liberals and New Democrats compared to the vexed question of separate-school funding. And on this issue the Conservatives continued to give the accord partners good cause to draw together.

Although Frank Miller had rejected the temptation to renege on Bill Davis's promise of full funding to separate schools, members of the Conservative caucus were clearly attempting to distance themselves from a decision that had cost so many votes. Miller himself announced his party would insist on full public discussion before any legislation could pass, an unnecessary commitment, since the bill introduced by the Liberals was already being sent for public hearings before a committee headed by New Democrat Richard Johnston. Next, Norman Sterling, previously a closet objector, made public his opposition to full funding. And during the committee hearings, Dennis Timbrell announced he would oppose the Liberal bill unless access to the separate system was guaranteed for non-Catholic students and teachers.

Peterson entrusted carriage of the most volatile issue facing his administration to Sean Conway, the 34-year-old education minister and MPP from Renfrew North. Conway came from an old eastern-Ontario Irish-Catholic family and was the grandson of former Liberal MPP Thomas P. Murray, who had been deeply disappointed when Mitchell Hepburn's Liberal government backed away from a promise to increase funding to Catholic schools. Ian Scott, with whom Conway soon formed a friendship, was the great-grandson of the elected member from Bytown in the Parliament of Canada who sponsored the Scott Act, which later became the foundation for Section 93 of the British North America Act, providing for Catholic school funding in Ontario and Protestant school funding in Quebec. For them both, Davis's announcement had been the righting of an historical wrong. Conway was strongly committed to full funding and wary of attempts to use money as a wedge for secularizing Catholic education. As a student educated in the separate-school system himself, however, he had appreciated the social advantages of mingling with the general community during his last three years in a composite high school in Renfrew.

Conway's approach to separate-school funding was cautious. He quickly introduced Bill 30, legislation that was closely based on the principles enunciated by Davis, but in a manner so mundane as to depress controversy. This was unusual for Conway, who until then had been one of the more colourful speakers in the legislature. But, overnight, the cabinet oath of office transformed the witty, self-assured Conway into a stuffy politician. Reporters were unable to get colourful quotes out of him even when he broke the news that Bill Davis's full-funding cost estimate of $40 million for the first year was a mistake, and the actual cost would be closer to $80 million in 1985-86, $130 million the second year, and $150 million a year thereafter. Answering excited queries, Conway said mildly that Davis had apparently mistaken a partial-year figure for the cost of a whole year. He uttered no criticism of previous Tory education ministers Keith Norton and Larry Grossman, who had known of the error but concealed it. In the following months, the media continued to find Conway a dull interview. He played his new role so warily that he successfully "low-bridged" himself right out of the headlines, in a performance worthy of Bill Davis. Conway would need those skills in the months ahead. The Catholic school issue was quiet, but far from over. In May 1986, pollster Martin Goldfarb, in a survey for the *Star*, found fifty-two per cent of Ontarians now disapproved of full funding, while only 45 per cent approved. "This is an issue that has not gone away," Goldfarb warned. "It is an issue that has the potential to create additional problems for the Liberal government."

But that was a future problem. As the summer of 1985 slipped by, Frank Miller resigned, the Conservatives plunged into their second vicious leadership race within a year, and life in government appeared rosy for the Liberals. David Peterson had warned that his party was bound to make mistakes during the adjustment to government – and it did – but nothing disturbed what was becoming a prolonged honeymoon with the public.

In late August, while Peterson was attending the annual premiers' conference in St. John's, Newfoundland, the media caught the scent of some dubious new fund-raising techniques devised by Liberal party headquarters. Don Smith, president of the Ontario Liberal party and president of the giant Ellis-Don construction firm, had leaped to take advantage of unexpected success and drag his chronically indebted party into the black. Already he had been trying to whip an antiquated party organization into modern competitive shape by hiring five full-time regional organizers, tripling the staff to fifteen working out of headquarters, installing a computer, and moving into larger, brighter offices on Toronto's St. Mary Street. But as the construction magnate was aware, big-time operations require a big-time budget.

Smith turned to Judd Buchanan, a former federal Liberal cabinet minister and party bagman, and together they came up with a plan patterned on the federal Liberals' Rideau Club, and on Brian Mulroney's 500 Club, both of which charge $1,000 a year for memberships. Smith mailed out 15,000 letters to officials of small companies, offering them $1,000 member-ships in a Liberal Economic Advisory Forum. But he went a little further than the federal clubs, and came precariously close to peddling influence by offering LEAF members "reg-ularly scheduled meetings with Premier Peterson and his most senior cabinet colleagues" in return for their donations.

The press pounced and soon came up with more examples. In London, Joan Smith, the newly elected MPP for London South, and Don Smith's wife, held a cocktail party at which doctors and health administrators were invited to meet the new health minister, Murray Elston, at $150 a head.

Peterson was clearly uncomfortable with the revelations, but he didn't denounce them with the vigour the media anticipated. An expectation of strict probity had been created by Peterson's treatment of his former election campaign manager, Ross McGregor. When the media learned that McGre-gor's consulting firm had sent out letters offering clients assistance in getting the ear of the government, McGregor was swiftly cast out of the premier's inner circle. But Peterson didn't feel he could treat Smith in that fashion. The party president was an old London friend and a loyalist who'd raised money and supported Peterson when he was at his political nadir. In his case, Peterson merely sent out quiet instructions that future soliciting should adhere to the party's code of ethics.

Smith was not asked to resign as party president for the fund-raising gaffe or later when he presented a potentially far greater embarrassment. That fall, Smith's Ellis-Don firm won the bid for construction of Metro's $225-million Dome

Stadium. He was at once party president and winner of the biggest single contract with the new Liberal government.

This potential scandal was defused by, of all people, former Conservative premier William Davis. Peterson and Davis had established a new friendly rapport in the last weeks before the Conservative fall when Peterson was still Opposition leader but was clearly poised to take power. They met at a downtown hotel for two and a half hours, during which the seasoned leader of government instructed the novice in the niceties of being premier – how to decide which invitations among many he had to accept, and how to protect his family from the public spotlight. After that the two men talked whenever Peterson wanted advice – on separate-school funding, on extra billing by doctors, and on the Dome. Davis, appointed vice-chairman of the Dome Corporation by Miller, offered to make public his view that Ellis-Don won the Dome contract fair and square. He went on television and said the bid had been the best and that favouritism played no part in the choice of Smith's firm. After that, when the Conservatives tried to raise the issue in the legislature, Peterson was able to quote Davis back at them.

Peterson's luck held, but so did his own performance. In November, when the Ontario contingent arrived in Halifax for a federal-provincial conference, Ottawa Gallery reporters, accustomed to the tight lips around Mulroney, were surprised and delighted by the informality of Peterson's crew. Reporters, therefore, were ready to cheer when Peterson took Mulroney on in a live television duel by accusing the prime minister of a breach of faith in reducing federal transfer payments to the provinces. Mulroney, red-faced, remarked huffily that the new premier displayed "an unbecoming degree of temerity", but Peterson threw the phrase back at him, saying it took unbecoming temerity to cut promised increases in payments for universities and health care. This little exchange was all it took for the media to proclaim that Peterson had won his spurs. He'd played in the national league with the big boys and come away with a stature as premier that Frank Miller had been unable to achieve.

The careful introduction of the new Liberal government was completed, and no disasters great or small had attended the end of what had seemed to be perpetual Conservative rule. Ontarians liked what they were seeing of Peterson, as pollster Michael Adams discovered. Environics' second Focus Ontario survey showed that almost two-thirds of Ontarians were satisfied with the Liberal government. The October survey found that 47 per cent of voters were ready to support the Liberal party in an election, a jump of 10 per cent over Liberal strength in the May election. Bob Rae, at 22 per cent, noted happily that his party had not suffered voter disapproval for its role in the accord. The Conservatives, at 31 per cent, finally stopped saying that the election had been a fluke and that the public regretted throwing them out of office.

9

The Tories Lock Horns

On August 13, when he was supposed to be touring the province to unite grass-roots Conservatives behind his leadership, Frank Miller slipped quietly into Brampton to talk to Bill Davis. Not even his wife, Ann, or his closest friends knew of his visit to the Davis family home – or its purpose. Miller was thinking of resigning as party leader.

In the aftermath of the election, Davis had declared himself a "committee of one", ready to give Miller advice whenever he needed it. Now Miller put the most difficult question: Would it be better for the Conservative party if he stepped down as leader? Davis's reply was, as always, hidden in a smoke-screen. He listened, nodded, spoke non-committally, and promised his support whatever Miller decided to do. Miller knew his former leader, however, and interpreted Davis's attitude as a clear yes.

Through the tortured weeks that had followed his fall from power, Miller had been determined to hang on. Ann told the media her husband was no quitter, and Miller comforted himself with the notion that he hadn't been rejected by the people, but cheated of power by the Liberals and New Democrats. Once, in the privacy of his office, he'd done the calculations to assure himself that he wouldn't replace Harry Nixon in history's footnotes as the shortest-reigning Ontario premier. But it was little comfort: Miller couldn't bear the idea that he would be remembered as the man who sank the Tory regime.

After the summit in Bracebridge, Eddie Goodman had advised Miller to give himself a few months to discover whether he could repair the party and one day regain the government for the Conservatives. First, he had to gain control of the caucus, the party executive, and his staff, and recapture the affection of the alienated right-wing core in the party. As he moved into the Opposition leader's office, Miller determined that he would start to do things his way. He dispensed with John Tory, who'd been his principal secretary, and brought in his Muskoka friend Hugh Mackenzie as chief of staff. He placed Larry Keech, his loyal eastern-Ontario organizer, in party headquarters as executive director, pulling Bob Harris up to Queen's Park, where he hoped Harris's friendly personality would help smooth relations with the Conservative caucus.

The caucus was Miller's immediate problem. Most of the Conservative MPPs were taking defeat hard, and angrily blamed Miller for their loss of power. Robert Elgie almost immediately took an appointment from the Liberals as chairman of the Workers' Compensation Board, thus creating a by-election, and other disgruntled Conservatives either talked of resigning or were disinclined to carry their load as Opposition critics.

Larry Grossman, Miller's nemesis, stalked the Opposition offices like a chained tiger. He was convinced that the Conservatives would continue to lose popularity with every day that Miller remained as leader. He knew his own chances of winning the leadership were best before Dennis Timbrell or any other rivals could build an organization equal to his. Grossman also knew it would be fatal to be openly disloyal, and advised his supporters accordingly. But when Hugh Segal accepted Miller's request to prepare the party for a possible election, Grossman was upset with his old henchman, and even more offended when Segal told him, on Miller's behalf, to be a better team player.

As part of his determination to do things his way at last, Miller decided that he would not appoint Grossman as the Opposition House Leader, although Grossman's position as head of the Tory negotiating team made him the obvious choice for a post that involves constant dealings with the other two parties. Miller was convinced he had made a big mistake in embracing Grossman after the election, and should instead have cleaned his house of enemies. Before Miller revealed his intentions, however, Hugh Mackenzie intervened with some unpalatable but level-headed advice. Mackenzie warned Miller that he would give Grossman the needed excuse to openly challenge his leadership, and that Grossman might well win because he was generally well regarded in caucus. As well, by spurning Grossman, Miller would alienate Hugh Segal and Eddie Goodman, whose help he needed to survive.

Miller relented and asked Grossman to be House Leader, knowing as he did so that he was giving his most dangerous rival the opportunity to work on a daily basis with the members of caucus. The House Leader's job is an internal role, unseen by the public, but second only to the leader in sway over fellow MPPs, who get their committee assignments, opportunity to ask questions in the House, and legislative duty shifts from the House Leader's office. Almost immediately, Miller was confronted with complaints from the other potential contenders, Alan Pope and Dennis Timbrell, who argued that he had given Grossman an unfair advantage. Timbrell and his fund-raiser, John Bitove, met with Miller to point out that Grossman's organizing activities were forcing Timbrell into the field, since he dared not let Grossman get too far ahead.

So, in early July, Miller summoned Alan Pope, Dennis Timbrell, and Larry Grossman into his office and asked them to stop campaigning against him for a year and to work together on reuniting the party. Afterwards, Miller's staff told inquiring reporters that all three had pledged to give Miller a year's grace. Grossman and Timbrell had a different version, however. They said they'd agreed only to knock off visible campaigning, not to cease altogether.

The war of nerves continued as Miller assigned critics' spots to his former cabinet ministers. To Grossman's fury, the leader gave the high-profile job of education critic to Dennis Timbrell. The next-best showcases, health and Treasury, went to Alan Pope and Bette Stephenson. Grossman confronted Miller in his office, arguing that he was the party's best spokesman and should be up front. Miller offered to make him critic of the attorney general's ministry, a minor critic's post which Grossman rejected.

Grossman then found himself in the unaccustomed position of sitting silent in the legislature while the TV lights shone on his rivals. The New Democrats caught on and made a daily game of shouting, "Where's Larry?" as Miller tried to ignore the taunts from his left. Grossman privately accused Miller of putting his "own ass before the interests of the party". By the end of the first week, Miller said the tension in caucus was "so thick you could cut it with a knife". So he talked once more to Grossman and they agreed he could be a sort of roving ambassador, free to ask questions on a wide range of topics in the House.

As the legislature adjourned for the summer, Miller and Mackenzie turned their attention to wooing the party executive. Grossman supporters were calling for a leadership vote, which the executive had the right to convene any time once the Conservatives lost the government. To ward off the convention threat, Miller made common cause with Pope and Timbrell, who knew their chances were better if the leadership contest came later. Allies of Miller, Timbrell, and Pope on the executive combined to hold off the calls for leadership review.

As the days went by, Miller realized his year of grace was an idle fantasy. Everywhere he went in a series of tours to talk to local riding organizations, and as he sounded party opinion on the telephone, he found signs that Grossman and Timbrell were organizing. His core supporters, offended both by the purging of Perik and his replacement by Tory and Segal, and then by the Throne Speech, were drifting away. They had given up on Frank Miller and were looking for a new standard-bearer. John Balkwill and Ted Matthews, the two hard-nosed organizers who had been so vital to Miller in his leadership victory, offered their services to Timbrell. Balkwill became deputy chairman of Timbrell's campaign and Matthews again was in charge of delegate selection and tracking. Their motive was not love for Timbrell but dislike of Larry Grossman and the Big Blue Machiners who were working so hard behind the scenes for him. Balkwill organized new Conservative campus clubs, groups of right-wing youths who wouldn't have qualified for the campus association except by signing up for college courses to study light subjects, such as wine-tasting, so they would be able to send Timbrell delegates to the convention.

Miller found the party youth relatively truthful about his prospects for remaining leader. When he was flipping hamburgers at a fund-raising party in Huntsville, young Tories told him about recent efforts by the Timbrell people to organize their support. On the telephone, a Grossman youth bluntly told Miller that they'd give him until October, and if he hadn't resigned, they'd push him out. Miller probably could have used the leverage of his office to thwart the pretenders, but the prospect of continued nasty infighting was repugnant to him.

One morning the increasingly despondent leader of the Opposition told his executive secretary, Laura Mayne, that the Conservative party reminded him of a Ukrainian Easter egg, beautifully and intricately scrolled on the outside, and inside empty. The party's fabled organization was in a shambles as Conservatives lost heart at unaccustomed defeat.

The party debt stood at a stunning $5 million, reflecting the accumulated deficit of the Davis years and the desperate spending in the last days of the election. Now that the party was out of power, generous donors were hard to find.

In early August, before Miller talked with Davis, Hugh Mackenzie had visited him at his island cottage near Bracebridge, and had found the leader's demeanour worrisome. "Are you sick? Are you thinking of quitting?" he asked. Miller said that he was having "very private discussions" with himself, and he mentioned that he had been seeing a doctor. Mackenzie discovered that the former premier was on medication for high blood pressure and unevenness in his heartbeat.

The pressures were piling up on Miller. The day after he saw Davis in Brampton, the Conservative MPPs met in caucus at Queen's Park and Susan Fish and Phil Gillies, both Grossman supporters, demanded the results of Decima polling done for the leader's office right after the election. Gillies said the MPPs needed to know how bad things were before deciding whether to run again. Hugh Segal, as chairman of campaign readiness, fought off the demands, saying the poll was a tool for the leader's use and that sharing it widely would be "political folly". Segal confessed later that defending Miller against Grossman troops had been "an out-of-body experience". He was furious at being embarrassed by Grossman people after the hard work he had done for Grossman in the leadership.

A day later, the *Globe and Mail* gave the Grossman supporters the ammunition they wanted by publishing a poll by Michael Adams. In a survey done between August 2 and August 11, the pollster found that the Liberals had the support of 47 per cent of the population. The Progressive Conservatives had tumbled to 29 per cent, and the New Democrats held steady at 23 per cent. There was even worse news for Miller: he was now the last choice of Ontarians for premier, behind both Peterson and Bob Rae.

Miller had given himself a week after his conversation with Davis to make a final decision on retirement. The last straw came at a backyard barbecue thrown by the Erie PC Association, which had supported him in January. Here, as everywhere, Miller's friendliness and candour won him a good reception. But, as always, there were the behind-the-scenes murmurings. Miller learned that both Grossman and Timbrell were down Niagara way campaigning that weekend. Timbrell, in fact, was still at the barbecue when Miller arrived, while Grossman had been and gone. One of the party-goers told Miller she'd overheard a local Conservative pledge to stand as the riding's candidate in the next election, but only if Grossman were leader. And, she said, Grossman had replied, "I'll be there."

Miller decided he couldn't continue with two aspirants so close on his heels. He went home to Bracebridge and on Sunday night told his wife that he was going to retire. The next morning in Toronto he met at his Sutton Place apartment with Bill Davis and two people Davis felt could help – Eddie Goodman and Hugh Segal. "If I decide to resign, will you tell me how?" said Miller in a final act of surrender.

Segal wrote a draft of a resignation statement and a letter to party president David McFadden instructing him to call another leadership convention. Goodman polished the statement and sent it off to Miller's office by courier. On Tuesday, August 20, Miller told Sally Barnes he was stepping out, and gave her the statement and the letter. Feeling that Segal's version had Miller casting too much blame on himself, she performed yet another set of revisions.

Miller's resignation burst dramatically at a news conference that afternoon. Nobody in his caucus, his party, or the media had any idea that he was thinking in such drastic terms, or that he would acknowledge party schisms so openly. Miller said he could not unite the Progressive Conservatives because "in the final analysis there would be pretenders to the throne, working hard not for party unity, but for themselves. . . . therefore I had to make way for someone who could unify the party."

Miller saw his resignation as a personal sacrifice for his party. He had been leader of the Conservatives only 207 days, and premier for 139 days. By stepping down, he lost all opportunity to recoup his reputation and save himself from history's footnotes. But he believed his retirement, with a November leadership convention, was one way to prevent David Peterson and his Liberals from breaking the accord and calling a snap election while the polls were so favourable to the government. In fact, Peterson had observed the rebuff that voters had given both federal Liberal leader John Turner and later Miller for rushing to the hustings – and he had no intention of repeating their mistakes that fall.

Ironically, by fearing Liberal opportunism, Miller lost leverage over the Conservative succession. What Miller wanted most was to prevent Grossman from succeeding him, but Grossman was best organized to benefit from the leader's sudden departure.

Still, to everyone's surprise, Grossman took his time about jumping into the ring. He didn't want to appear over-eager, and there was also part of him that wondered whether he really could stand to go through all those Legion Hall meetings once again. He felt he had put doubts about whether a Jew could win behind him when he came such a close second to Miller at the first convention. But polling done for him by Allan Gregg showed that, while potential delegates rated him highly for intelligence and competence, he still had to overcome the perception that he was too slick and aggressive. Grossman's father, Allan, the former Robarts cabinet minister, didn't want his son to run again. Grossman, Senior, had long argued that Larry needed a second career, because politics was too insecure a profession, and he'd be sorry one day that he had never practised law for any length of time. After listening to his father, Grossman pondered briefly the advantages of a private-sector job that would give him an income to support his Forest Hill lifestyle and would guarantee future financial security.

The former treasurer decided he wouldn't go for the leadership without strong assurance that he would win this time, and that he wouldn't come out bankrupt. He and Timbrell were both about $250,000 in debt from the first campaign, in which the four candidates had each spent more than a million dollars. Now, the party put a limit of $500,000 on each campaign – still a ludicrously high amount, particularly for a deeply indebted party that was now in Opposition. So Grossman had good financial reason to hesitate. Alan Schwartz, Grossman's friend, adviser, and fund-raiser, persuaded twenty of Grossman's supporters to set up a $150,000 line of credit for the campaign: each signed for $7,500 on assurances they'd be repaid after the leadership was over. Schwartz promised Grossman that at the end of the second campaign he'd be no worse off financially than he already was.

By then, Grossman's prolonged flirtation with running had had the desired effect of convincing prominent members of his party that if they wanted him in the race they'd better get a large contingent on board. The vast majority of caucus quickly rallied to the side of the man they rated most able,

Who Knows? Bob Rae responds with a shrug when he is asked whether his party will throw the balance of power to David Peterson or to Frank Miller. With Rae are the NDP negotiators Ross McClellan (with mustache) and Michael Breaugh. (TORONTO STAR)

Ross McClellan and Larry Grossman wear false smiles as they enter negotiations for NDP support of the Conservatives. Both knew the game was really going to the Liberals. (TORONTO STAR)

Norman Atkins, chief of the legendary Big Blue Machine, holds the tally sheet of the final vote at the second Tory leadership convention, and reacts exuberantly as Larry Grossman is elected leader of the party and of the official Opposition in the legislature. (CANAPRESS PHOTO SERVICE)

Health minister Murray Elston and Premier David Peterson confer at a cabinet meeting during the Spring, 1986, confrontation with the province's doctors over the Liberal/NDP promise to end the practice of billing patients more than medicare allows. *(TORONTO STAR)*

This cartoon by John Larter, which ran in the Toronto Star on April 22, 1986, so infuriated doctors that government spokesmen said a settlement became more difficult. Peterson clangs the triangle, calling doctors to dive into his offer of a special fund to recompense physicians for excellence. *(TORONTO STAR)*

Members of the Ontario Medical Association rally at Queen's Park in May 1986 against the Liberal legislation to end extra billing by doctors. A month later they went on strike, closing doctors' offices and some hospital emergency wards.

(TORONTO STAR)

and most likely to win. The overall poll results were favourable, and he had the solid backing of the Big Blue Machine.

With those assurances, Grossman finally kicked off his leadership bid at the Convention Centre, promising to make Liberals, not other Conservatives, the target of his campaign. The January before he had run a catch-up campaign, aimed at upsetting party complacence by warning that Conservative hegemony was fragile and could be easily lost. Nine months later, Grossman waged a cautious campaign in observance of campaign chairman Norman Atkins' rule that front runners must avoid mistakes that could blow their lead. Grossman's managers counted on the party to remember his prophetic January warnings and to rectify its error by choosing, instead of a right-wing, small-town businessman, an urban Jewish lawyer who could appeal to an increasingly multicultural province.

Grossman presented himself as the leader who could reunite the party, devastate the presumptuous Liberals and their NDP allies in the House, and then regain the province for its rightful rulers in the next election. "I believe we can beat the Liberals. . . . We stand ready to turn the indecision of May 2nd into a Conservative victory at the very next opportunity," Grossman said at his kick-off.

This became the battle of the second leadership contest: Who could best reunite the party, and how fast? The divisions in November were much less along ideological left Conservative and right Conservative lines. In Grossman's camp, his faithful loyalists like Toronto Red Tory Susan Fish held hands with Ottawa's right-wing Claude Bennett, who had supported Miller in January. The ideological split, perhaps always overrated by the commentators, had disappeared with the voters' firm rebuff of Miller's small-c conservatism. But the emotional aspects of January's party infighting remained, and were magnified by the blame each side laid on the other for the fall from power. November's contest was a struggle by the Big Blue Machine to regain mastery over the Ontario Conservatives against all the forces in the party that had felt excluded. Alan Pope called it a fight by northern, eastern, and southwestern rank-and-filers to break the grip of the Toronto Old Guard.

Dennis Timbrell moved quickly to rally the "outs". Announcing his candidacy on September 13, Timbrell said the party should be returned to the rank-and-file – the people who really won the past elections – not run by a "group of strategists working out of the Albany Club". He called the party hurt, confused, and divided, and admitted it was not "at this point in time an opposition party that is ready to govern". A week later, he described Grossman's kick-off statement as dead wrong. "On the 2nd of May, the people of Ontario sent us a message, a message that certain elements within the party still refuse to hear. The message was simple – you're arrogant, you're out of touch, and you don't stand for anything," Timbrell said.

This was not bland old Davis-clone Dennis, but a fighter. He'd been persuaded to recast his image by the trio of Peter Regenstreif, Skip Willis, and George Boddington, partners in Policy Concepts consulting firm. Regenstreif and Willis had run right-winger Peter Pocklington's flashy losing campaign for the federal Conservative leadership. They despised the Big Blue Machine, which they felt had cut them out of consulting jobs, and sensed that Timbrell could strike a receptive chord in the party by casting off the Davis years. Timbrell began by announcing that he would not support the Liberal separate-school legislation, although it was so closely based on Davis's announcement, unless amendments were introduced to guarantee entry to Catholic schools for non-Catholic teachers and students. This stance won him some points among hard-core Tories, but alienated others. Norman Sterling, the foe of separate-school funding, who had supported Timbrell in January, went over to Grossman, denouncing Timbrell as an opportunist for making his criticism of full funding part of his leadership bid when he hadn't dared to oppose Davis at the time. Bill Davis himself watched Timbrell's performance with chagrin. The former premier regarded the anti-Big Blue Machine campaign as misconceived and dishonest: there were members of the party's Old Guard in every camp, and Timbrell himself had been an eager attender of the old Tuesday Park Plaza breakfasts.

Timbrell's biggest problem was his third-place showing in January. Delegates felt he had blown his chances by poor organization and doubted whether he could ever be a winner. Yet, within weeks, Timbrell was neck-and-neck with Grossman. His performance was strong, his message had deep appeal in the grass roots of the party, and this time his organization, under campaign manager Ruth Archibald, worked smoothly. He felt, besides, that he held an ace in the candidacy of Alan Pope, the former minister of natural resources, who entered the race urging delegates to choose a fresh face, someone who had been above the fray during the struggle the previous January.

Timbrell and Pope had once been casual friends, and their wives liked to get together for regular chats, although their relationship had been strained, first when Pope supported Miller in January, and then when Pope entered the second leadership. None the less, they had an obvious common interest in stopping Grossman, and more than once Pope and Timbrell organizers combined efforts to embarrass the front runner. Early in the leadership contest, Timbrell and Pope met secretly, once at Pope's apartment and once at John Bitove's place, to discuss their mutual reservations about the Big Blue Machine and the need to open up the party. Pope gave no firm undertakings, but both Timbrell and Bitove came away from the second meeting certain that Pope would swing his support to Timbrell after the first ballot on voting day, November 16.

Pope, in fact, had no such intentions, even though his own campaign was not going as well as he'd expected. He entered the race with an advantage over his indebted opponents – some $250,000, raised for his possible candidacy in January and saved since that time. But his early organization was weak and he parted with his campaign manager, John Thompson, because Thompson believed Pope would run third and because he didn't want to admit others to positions of authority.

Pope then put his campaign in the hands of Gordon Walker,

the former London-area cabinet minister, Donald Martyn, a former executive assistant to John Robarts, and Cam Jackson, one of the few newly elected Conservative MPPs. Pope believed that, although he was a long shot, he had a chance at the leadership. He was in the race to win and used the fractured state of the party to good advantage. "Don't take sides, take Pope," his buttons said. At the Convention Centre, his supporters handed out a pamphlet bearing a picture of two locked moose antlers still attached to the skeletal remains of the one-time antagonists.

However, Pope's campaign was marred by a series of bloopers that prevented him from ever gaining momentum. The worst occurred when one of his telephone delegate-trackers asked party members whether the religion of the candidates would make a difference in the race. The story hit the press, and Pope, appalled, made a public apology to Grossman. The only role left for him to play was kingmaker, but that he publicly said, time and again, he would not do. Timbrell was still counting on the understanding he'd had that night at Bitove's place, but was a little dismayed when repeated attempts to reach Pope in the final days fell through.

The convention itself was a tense, bitter affair. Frank Miller's little band was a lonely sight as they walked him to the podium for his farewell speech. The majority of the previous January had dwindled to Miller, his wife, Ann, and his friends Hugh Mackenzie, Tony Brebner, and Doris Pun, all with tartan scarves defiantly round their necks. Miller talked of the divisions in the party, of its failure in recent years to reach out to young urbanites, to women, and to people of different cultural and racial background. He accepted responsibility for the poor election campaign, but urged Ontario Conservatives to make a fresh start, to no longer be "a party sustained and driven by legend".

"I worked hard to win the leadership of our party last January. It was one of the proudest achievements of my life," he said. "I am a competitive person and it is not easy for me to step aside and let someone else carry on the job I had hoped to do. But I made my decision as an act of faith to you and our party. What I was unable to give you by remaining leader of our party I give you now by stepping aside."

What Miller did, in effect, was make room for the big generation of post-war baby-boomers who were coming into leadership in Ontario society when he took power – and with whom he'd been unable to identify. The candidates vying to succeed him were a generation younger: Grossman 41, Timbrell 39, and Pope 40 years old.

The convention delegates were younger this time, too. Many of the older Conservatives who still dominated local riding associations hadn't the heart, or the cash, to attend a second convention in a year. But, once again, the party executive had elected to cut off memberships as of Miller's resignation, so there had been no substantial infusion of new blood. The delegates were still mainly white, Protestant, small-town, and wealthier than the population at large.

This time, the venue was the new Metro Convention Centre, at once snazzier, warmer, and more convenient to hotel rooms, bars, and restaurants than the draughty Coliseum that had quartered January's misadventure. Throughout the convention there were youth parties, special breakfasts, blaring bands, waving signs – delegates were cornered, much flesh was pressed, and somehow it was all no fun. The race between Grossman and Timbrell was too close. Either was a potential two-time loser of the leadership – and of the nearly $1.7 million each spent reaching for the now-tarnished prize. People still spoke bitterly of the loss of power, and several delegates wore buttons proclaiming their opposition to Bill Davis's promise of full funding for Catholic high schools.

Before the voting, Pope's manager, Gordon Walker, a defeated politician whose own leadership aspirations had been crushed by the Davis circle, exerted intense pressure on Pope for an alliance with Timbrell. Walker asked Hugh Mackenzie to arrange a meeting between Frank Miller and Pope, so that the retiring leader could ask his young friend to take his support to Timbrell. Miller was torn: leaders traditionally stayed neutral over the succession, but he dearly wanted to stop Grossman. He agreed to talk to Pope, but not in specific terms. If Grossman should win, Miller didn't want him to have any excuse to veto his attempts to win a Senate seat. Davis was sponsoring Miller for the seat, but Brian Mulroney was unlikely to make an appointment over the opposition of the party's Ontario leader.

At 4 p.m. on Friday, Miller went to Pope's suite in the adjoining hotel and pleaded with him not to stay neutral in the race. Miller didn't say where Pope should tell his delegates to go, but Pope knew what was wanted. Pope was non-committal, but Walker remained hopeful, and that evening he arranged for Timbrell and Bitove to wait in Timbrell's suite on the promise Pope would be there. He was unable to deliver: Pope simply said he'd let Walker know his decision in the morning, and Timbrell and Bitove waited in vain. In the morning, Pope confirmed what he'd said publicly all along. He would not throw his support to anyone because to do so would be to take sides in the war in the party, instead of standing above it as he had promised in his campaign.

The first ballot made it clear that Pope's choice was decisive. Grossman's over-managed, uninspired campaign had cost him, and he fell short of victory, with 752 ballots. Timbrell had 661 votes – but what had happened to him in January began again. The momentum he'd enjoyed in the last days of the race stalled on the convention floor as disappointed supporters realized he was further behind Grossman than they'd been told. Pope had 271 votes, in part a tribute to the dramatic speech he'd given the evening before, during which he had spoken from the convention floor rather than from the platform.

Turned loose without instructions, many in Pope's camp went with Gordon Walker to join Timbrell's forces, but another large group, including financier Hal Jackman, wrapped scarves in Grossman's colour around their necks. A core around Pope sat tight, blocking access to their area to keep the strong-armers at bay.

At this moment, Miller made a last attempt. His emissary Hugh Mackenzie quietly appeared behind Pope lines and asked Don Martyn, the former Robarts aide who was helping Pope, to carry the message that the outgoing leader didn't want Pope to remain neutral. Pope nodded receipt of the message but didn't budge. There's no question Pope could have carried a couple of dozen votes wherever he went, but instead he let his delegates decide – and allowed Grossman victory.

While Pope's remaining supporters were still deciding what to do, Grossman's campaign gleefully flashed a message on their lighted scoreboard saying that Timbrell's pollster Peter Regenstreif had just said on television that his man didn't have the numbers to win. It was true; acting as a commentator on CBC-TV, Regenstreif had momentarily forgotten that what he said on television would get back fast to the convention floor. Before the first ballot was counted, he said Grossman would likely win. "I think he's got us by 20 to 25," the pollster said. Regenstreif wasn't the only Timbrell worker to lose his cool in the heat of balloting. Alan Eagleson, co-chairman of Timbrell's campaign, appeared on screen telling a television interviewer it would "take a miracle to pull it off now." Their pessimistic remarks must have hurt Timbrell's chances at this crucial point. Grossman, in fact, was leading by a slimmer margin than any of his campaign managers had anticipated. When the final ballot was counted, Grossman had 848 votes and Timbrell 829 – a difference of only 19 votes.

Grossman's long struggle to be leader was at last rewarded, and the Big Blue Machine was back in charge of the Conservative party. Whether the convention made the right choice was not immediately clear. Shortly before the voting, pollster Martin Goldfarb had produced a public survey for CFTO-TV showing that Grossman would do better against the Liberal premier David Peterson than would Timbrell. The poll may have helped Grossman at the convention. No doubt it also caused Liberal backroom boys to raise a glass to Goldfarb. They knew the Liberal pollster had found different results when he polled privately for the Ontario party a couple of months earlier. For the Liberals, Goldfarb had tested Timbrell and Grossman as possible election contenders against Peterson, and he had found then that Timbrell was the greater threat. Timbrell was viewed as trustworthy and non-confrontational in style, and he showed considerable strength across the rural stretches of the province. Grossman, by contrast, was seen as feisty and aggressive, with strength in Northern Ontario and in Metro. Adding that up, Timbrell looked more dangerous as a potential premier. But, for all the public talk about regaining government, the Conservatives had apparently decided that what they wanted for the moment was a strong Opposition leader. They needed Grossman's hard drive to put life back in a demoralized party – and that was what Goldfarb's television poll had picked up.

Grossman's immediate actions quietly acknowledged his recognition that he had to rebuild the Ontario Conservatives before he could hope to retake the government. The first thing he did was to postpone the party's annual meeting, slated for February 1986, even though there hadn't been a meeting since the fall of 1982 and the party's officers were anxious to be released from duty. Grossman knew his party was still too badly divided, and an election of officers so soon could turn into a contest between his forces and the people who had supported Miller and then Timbrell.

The new leader put election readiness to one side for the moment, and concentrated instead on organizing regional policy meetings, where his party would attempt, for the first time since George Drew wrote his twenty-two points of progressive reform in 1943, to work out a new campaign platform. The party that had ruled by pragmatic compromise now had to find out what it stood for. Grossman's plea, articulated in January at a symposium at the University of Toronto, was for a return to the Conservatism of Benjamin Disraeli, the British prime minister who is Grossman's personal hero and whose portrait hangs on his office wall. "The conservatism that makes politics for me something other than the day to day pursuit of tactical advantage, is the conservatism of Benjamin Disraeli, Sir John A. Macdonald, and those in the British and Canadian tradition who see an activist agenda for Conservatives, one tied to the integrity of the state, the

interdependence that must exist between liberty and responsibility, and the collective expression of those values that
represent the highest calling of government in the conservative
mode," he said.

"We have in this country been, of late, far too influenced
by the development of neo-Conservatism in the United States –
conservatism which in my view has, despite its many positive
aspects, really been little more than a shallow reconstitution
of laissez-faire liberalism. . . . There is little of importance
to Canadian Conservatives in the rediscovery by American
Republicans of classical liberal roots. The fact that those roots,
when reconstituted, conform to the present materialism that
strides across American politics like a colossus is fortuitous
for our American friends, but of no particular philosophical
or instructive value to those who call ourselves Canadian
Conservatives."

Frank Miller, the Ronald Reagan of the north, retired in
sad chagrin. "There was no real testing of me in the time
I was leader," he said in an interview the next spring. "I was
branded as a right-wing Tory in the leadership and that
reputation hung over into the election. Then there was the
school issue and my poor campaign, and a stronger desire
for change among the voters than any of us could measure."
In a way, he felt he paid for the fact that his party had been
in power so long. And when he voluntarily retired, clearing
the way for someone else to rebuild, the party showed no
gratitude. His kindest helping hand came from David Peterson,
after a plea from Miller's friend Hugh Mackenzie that Miller
not be left dependent on Larry Grossman for his office
entitlement at Queen's Park. The Liberal government assigned
Miller a set of spacious offices, and a limousine and driver,
for as long as he represented Muskoka riding. By comparison,
Miller felt his own Conservative party was letting him down.
The senatorship for which Davis had recommended him to
Brian Mulroney appeared to be eluding his grasp. Miller lent
his name to a consulting firm set up by his loyalists, Sally
Barnes, Hugh Mackenzie, and Doris Pun, but otherwise had
little to do but wait, in increasing bitterness, for offers of

public employment which didn't appear to be forthcoming.

He tried not to think too much about what he had lost. He had decided, he told a reporter, to "protect myself from becoming insane" by avoiding the thought that he might have won if he hadn't called the election so quickly. But the "what ifs?" made Miller a haunted man.

Bill Davis finished his first task for Brian Mulroney to little public accolade. As Brian Mulroney's envoy on acid rain, he and Ronald Reagan's envoy, Drew Lewis, produced a compromise report on measures for acid-rain reduction that on one hand was sharply criticized by environmental groups, and on the other seemed unlikely to meet its purpose of wringing more spending on acid rain out of Reagan. Davis by now had accepted invitations to serve on boards of a dozen large companies, which gave him a pleasant lifestyle, hobnobbing with business magnates, and a hefty income. He also became a partner at Tory, Tory, Deslauriers and Binnington, the law firm headed by John Tory's uncle, James Tory. The former premier's offices soon looked much like his old set-up at Queen's Park, with Laird Saunderson, his former appointments secretary, still answering queries, and John Tory, his former principal secretary, installed next door as a member of the same firm.

Dennis Timbrell formally buried the axe with Grossman and, whatever he may have thought privately, maintained a dignified silence about his two-time rival's running of the Conservative party he'd wanted so badly to lead himself. He was less emotional about his second loss than about the first – the prize had been worth less, after all, and he felt that he'd run a better campaign and lost fairly, rather than being out-manipulated on the convention floor. Both Timbrell and Keith Norton, the defeated former cabinet minister from Kingston who'd worked on Timbrell's first leadership campaign, earned extra income as consultants on government-business relations at Policy Concepts consulting firm. In the spring, Timbrell made public what he'd already quietly told his Don Mills riding association: he would not stand for re-election and soon would be leaving provincial politics.

Alan Pope bought back into his Timmins law practice, where he spent two days a week. Pope maintained that he intended to contest the next election in Cochrane South, but he had much less time for the legislature. Left with only a part-time health critic during the doctors' dispute with the government over extra billing, Grossman responded with the deal he'd once had with Miller. Pope could be critic-at-large, with no specific responsibilities in the Conservative caucus at Queen's Park.

10

Liberal Honeymoon

The doctors couldn't believe that David Peterson really meant it. In the fall of 1985, while health minister Murray Elston was preparing his legislation to ban extra billing, leaders of the Ontario Medical Association assumed that by making enough trouble they could force the government to back off. Dr. Ed Moran, general secretary of the OMA, boasted that in 1982, when Larry Grossman was health minister, the doctors had only to stage rotating one-day protests and the former government had suddenly come up with hefty increases in doctors' fees. Moran told government negotiators that they had wrestled Larry Grossman all the way to the ceiling, implying that they would do the same to Elston.

Not long after, Elston came into a fall cabinet meeting looking upset, drew Peterson aside, and said that Moran was telling OMA members that the premier would not back the health minister on the extra-billing ban. The OMA didn't believe Peterson was personally committed to banning extra billing, and assumed he'd drop the bill rather than proceed in the face of strong opposition from the powerful medical profession. Peterson arranged a meeting with Moran and OMA chairman Hugh Scully in the premier's office. "Just so you guys understand," he said. "The government is committed to this policy and it is not something you can negotiate away." Moran appeared stunned, and it seemed to Peterson that until that moment he hadn't believed at all that the government would go ahead.

The doctors were about to join the growing list of powerful interest groups to be offended as the Liberals gained confidence and moved quickly on several fronts at once. Businessmen, too, were upset by the government's promises to introduce pay equity and assist new unions; pharmacists were annoyed by Elston's bills to regulate drug pricing; professors at the Ontario Institute for Studies in Education were fighting Nixon's plan to put OISE under the control of the University of Toronto; and even lawyers, the profession with the closest links to politics, felt their privileges were threatened.

In November, Attorney General Ian Scott brought to cabinet a proposal to abolish the honorary title of Queen's Counsel, a distinction with which the former government had rewarded members of the legal profession. Scott himself was a QC; so was Peterson, although he had never practised; and they knew the emptiness of the honour. Scott peered over his bifocals at his colleagues around the cabinet table and wondered why lawyers should be singled out for recognition. Why not have Queen's Chiropodists and Queen's Podiatrists as well? he asked scathingly. Nixon was delighted: like most of the rural members of cabinet, he had a strong populist tinge. Over the years, the powerful professional groups – particularly lawyers and doctors – had been allied to the Tories, and were no particular friends of Liberals. Nixon had once suggested a new honorary title for lawyers, Senior Ontario Barristers – SOBs.

Yet the time for the yearly New Year's list of new Queen's Counsels was approaching, and lawyers with Liberal connections were clamouring for their rewards. Peterson, who had promised to clean up the old Tory patronage system by awarding on merit rather than political hue, found the growing list unseemly. "The second I do this [award QCs], I am tainted," he said. On December 10, Peterson announced that the government was abolishing the title of Queen's Counsel and revoking the honorific from 2,800 Ontario lawyers who used it on their letterhead.

This action was a relatively harmless little blow at entrenched privilege, but from the favourable public reaction the Liberals concluded it was a successful demonstration of popular politics. Revoking old QCs soon proved more troublesome than anticipated, however. Scott found that he couldn't do it simply by cabinet order, but that he had to introduce special legislation. And there was a price to pay: many senior lawyers felt demeaned by the suggestion that their QCs had not been earned. The Liberals were making some powerful enemies.

That fall the province saw active government for the first time in recent years as the Liberals moved to implement the commitments in the accord with the NDP. Environment minister James Bradley gave the province's four biggest acid-rain polluters – Inco Limited, Ontario Hydro, Falconbridge Limited, and Algoma Steel – an eight-year period to cut the 1980 levels of sulphur dioxide emissions by 67 per cent. After the spills bill was proclaimed in late November, Bradley also persuaded the insurance industry to pool liability, enabling it to provide coverage to polluters. Health minister Murray Elston announced subsidies for northern residents who had to travel to reach necessary medical care; introduced the bill to ban extra billing by doctors; and told pharmacists to push lower-cost drugs under the Ontario drug-benefit plan. Natural resources minister Vince Kerrio approved an independent audit of the province's timber stocks. Labour minister William Wrye provided automatic yearly adjustments for workers'-compensation benefits to keep in step with the consumer price index; promised stricter regulation of toxic workplace chemicals; and introduced bills to bring pay equity to the civil service and to offer arbitration of first-contract labour disputes. Attorney General Ian Scott announced a $16.7-million settlement for the Indian bands at Grassy Narrows and Islington on the mercury-poisoned English-Wabigoon river system. Soft-drink containers made of plastic glass and aluminum were made legal in return for greater recycling efforts by industry. And housing minister Alvin Curling extended the four-per-cent rent-control guideline to all rental units and announced a $500-million housing program.

Throughout this dramatic increase in government activity, Environics, in its Focus Ontario report, found the allegedly sleepy province welcomed the new government's energetic performance. "This is not the traditional post-election honeymoon enjoyed by parties which have received majority mandates. Rather we see a government creating its own honeymoon and winning public confidence," Environics' president Michael Adams said in a letter to subscribers in mid-December. Although the Liberals had raised some hackles, they were also gaining friends. Alvin Curling's surprising entente with the housing industry was only one of several examples of skilful Liberal politicking.

Curling, a new Liberal MPP from Scarborough who'd been named housing minister, had gotten off to a rocky start as he tried to introduce the accord's rent-review promises through a housing ministry used to dealing with landlords and builders but not with tenants. Then, in August, Curling hired Sean Goetz-Gadon, a well-respected activist from Metro Tenants' Legal Services, as his knowledgeable executive assistant. Developers were horrified to learn that a tenants' advocate had the minister's ear, but by adding him to the mix, Curling had balanced his ministry. Gardner Church, assistant deputy minister of housing, welcomed the young activist with disarming frankness: "We need you here," he said. "You represent the tenants – and I represent the developers."

The two worked with Curling to persuade the warring interest-groups in housing to abandon rigid stances and negotiate toward a compromise. Landlords and developers who had insisted that new units would not be built under rent controls decided they could manage after all if a satisfactory rate of return were guaranteed under the new legislation. Tenants accepted landlord profits in return for increased protection from rental gouging through the new rent registry. The government, addressing the severe shortage of rental accommodation, agreed to put more millions into subsidized housing. Tenants and developers together helped write the new rent-control and housing program announced by Curling on December 16.

The Conservatives watched the growing co-operation between developers and the government with resentment and mortification. Parts of Curling's new housing program had in fact been developed under the Tories. Party president David

McFadden, the MPP for Eglinton, had been working with Gardner Church on housing initiatives, but they had fallen victim to Frank Miller's decision to run a limited, business-oriented election campaign. Now McFadden had to watch the new government introduce some of his ideas.

In fact, the whole concept of "multi-stakeholder consultation" – getting the parties to a dispute to work out their own compromise solutions – was not new to the Liberals, although they liked to pretend it was. The Conservatives had first experimented with the technique when Susan Fish, then minister of the environment, accepted a suggestion from Pollution Probe that new methods of consultation being used to solve environmental conflicts be applied to the dispute over pop cans. With the ministry of environment supplying a mediator, the canning companies, bottling companies, recycling companies, retailers, and environmentalists had worked out a compromise just before the Tories fell from power. The Liberals inherited the solution to a problem which had been festering under the Conservatives for a decade, and announced it as theirs.

Small wonder then that the Conservatives felt a bit robbed. In February, Larry Grossman startled members of the Albany Club by saying that Conservative passivity in the last years in office – and the battering of the old government in the election – had been due in large part to the intractability of the party's support groups in preventing action while the Tories were still in office. The party – and those at the Albany Club – represented many insurance agents, real-estate developers, businessmen, and others who had lobbied hard against even mild reform attempts by the Conservatives.

Grossman noted that the insurance industry had threatened that no company would agree to cover polluters against the absolute-liability clauses of the spills bill. So the bill remained unproclaimed until the Liberals came to power. Then, suddenly, the companies co-operated with the new government to create pool coverage and the bill was proclaimed. Landlords and developers had insisted that they could not afford to build, and the housing shortage would worsen, unless the government

retracted its rent-control legislation. The Liberals streng-
thened the legislation, Grossman said, and the developers
found they could build after all. Inco Limited said it couldn't
afford to reduce acid-rain emissions without firing thousands
of workers, but the Liberals imposed tough controls and Inco
did nothing but yell.

Grossman concluded that the Conservative mistake had
been to respond too faithfully to the wishes of its corporate
supporters. The result had been a policy vacuum which the
Liberals had quickly filled. "This new Liberal government is
dangerous," Grossman said jealously. "It is going ahead full
steam with all the things you cautioned us against for years."

The only interest group that lived up to Grossman's expectation of loyalty was the Ontario Medical Association, which
steadfastly refused to compromise with Peterson's government
over extra billing. This was the one case where Grossman
didn't apologize for past Conservative inaction. Instead, he
accused Peterson of oppressing the doctors and trying to turn
them into civil servants. "His stubborn approach has transformed the harmony and co-operation that built our health
care system into suspicion and bitterness," Grossman said
in a February 19 speech in Hamilton. He attacked the Liberal
cabinet for ham-handed incompetence, arguing that the Conservatives should be returned to power because they were
experts at the smooth management of tough issues.

Although the Liberals introduced their Health Care Accessibility Act on December 19, officials of the Ontario Medical
Association wouldn't even talk about it until March, when
the two sides began a series of "negotiations", which appeared
to consist mainly of statements of their diametrically opposed
positions – exchanged over restaurant dinners of steak and
wine. Health minister Murray Elston, a 35-year-old former
municipal solicitor from Wingham, was backed at these dinner
meetings by Attorney General Ian Scott, who had once been
legal counsel to the OMA, and on occasion by Peterson himself.
But by May, no settlement was yet in sight and the medical
association called a rally at the doors of Queen's Park to
demonstrate to the government by a show of mass strength

that the doctors were united enough to pull off a strike if extra billing were banned.

The rally, on May 7, 1986, came slightly more than a year after the fateful election that led to the fall of the Tory regime. Once again, as it had been for the Liberal cabinet's swearing-in, the weather was balmy. About 3,000 of the province's 17,000 doctors, most of them in white hospital coats, spread over the sunny Queen's Park lawns, greeting old pals not seen since college days and chatting good-humouredly. The signs they carried, and the sentiments expressed by their speakers, were far from amiable, however.

Months of propagandizing by the OMA leadership had convinced the doctors that what was at stake was not just the right to bill their patients more than the amounts covered by public medical insurance, but the freedom of the profession itself. Like cowboys being asked to hang up their guns at the door, the doctors were ready to fight for their manhood. They saw themselves as a last bastion of free enterprise against creeping socialism. "We're doctors, not civil servants", the signs read. "Down with Socialism" and "If you like the Post Office, you'll love state-controlled medicine". Dr. Earl Myers, the grey-haired president of the OMA, said the government had "insulted and denigrated" doctors at a time when much more important reforms were needed to health care than the trivial question of extra billing.

Health minister Elston was not invited to address the rally, and Peterson pointedly declined an invitation, saying the confrontation tactics of a rally would solve nothing. But Conservative MPPs were out in full force, attempting to profit from Liberal discomfiture. Bette Stephenson, herself an opted-out general practitioner and a former medical association chief, savoured her role, denouncing the Liberals from the back of the flatbed truck which was the OMA platform. She had been the victim recently of one of the Liberal premier's occasional lapses into personal nastiness. When Stephenson was asking questions in the legislature about extra billing one day, Peterson remarked that she was "living proof that opted-out doctors have nothing to do with any kind of expertise" – an unkind reference to the OMA claim that extra billing was a kind of merit pay for the finest doctors. Stephenson now called Peterson a "thoughtless politician" and warned there "is a penalty for bad bill-pushers". Larry Grossman climbed up on the flatbed and reminded the crowd that Elston had described the OMA leadership as "living in an ideological time-warp" and had accused the extra-billing doctors of putting a "tollgate" on medical care. Grossman won cries of "We want Larry" from the medical crowd by urging them not to give up their fight.

For his part, Peterson showed no sign of breaking down, although Bob Rae was sharply critical of his failure to move faster against the doctors. This fight was proving the greatest test of his fledgling government so far. Peterson was anxious to avoid a doctors' strike, which – if prolonged – could make voters question the Liberals' ability to handle tough issues. Yet, he risked the defeat of the government if he broke the promise he had made in the accord with the NDP to ban extra billing, and he could not afford to enter an election appearing weak on a major commitment to the Ontario people.

The premier told reporters that he hoped his epitaph would be a simple one: "Peterson did what he said he would do." He worried about the powerful interests ranged against the major promises of the accord, but he was still too new a premier to be consumed with office as an end in itself. There was, of course, pressure from the New Democrats, but aside from that there was no point being premier, he said, unless he could make important changes. While it might seem astute to slow the early pace of reform, he would not. He believed he would never have a better chance to tackle tough questions than during his first months in the premier's chair.

Through the spring of 1986, the accord with the New Democrats functioned so well that Peterson said publicly that – quite apart from his intention of keeping his word to his legislative partners – he had no reason to contemplate an early election. Government business was moving smoothly through the House, and the Liberals were too happy with their taste of power to risk losing it prematurely. The main time constraint on the new government was the Ontario Liberal party's wish to go to the people before a federal election. Brian Mulroney's Conservatives continued to plunge from scandal to scandal – up to this point five federal ministers had been forced to resign – and provincial Liberals across the country were enjoying an upsurge. In Quebec, Liberal Robert Bourassa had taken the government from the Parti Québécois, and shortly thereafter the newspapers had been full of pictures of Bourassa and Peterson celebrating a new Ontario-Quebec axis with raised glasses. Peterson continued his policy of distancing himself from the federal government, criticizing Mulroney's attempts to win a free-trade deal with the United States and accusing him of trying to shift the federal deficit to the provinces by reducing the rate of transfer payments. In the next provincial election, Peterson no doubt would run as much against Brian Mulroney as against Larry Grossman.

Once the Ontario Liberal accord with the NDP expired in June 1987, Peterson said he doubted there would be another. His aim, despite the public success of the pact with the NDP, would be a Liberal majority government. In seven months after the May election, the Liberal party had more than doubled its membership to 65,000. Indeed, veteran riding presidents were complaining that, with the appearance of so many instant Liberals, Peterson wasn't making them feel as needed as he had in the years in Opposition. President Don Smith reported that the party was in good financial shape for the first time in decades. He had raised $2.3 million in 1985 and anticipated $3.5 million in 1986.

The Liberals' greatest weakness remained Northern Ontario. During the reign of Liberal Mitch Hepburn, the northern ridings had been a bastion of strength, but by 1985 the north was a Liberal desert. Peterson had managed to get only one Liberal elected in fifteen northern ridings – René Fontaine in Cochrane North. He had promptly named Fontaine minister of northern development and mines in an attempt to build northern allegiances, but otherwise the vast region remained evenly divided between the New Democrats and the Conservatives.

By contrast, the Liberals had made strong inroads in Tory eastern Ontario, gained in the Niagara Golden Horseshoe, and broken through dramatically to win 9 of 29 Metro Toronto seats. The solid Liberal base remained the old Clear Grit territory in western Ontario, where Liberals won, often by smashing majorities, in 21 of 34 seats, contributing a cautious rural contingent to the Liberal caucus that was suspicious of the urban activists dominating the premier's office.

For the Liberals, the political situation remained extraordinarily fragile. The pollsters agreed that Peterson was in the same position as Miller had been a year earlier: his overall support in the polls was good but easily changeable, because voters didn't yet feel they knew him or his government. The Liberals now were the party with support a mile wide and an inch deep. Peterson regularly warned his MPPs that honeymoons don't last. The Conservatives, with 51 seats, could still be a powerful challenger in the next election.

For that to happen, the new Progressive Conservative leader, Larry Grossman, needed luck on his side, and a great deal of hard work. In June the Conservatives were elated when a little sleuthing turned up a jackpot. Both René Fontaine, the only northerner in cabinet, and Elinor Caplan, one of Peterson's most senior and trusted ministers, were forced to resign while separate legislative committees investigated conflict-of-interest charges arising out of their personal lives. Caplan's husband, Wilf, a business consultant, had been involved with a hi-tech company which won a $3.5-million investment from the IDEA Corporation, shortly before the Crown agency was wound down by the Liberals. Wilf's blunder appeared likely to blemish Elinor's career. Fontaine resigned his seat as well as his cabinet post over Tory charges that he failed to disclose shares he held in Golden Tiger mine – and the Liberals faced a by-election which the other parties refused to contest. The Liberal honeymoon with the media cooled, but the polls showed little impact on the government's continued high public rating.

In the past, the traditional stability of Ontario politics has meant that incumbent governments could count on re-election, unless they defeated themselves by serious blunders. David Peterson so far had made minor slips, but nothing seriously damaging to his minority administration. And, for the moment, the Progressive Conservative party was in a dangerously weakened state. Larry Grossman inherited a party $4.5 million in debt, fractured by a year of bitter infighting, and led by a caucus ill-suited to the fight from Opposition. At least ten MPPs talked of not running again, and others, including former cabinet ministers, remained in their seats only because there were no greener pastures. Grossman himself found the adjustment difficult, and his early performance in Opposition was less dynamic than expected.

But the Conservative leader's real problem was his party's unrepresentative nature at the riding level: the membership base was too old and too uniformly Anglo-Saxon-Protestant. Grossman set out to attract young people between twenty and thirty-five, working women, and ethnics. However, when he made the appeal for wider membership in regional policy meetings, he was treated roughly by representatives of his target groups, who condemned the party's past record. Grossman told the riding executives they had to work harder to diversify the audiences at membership meetings before his next visit.

The Conservatives had taken existing patterns for granted in the May election, and had weakened their prospects by failing to mount strong campaigns in at least 25 Opposition ridings where they felt they couldn't win. Grossman needed to revivify those riding associations and strengthen others that had managed only narrowly to stay Conservative during the Miller slide. Of 52 Conservative seats, 24 were "at risk" because they were won by margins of less than 10 per cent. The Liberals had similar narrow margins in 14 seats and the NDP in 10. In the next vote, the Conservative party would be the most vulnerable of the three.

Grossman's henchman Hugh Segal felt that future Conservative opportunities rested largely on the fortunes of the NDP. If the NDP vote collapsed and went Liberal, the Conservatives would be in big trouble. In Opposition, as in government, therefore, the Conservatives saw an advantage in propping up the NDP. That old symbiosis was not easy to translate into renewed alliance, however. Grossman, trying to occupy the moderate middle, with one foot planted firmly on the right, felt compelled to cultivate the groups alienated by the accord's active agenda. He persuaded his caucus to vote against the Liberal first-union-contract legislation – despite the protests of Tory labour critic Phil Gillies – to maintain the goodwill of the Canadian Organization of Small Business, the Canadian Federation of Independent Business, and the Chamber of Commerce.

Grossman was also eager to distance the party from Bill Davis's separate-school promise. He and Segal had wanted to fudge the commitment in the Miller Throne Speech, but had been thwarted by a backroom majority which felt it was too soon to renege on Davis's commitment. When he became Opposition leader, Grossman promised not to play politics with the issue. His intention was to remain silent, hoping that blame would eventually be transferred to the Liberal government. But, in the York East by-election the Conservative candidate, Gina Brannan, campaigned openly against full funding for separate schools. Brannan lost, but by a narrow margin. Her pollster, Michael Adams, found opinion was still simmering on the vexed school question, with York East voters about equally divided for and against full funding for separate schools. Adams also noted, however, an impatience among the public for the dispute just to be over with – the issue was divisive and people wanted it behind them.

So did all the politicians involved. Sean Conway, the Liberal education minister, accommodated several Opposition amendments to his bill, guaranteeing hiring rights for non-Catholics, protecting public education in communities with only one high school, and freeing non-Catholic children from compulsory religious education in separate high schools. Suddenly that spring, Conway's legislative ally, Bob Rae, faced a strong minority movement within his party of New Democrats opposed to public funding for private schools. As the NDP's annual convention loomed in mid-June, 1986, there appeared a bare possibility that the dissidents would win over the delegates and reverse the New Democrats' historic support of full funding, cutting Rae off at the knees just days before the bill was to pass. Rae won the issue at convention, however, causing all the partners in the accord, of which full funding was a major plank, to draw sighs of relief.

As the day for the final vote on the bill approached, Larry Grossman met a fractious caucus. The majority of Conservatives – and in his heart Grossman himself – were opposed to full funding. Only a few – Norman Sterling, Reuben Baetz, and Jim Pollock – had dared express their doubts publicly. Bill Davis's ghost still hung too closely over the heads of his party members, and a reversal of his decision would enrage Catholic MPPs, or representatives of largely Catholic ridings, who expected the party to live up to its former leader's promise. Even so, Grossman had to fight a hard internal battle to get his troops in line and voting in unison with the Liberals and New Democrats to finally pass the full-funding legislation – a little over two years after Davis had made his historic announcement.

On this occasion, as on others, the opportunities for Grossman to differentiate his party from the government were slender. He felt it would be fatal for the Conservatives to move to the right as Frank Miller had done. Miller disagreed, convinced he had been defeated only by the inept mechanics of his campaign. But Grossman was determined to regain the middle ground that had proved so fruitful for four decades. David Peterson already inhabited much of it, so Grossman laboured to find a centre-right approach to the issues. The fine points of the Opposition's stance on extra billing ("fight but don't strike") or on first-contract labour disputes ("we're opposing the legislation because it isn't good enough") mattered little, however, to anyone but those directly involved, and that left Grossman with only one resort: to attack Liberal competence. That was a gambit that was unlikely to succeed while the Liberals were sustained by recovery in the economy. Grossman kept calling the Liberals "inexperienced and inept", but as long as the public felt Peterson was doing well, the Opposition leader's attacks went unremarked, even by the media. Unable to make progress by saying he could do the same thing better than Peterson, Grossman was likely to be forced to differentiate himself in the only way possible – by moving right. He was beginning to understand the problems the Liberals had had in their long years in the political wilderness.

Bob Rae and his New Democrats, on the government's left flank, were in a philosophic and political quandary similar to Grossman's. Rae took a huge chance when he decided to negotiate the accord with the Liberals. He was gambling that instead of punishing the junior partner of a minority government in the usual Canadian way, voters would see the benefits of re-electing a strong contingent of New Democrats in the next election. The young NDP chief was convinced that old Ontario voting patterns could change even further and that, for once, the electorate would consider a New Democrat government, provided it were responsible and moderate. Others in his party feared that the result of the accord would be a further dilution of social-democrat ideals – and extinction at the polls. Major figures on the left and right of the party warned that the accord simply made the Liberals look good, and the short-sighted voters would reward the government for its reform program at the expense of the NDP.

During the first year, Rae's optimistic judgment appeared to be borne out by events. The Liberals honoured the major terms of the accord, and the NDP suffered no significant drop in the polls. New Democrat MPPs took different approaches in assisting the new Liberal ministers with difficult issues. Education critic Richard Allen helped the government avoid unnecessary mistakes on the issue that sparked the accord – full-funding legislation for Catholic schools – in numerous behind-the-scenes meetings with education minister Sean Conway. Others, such as Richard Johnston, critic to social services minister John Sweeney, preserved their distance by declining a backroom role. Johnston attempted to play an independent part, feeling that it was not in the NDP interest to push the government too far left. He wanted to keep that territory for the NDP.

There were other, deeper dangers for the NDP in the accord. The third party risked neutralizing or losing social-activist supporters as they joined the government. Sean Goetz-Gadon, for example, surrendered both his public role as a champion of tenants and his riding work for the NDP when he went to work in Alvin Curling's office. A number of young labour activists and representatives of injured workers were hired by the Liberals, often on NDP recommendations, to help establish the workers'-compensation appeal system. High-profile New Democrats, among them former MPP Eduardo di Santo and labour leader Wally Majesky, took on labour ministry tasks for the Liberals. Former leader Donald Mac-Donald was appointed chairman of the Electoral Expenses Commission. Both the individuals and the NDP leadership were left to wrestle with the question of whether they were making an important difference to public policy and whether the reform process was sufficiently worth while to warrant the risk to the future of their party. Bob Rae believed it was. He felt the NDP could only gain credibility if its activists learned to play a governing role. Others feared the party was losing its most vital members.

As the months passed, that danger sparked increasing debate within New Democratic Party councils. Gradually the moderate-partner stance began to change as the party considered what to do when the accord came to an end. The majority felt the time had come to put a greater distance between themselves and the government. That meant gradually phasing out meetings of the NDP/Liberal liaison committee, in preparation for the day when the NDP would pull the plug on the minority government. The more militant MPPs favoured forcing an election as soon as the accord expired in June 1987, rather than allowing the Liberals even more time to woo the voters while governing solo.

However, there were obvious dangers in a quick election for an indebted and still disorganized third party. New

Democrat strength in the province was sketchy outside the party's strongholds in Metro Toronto and Northern Ontario. The party was lumbered with a $1.2-million debt and was obliged by fund-raising difficulties to pare organizing efforts at a time when it needed to expand them. After the election, Rae had swept away some of the staff and party officers blamed for his lack-lustre campaign and appointed Robin Sears, a former executive director of the federal NDP and deputy secretary of the Socialist International, as his new chief of staff. Sears' arrival at Queen's Park signalled just how worried the federal New Democrats had become about potential losses in their Ontario base. At headquarters, Brian Harling, a former Hydro employee, replaced a tired Michael Lewis as party secretary. The NDP was beginning to regroup, but was far from ready for an election.

Like Grossman, Rae was searching for a new policy agenda. The New Democrats needed election planks that the Liberals wouldn't be able to steal, and agreed on the general topics of universal accident and disability insurance, fairer taxation, reduced working hours, fully indexed pensions, and protection of workers against technological change that would displace them from their jobs. Within those subject areas, however, there was disagreement. The NDP, like the other two parties, was a consensus party, encompassing a wide ideological spectrum. There was a continuing tug between moderate reformers and hard-line socialists.

For the new government, too, the challenge was planning for life after the accord. Peterson and treasurer Robert Nixon had already discovered the frustrations of trying to effect real change. In Opposition the Liberals had been part of the chorus criticizing the chronic under-funding of major institutions. Now, in government, Nixon was determined to do more than just throw new tax dollars on top of the basic structure that had been built during the preceding decades. But he was already worried that his October 1985 budget had increased the rate of Ontario's provincial spending faster than that of any other province. He didn't like deficits, nor did he want increased taxes to become a part of every year's budget.

On taking office, Peterson had challenged the bureaucracy to find creative new approaches to four long-term problems: restructuring Ontario's industrial base to meet the high-tech competition on world markets; changing the school curriculum to produce the highly trained workers needed in the new era; containing escalating health costs, without reducing the quality of care; and planning for an aging society. The premier said he did not want his bureaucracy tied up only in day-to-day issues, providing the missiles that would allow the cabinet to be artful in shooting down the Opposition at Question Period. He wanted serious work on long-term problems, and he wanted to consult the communities and the public as much as possible.

Peterson displayed a startling naivety about brainstorming in public when he mused to a Kitchener newspaper's editorial writers about the advantages of a health-care tax on higher-income Ontarians to help pay for their medical costs. When what he later claimed had been only "an academic discussion" hit the news in late March 1986, there was an outcry, led by Robert Rae, about how Peterson himself was now threatening the principle of universal public health-care insurance. The premier quickly backed off, and said later he'd learned a lesson about blurting things out – there was a fine line between openness and letting things slip that he shouldn't, and he had not found that line yet. "I've got myself in lots of trouble and probably will again," he admitted. Yet, this slip aside, there was method behind Peterson's open attitude. The more he could share the big problems with the public, he felt, the better were his chances of survival.

In the spring of 1986, Peterson's chances of lasting in office appeared promising. On April 17, Liberal candidate Christine Hart won the Tory stronghold of York East in a by-election caused by the decision of former cabinet minister Robert Elgie to take a provincial appointment as chairman of the Workers' Compensation Board. The Conservatives fielded a strong candidate in lawyer Gina Brannan, and so did the New Democrats, who had high hopes for East York alderman Gordon Crann. But Peterson's growing personal popularity overcame a weak local Liberal organization – whose past candidates had run a distant third – and Hart rode his coat-tails to victory.

However, the Liberal riding association's sluggish performance at the beginning of the York East campaign pointed to the Ontario Liberals' continuing organizational weakness at the local level. Shortly after the by-election, Peterson appointed his sister-in-law, Debbie Nash, and former federal Liberal David McNaughton, the business partner of Tory pollster Allan Gregg, to put together the organization for the next election campaign. The small crew that helped Peterson into office a year earlier had been replaced by a big-business professional.

The Liberal premier now deliberately slowed the pace of his administration – distancing himself from his NDP partners just as they were distancing themselves from him – and reached out to the wary business community. In April, he introduced a Throne Speech intended to give Ontarians a glimpse of what Liberals would be like unencumbered by NDP allies. There were further commitments to a tough stance on environmental protection, to more money for cancer treatment, and to home care for seniors, but the focus of the Throne Speech was on industrial restructuring. The centre-piece was a billion-dollar fund, half of it new money and half from old programs, to be spent over the next ten years to spark technological innovation. The fund, administered by a Premier's Council headed by Peterson himself, would direct money to university research departments and businesses for "leading edge" inventions with practical applications in Ontario industry.

With a red carnation in his lapel and his red tie neatly in place, Peterson met the locked-up media before the reading of the Throne Speech, and defended his emphasis on high-tech by arguing that Ontario faces increasing world competition for its traditional resource and manufacturing products – and must pick a new area of excellence. "Our alternative is to drift in mediocrity," he said. The first $15 million from the fund was allocated the next month to university research programs, an infusion welcomed by those cash-starved institutions. But just how much difference $100 million a year would actually make to the Ontario economy was open to question.

The billion-dollar council had a more immediate and political purpose. Peterson knew he was unlikely to win support from the older business interests that had supported Bill Davis. The council now gave him his own network in the business, labour, and university communities. It was to be made up of major players from all three sectors, and Peterson would use the opportunity to repair some of the relationships damaged by his government's first year of reform action.

A month later, Robert Nixon's first full-year budget was presented with the same careful political calculation. Gabor Apor, the expert on getting a message across on television, stood on the sidelines admiring his handiwork – a huge red trillium backdrop. He winced when the treasurer turned up for this formal occasion in bright-red argyle socks, but Nixon's footwear was the boldest thing about him that day. Despite extra revenue from a burgeoning economy, the Liberals moved with caution and the biggest chunk of new spending was $850 million allocated over five years for hospital expansion. This was meant to silence the growing public outcry over under-funded health services and to undermine the Ontario Medical Association's claim that government parsimony was doing more harm to medical care than was extra billing by doctors. More money went to programs in the north, where the Liberals needed to win seats if a majority government were to be possible, to eastern Ontario, another weak spot for the party, and to quiet restless farmers who were hit hard by low prices for their produce.

What the media noticed most was that, unlike his first budget in October 1985, Nixon's 1986 budget included no tax increases. He had moved "incrementally" – to use his word – on the most expensive promises of the Liberal campaign platform: allowing a few thousand more low-income Ontarians to escape paying OHIP premiums, instead of abolishing the premiums altogether; providing dental care for needy children, when the election promise was denticare for all children and for the aged; fiddling with tax reform, instead of engaging the problem of unequal tax burdens in a serious fashion. The accord promise of universally accessible day care was honoured in spirit. Nixon publicly acknowledged that child care is a basic public service – but not with cash.

It was, as Nixon said, a businesslike budget, based on the Liberals' overriding need to gain a reputation as prudent managers like the Tories. Nixon repeated his commitment to funding education and health at improved levels, but he was also determined to achieve "pay as you go" deficit-free management. The budget would not regain Ontario's Triple-A credit rating, but the deficit was reduced and the goal was clearly in sight.

Bob Rae denounced the Liberals for "coasting" when they ought to have been getting on with major reform. Rae's finance critic, Jim Foulds, remarked that Peterson and Nixon had obviously taken to heart Bill Davis's observation that "bland works". In the same spirit, Larry Grossman accused Nixon of "rummaging around in the cemeteries of former Conservative treasurers" and coming up with a budget suitable for an earlier decade. Television commentators that night announced that Peterson's government had turned conservative, and nothing had changed in Ontario after all.

It was true only in part. The Peterson government was moving slowly on reforms that involved major spending – day care and pay equity – but it *was* moving. Environment minister James Bradley was going about the business of pollution clean-up with a vigour not seen before in the province. The Liberal broom was sweeping out the patronage system, cleaning up the letting of advertising contracts, and shaking up a tired bureaucracy.

And on June 20, 1986, David Peterson did the one thing the Tories might never have done – pressed through the law banning extra billing by Ontario doctors. He acted late for his accord partner, Bob Rae, who had been demanding action all spring, but too soon for the Ontario Medical Association, whose leaders accused the Liberal premier of tyranny. Angry doctors closed their offices, conducted rotating strikes at emergency departments, and threatened to close whole hospitals.

Ontarians were astonished at the furious response of a normally staid profession, and no doubt a little of the bloom came off the Liberal rose. Larry Grossman liked to think so. When the Liberals, supported by the New Democrats, finally invoked closure to force final passage of the bill over Conservative objections, Grossman said to Peterson, "Let this hang around your neck." An important sector of the Tory constituency had gone to the mat with the new government, and lost. After twenty-five days, in which doctors closed offices across the province, but never more than a minority of hospital emergency wards, the OMA conceded defeat. Too many of the profession, including Hugh Scully, the OMA leader who was chief of staff at Toronto General Hospital, believed a strike that affected emergency health services was wrong. The doctors gave up the strike, but vowed to continue the struggle in the next election. Peterson expressed his concern at alienating a substantial profession, but, he said, a principle was at stake – equality of medical care for all, regardless of income. Doctors would probably never vote for him, but then they never had. A new coalition was in charge in Ontario, and the old power groups who had supported the Conservatives were suffering the consequences.

But the most noticeable change, after a year of Liberal government, was the new vigorous style. Unlike Bill Davis, or John Robarts or Leslie Frost, David Peterson had come out of Opposition. After a decade of watching what he thought were the old regime's mistakes, Peterson promised himself not to allow his government to run out of ideas and energy as he felt Davis had during the last years. "When I can't drive the system any more, I'll go grow pumpkins," he said.

Beyond that, it would be difficult to differentiate between David Peterson's Liberalism and Bill Davis's Progressive Conservatism. Peterson and Davis were fundamentally pragmatic politicians, rejecting what Davis once called "the ideological prisons of left and right". Both claimed that attempts to classify them on the political spectrum were fruitless, because they would respond to practical needs as they arose. At this point, the new government could best be compared, not to the dying Tory regime, but to the dynasty at its beginnings.

Like the old-time Progressive Conservatives led by George Drew, David Peterson's Liberals came into office with an attractive reform platform, spent their first months in vigorous activity, and benefited from economic recovery. They have been progressive on social issues and conservative about fiscal management. They recognized new forces in the electorate and then set out to build broad support across the moderate middle of the Ontario political spectrum. The next ballot will show whether they can balance on that golden mean as the Conservatives did, election after election, for more than four decades.

A Note on Sources

As indicated in the acknowledgements at the front of the book, my main source of information was the politicians, their aides, and their party workers who were active in the months before and after the election. Little of value has been written on Ontario politics and history, but that is gradually changing, largely because of the efforts of the Ontario Historical Studies Series. George Drew's biography has been stalled because of his family's determination not to release his papers for several more years, but I was able to talk to historian Roger Graham about Leslie Frost, whose biography he is writing, and to Alex McDougall, who published his book about John Robarts in 1986. Another book in the Series which I found useful was Kenneth Rea's *The Prosperous Years: The Economic History of Ontario, 1939 to 1975*. I consulted Claire Hoy's biography of Bill Davis, which was published by Methuen in 1985; and, of course, the best overall look to date at the Ontario Conservatives was Jonathan Manthorpe's *The Power and the Tories*, published by Macmillan in 1974. Also useful were *The Government and Politics of Ontario*, edited by Donald C. MacDonald and published by Van Nostrand Reinhold Limited in 1980, and *Ontario: 1610-1985: A Political and Economic History* by Randall White, published by Dundurn Press. Peter Oliver's *Unlikely Tory: The Life and Politics of Allan Grossman*, published by Lester and Orpen Dennys Limited, provided some fascinating background on Allan's son Larry Grossman.

Where people are quoted in the book, the sources are usually newspaper accounts, the legislative *Hansard*, the texts of speeches, or notes that I took while covering public events. Quotes of things said in cabinet or in other private meetings have been cross-checked, either with the speaker, or with one or two other persons who were present. In certain cases, such as the private negotiations between all three parties after the May election, participants took notes and kept diaries, and I have had relevant entries read to me by both sides.

Senior Conservatives shared with me the polling results before and during the election, and I have discussed those findings with Decima Research's pollsters Allan Gregg and Ian McKinnon. Michael Adams of Environics was interviewed about the polls he did for the *Globe and Mail* during the election and let me study relevant polls taken after the election. Michael Marzolini kindly shared his election data. Martin Goldfarb gave advice on the public mood during the period, and I had access to polling for the New Democrats by ABM Research.

Index